T0244614

WALL STREET
the
NAZIS
AND THE CRIMES OF THE
DEEP STATE

WALL STREET
the
NAZIS
AND THE **CRIMES** OF THE
DEEP STATE

David A. Hughes

Skyhorse Publishing

Skyhorse Publishing books may be purchased in bulk at special discounts for sales promotion, corporate gifts, fund-raising, or educational purposes. Special editions can also be created to specifications. For details, contact the Special Sales Department, Skyhorse Publishing, 307 West 36th Street, 11th Floor, New York, NY 10018 or info@skyhorsepublishing.com.

Skyhorse® and Skyhorse Publishing® are registered trademarks of Skyhorse Publishing, Inc.®, a Delaware corporation.

Visit our website at www.skyhorsepublishing.com.
Please follow our publisher Tony Lyons on Instagram @tonylyonsisuncertain.

10 9 8 7 6 5 4 3 2 1

Library of Congress Cataloging-in-Publication Data is available on file.

Print ISBN: 978–1-5107–7985-3
eBook ISBN: 978–1-5107–7986-0

Cover design by David Ter-Avanesyan

Printed in the United States of America

Dedicated to all who are actively resisting
the global technocratic coup

LEGAL DISCLAIMER

CONTENTS

CHAPTER 1

INTRODUCTION

This book offers an updated and expanded version of my article "Wall Street, the Nazis, and the Crimes of the Deep State," first published in *Propaganda in Focus* on July 29, 2022 (Hughes, 2022b). That article quickly became the most read article in *Propaganda in Focus* and was translated into over half a dozen languages. The reason it struck a chord with readers, I think, is that it offers an attempt to make sense of the shocking resurgence of totalitarianism transnationally since 2020 by means of an historical materialist analysis of the class relations involved. Specifically, my article draws attention to the concrete actors and institutions responsible for covertly rehabilitating Nazism in the form of a transnational deep state that has been clandestinely cultivated since the late 1940s at least, and which today represents the most powerful entity influencing world affairs.

In addition to updating the original article with various minor amendments, this book offers several major additions. Chapter 2 massively expands upon the opening part of the article dealing with continuities between the early years of the Third Reich and developments in the global political economy since 2020. Chapter 3 significantly extends the discussion of Wall Street's role in aiding and abetting the rise of Hitler and the Nazi war machine. Chapter 7 considers where totalitarianism led in the case of Nazi Germany, and what we can expect to be the outcome if the global technocratic coup that is currently underway is not put down. Chapter 8 considers possibilities for resistance.

The Emergence of Global Totalitarianism

In 2020, as in 1933, constitutional guarantees were suspended in the name of "protecting" the public based on a false flag operation. Legislatures capitulated to executive power and began legislating tyranny, including legalized state crime, dangerously expanded police powers, and the criminalization of dissent. A revolution from above, known as the "Great Reset," was initiated, which seeks to remake the whole of society in the image of technocracy. The working and middle classes are under attack by a fusion of state power and Big Business. Individual rights are under attack from collectivism. *Gleichschaltung* (the production of ideological conformity) has resulted in a moral collapse across the citizenry, the professions, the churches, the "Left," and trade unions. *Ausschaltung*—being "switched off" (closed down, ostracized, censored)—has proven a powerful disciplining device. High levels of media cartelization and coordination are apparent, as is the use of propaganda to dominate the minds of the public. Health surveillance, in the form of "health passports" and mapping the population's biodata, is a characteristic of both eras. The health professions are subordinated to the state and used for biopolitical purposes, involving widespread violations of medical ethics, including euthanasia. Human beings are being experimented upon without their informed consent. Transhumanism is the latest iteration of eugenics, a pseudoscientific legitimation of "elite" rule. Conscience has been hijacked and morality rewired to make evil/harmful acts seem good/safe and vice versa. Ecopolitics is prevalent in both eras. Notwithstanding some important discontinuities, the affinities between the early years of the Third Reich and our own time prove too powerful to ignore.

That is not to say that liberal democracy has already collapsed into full-blown totalitarianism, any more than the early years of the Third Reich were synonymous with the atrocities that followed later. Many Germans, for instance, retrospectively referred to the 1933–1939 period as "'the normal years' of the Third Reich," when most Germans "disapproved of die-hard Nazis' coarse racist diatribes and pogrom-style tactics" (Koonz, 2003, p. 11). As explained in Chapter 2, the superficial continuities before and after 1933 were so strong that most Germans did not notice the tectonic shifts taking place politically. Similar is true today: most Westerners still believe they live in civilized societies where the rule of law prevails. In reality, liberal democracy is being systematically dismantled, and a novel, bio-digital architecture of oppression (technocracy) is being erected in its place (Hughes, 2024, Chapter 1).

For those with eyes to see, the warning signs are flashing red. We are at the thin end of the totalitarian wedge:

> Although it is hard to claim that—at least in the West—we find ourselves once again under the yoke of totalitarian regimes comparable to those we know so well from the 20th century, there is no doubt that we are faced with a global paradigm that brings forth steadily expanding totalitarian tendencies [. . .] (Alting von Geusau, 2021)

Indeed, we are dealing here with an emergent global form of totalitarianism, which in certain key respects is very different from twentieth-century (ultra)nationalist, imperialist, and Soviet forms of totalitarianism. However, Alting von Geusau is wrong to claim that those tendencies are not "planned intentionally or maliciously." They are by design, instigated by a transnational ruling class seeking recourse to totalitarianism in response to an acute crisis of capitalism—the same principle as in the 1930s. Then, as now, totalitarianism did not simply spring, fully formed, into existence. The descent into its worst horrors took place over many years (see Chapter 7).

The intended outcome of this process is global technocracy, a centrally managed totalitarian system based on energy usage rather than money (Hughes, 2024, Chapter 1). Rather than the unpredictable market forces of supply and demand determining price, humans are to be allocated a quota of energy certificates/tokens to be spent on goods and services priced according to the energy cost of production (Technocracy Inc., 2005, p. 230; cf. Wood, 2018, p. 13). The technology required to fulfil this vision—which essentially requires the constant monitoring and control of everything, plus digital currencies—was not available in the 1930s, when technocracy was first proposed, but it is now (it goes under the label "smart"). At the apex of the power structure (the Technate), the technocrats will control everyone and everything. It is they who get to manage and distribute all resources, right down to the individual level (Davis, 2022a). This implies, *inter alia*, eradication of private property, dependence on the Technate for all basic needs (food, housing, healthcare, transportation, etc.), and an inability to save for future needs, since energy certificates expire at the end of an accounting period (Wood, 2018, pp. 14–15). Central bank digital currencies represent a vital step towards replacing money with digitally programmable tokens: the state will get to decide when, where, how, and if those tokens are spent, enabling absolute financial control over citizens' lives.

Explaining the Resurgence of Totalitarianism

How is it possible that we find ourselves living in an era that displays evident similarities to the early years of the Third Reich? After all, the Nazis were ostensibly defeated in 1945, and the end of the Soviet Union was supposed to mark the definitive triumph of Western liberalism (Fukuyama, 1989).

The answer proposed here is that Wall Street—the apex of international finance capital and a "dominating complex" including "not just banks and law firms but also the oil majors" (Scott, 2017, p. 14)—has always been wedded to National Socialism as a ruthless means of crushing working class resistance. The Nazis, Loftus (2011, p. 17) notes, "were funded to keep the unions and Communists at bay: just a dog on a leash, or so they thought." Contrary to liberal and conservative myth making that conflates National Socialism and socialism in the Marxist sense, and which misleadingly portrays fascism and socialism as representing two opposing ideological extremes (the "horseshoe" metaphor), the historical reality is that Western capitalists funded fascist movements in the 1920s and 1930s to counter the threat of a politically organized working class (Elmer, 2023). Without their support, Hitler and Mussolini could not have come to power.

Who exactly are we talking about when we say "Wall Street"? Loftus (2011, p. 51) prefers the nineteenth-century term "Robber Barons" to include America's wealthiest families, e.g. Harriman, Bush, Rockefeller, DuPont, and Dulles, a collective which "funded both Hitler and Stalin." Higham (2007, xiv) refers to "The Fraternity" (eliciting secret society networks), i.e., US corporate giants entangled through interlocking directorates and financial connections, though certain red threads can be traced: "all were represented by the National City Bank or by the Chase National Bank and by the Nazi attorneys Gerhardt Westrick and Dr. Heinrich Albert," and all were linked to Emil Puhl of Hitler's Reichsbank and the Bank for International Settlements. This group has no party-political or national loyalty: it only believes in profit (Loftus, 2011, p. 51). It funded the Nazis and the Bolsheviks alike and is eager to destroy liberal democracy. Its only ideology is "Business as Usual," based on reactionism and a desire for a "common future in fascist domination" (Higham, 2007, p. xiv).

Having subverted the Bolshevik Revolution and turned the Soviet Union into a giant opportunity to acquire financial control over nationalized industries on a model previously established in Latin America (Sutton, 1981), Wall Street looked to do the same in Germany and the United States. The model was "corporate socialism," which involves centralizing power in the "pecuniary interests of the international bankers," something best achieved "within a collectivist society" (Sutton, 2016, p. 173). Stalin's "socialism in one country," National Socialism, and Roosevelt's New Deal were all forms of corporate socialism, in which the power of the state is made available to big business (Sutton, 2016, pp. 50, 121). Competition is thereby eliminated for an oligopoly of large corporations whose operations are financed (and thus ultimately directed) by Wall Street. Roosevelt and Hitler both took office in March 1933, and "both Hitler's New Order and Roosevelt's New Deal were backed by the same industrialists and in content were quite similar—i.e. they were both plans for a corporate state," a concept previously introduced by Mussolini (Sutton, 2016, p. 121). The New Deal was the outcome of the Swope Plan, named after the president of General Electric, Gerard Swope, whose company was also involved in financing Hitler and electrifying the Soviet Union.

From July 1933 through 1934, Wall Street financiers and wealthy industrialists planned a coup d'état in the United States. The "Business Plot," as it became known, was financed by Irénée du Pont, J.P. Morgan, and other wealthy industrialists including William Knudsen (president of General Motors), Robert Clark (heir to the Singer Sewing Machine Corporation), Grayson Murphy (director of Goodyear), and the Pew family of Sun Oil (Yeadon & Hawkins, 2008, p. 129).

Knudsen and du Pont instituted the speed-up system created by Charles Bedaux, which paid workers who exceeded average hourly production more and demoted or fired those who fell below. Working at unsafe speeds on the assembly lines to keep their jobs when few were available, many workers died from a combination of heat, stress, and fear (Higham, 2007, p. 166). Bedaux was appointed head of I.G. commercial operations in Germany in 1938. Du Pont, meanwhile, personally financed "armed and gas-equipped storm troops modeled on the Gestapo to sweep through the plants and beat up anyone who proved rebellious," to the tune of almost $1 million, as well as hiring the Pinkerton Agency to spy on leftists in the workforce (Higham, 2007, p. 166). There was no substantive difference between this kind of treatment of workers and what was taking place in Nazi Germany. The common aim was maximum exploitation of labor.

Had the "Business Plot" not been foiled by its intended leader, General Smedley Butler, the United States would likely have followed Nazi Germany and the Soviet Union on the path to totalitarianism, conceivably inaugurating the world of "garrison states" envisaged by Harold Lasswell in 1939, in which political opposition, legislatures, and free speech are abolished and dissidents are sent to forced labor camps (Lasswell, 2002, p. 146). The intrigue did not disappear: in 1937, US Ambassador to Germany, William E. Dodd, upon his return to New York claimed that "A clique of US industrialists is hell-bent to bring a fascist state to supplant our democratic government and is working closely with the fascist regime in Germany and Italy" (cited in Higham, 2007, p. 167). The plan to destroy liberal democracy in the interests of finance capital is, thus, approximately nine decades old.

Although the Business Plot and Nazi Germany were defeated, Wall Street representatives oversaw the recruitment of ex-Nazis to the United States after World War II. Through the national security apparatus they created in 1947—in particular through the CIA at the heart of a transnational deep state (Tunander, 2016; Scott, 2017)—they ruthlessly crushed working class resistance using methods derived from the Nazis, including death squads (Gill, 2004, pp. 85–6, 155, 255), torture (McCoy, 2007), false flag terrorism (Ganser, 2005; Davis, 2018), biochemical warfare (Kaye, 2018), surveillance-based targeting of political opponents (Klein, 2007, p. 91; van der Pijl, 2022, pp. 58–9), and the mass killing of civilians (Valentine, 2017). In the twentieth century, such methods were mostly reserved for non-Western populations to facilitate US imperialism under the pretext of a "Cold War" with the Soviet Union (Ahmed, 2012, p. 70).

The end of the Soviet Union meant that a new enemy had to be found for the securitization paradigm to continue to function (i.e. convincing the public that extraordinary measures, incompatible with democracy and the rule of law, are needed to deal with an alleged existential threat). In 1991, the Club of Rome proposed a new "common enemy against whom we can unite," i.e. "humanity itself" for its disastrous inference in natural processes (King & Schneider, 1991, p. 115). But while the green agenda—itself deriving from Nazi ecologism (Brüggemeier et al., 2005; Staudenmaier, 2011)—struggled to gain traction, Carter et al. (1998, 81) envisaged a transformative event that, like Pearl Harbor, would involve unprecedented loss of life in peacetime, necessitating a reduction in civil liberties, increased surveillance of citizens, detention of suspects, and use of deadly force. Similarly, the Project for a New American Century (2000) claimed that the rebuilding of America's defenses would be a drawn-out affair "absent some catastrophic and catalyzing event—like a new Pearl Harbor." 9/11 was duly used as the pretext, not only for imperialist wars abroad, but also for increased authoritarianism at home.

Rising social tensions in the West following years of "austerity" and surging levels of inequality resulting from the 2008 financial crisis (Chancel et al., 2022) were met with an escalation in the number of terrorist attacks (see Chapter 6) intended to reimpose discipline on populations between 2015 and 2017, especially in France (van der Pijl 2022, pp. 63–4). But when protests around the world began to assume a socially progressive form not easily assimilated by "populist" movements in 2018–19, it became clear that a new paradigm of social control was needed (van der Pijl, 2022, pp. 54–58).

"Covid-19" provided the pretext for inaugurating that new paradigm. Regardless of whether the "pandemic" was real or simulated, it was used a pretext for overhauling governance paradigms, implying that those paradigms were no longer fit for purpose (Agamben, 2021, p. 7). Liberal democracy, long since hollowed out by the "War on Terror," is now finished, and its intended successor is technocracy, a totalitarian control system based on data-driven scientific dictatorship (Wood, 2018). If successfully implemented, technocracy will be worse than anything envisaged by Hitler or Stalin, because it amounts to the digital *enslavement* of humanity through biometric nanotechnologies, constant surveillance and monitoring as part of the "Internet of Bodies," central bank digital currencies, and a Chinese-style social credit system (Davis, 2022; Broudy

& Kyrie, 2021; Wood, 2022). New technologies mean that the financial oligarchy's dream of global social control is on the brink of realization, unless, like the 1933–1934 Business Plot, the attempted global technocratic coup is defeated.

CHAPTER 2

ECHOES OF THE THIRD REICH

Developments in global political economy since 2020 call to mind the early years of Nazi Germany. In both cases, power was seized in a climate of fear triggered by a false flag operation, in which the people willingly surrendered their rights, and legislatures and judiciaries capitulated to executive power. A multi-year process of legislating tyranny was set in motion, its apparent lawfulness fooling most people into believing in the endurance of liberal constitutionalism. What is taking place, now as then, is a revolution from above—a top-down remaking of society to serve ruling class interests, conspicuous by its attacks on the working and middle classes. *Gleichschaltung*—the production of ideological conformity—is a striking feature of both ages, with the citizenry, the professions, the churches, the Left, and the trade unions all immediately falling into line with official ideology and offering virtually no resistance for fear of being "switched off" (fired, censored, shut down, etc.). Centralized control of the media in both eras has resulted in the people being barraged with propaganda; the media space has become a war zone. Health surveillance is another common feature, with so-called "health [vaccine] passports" forming part of an attempt to hoover up health data *en masse* for eugenics purposes. "Covid-19" witnessed the return of euthanasia and eugenics in novel forms, not least in the worldwide medical experiment that was the "vaccine" rollout—all premised on pseudoscience, like Nazi eugenics. Nazi propaganda created a "new moral order" that justified discrimination and persecution; similar was witnessed during the "Covid-19" era. A bogus ecopolitics is common to both eras. Notwithstanding some important discontinuities, the powerful historical affinities between the two eras are almost certainly not coincidental.

The Seizure of Power

The response to the "Covid-19 pandemic" has much in common with the birth of the Third Reich. Agamben (2021, p. 8), for instance, sees parallels between the emergency legislation passed in 2020, which involved the suspension of constitutional guarantees, and the Reichstag Fire Decree, issued by President Hindenburg on the advice of Chancellor Hitler on February 28, 1933, which invoked Article 48 to suspend numerous basic rights previously protected by the Weimar Constitution (Shirer, 1991, p. 194).

Although that decree "suspended all basic citizen protections" (Epstein, 2015, p. 66), this was done in the name of "protecting" the public: its proper title was the Decree for the Protection of People and State. Hitler justified curtailment of freedoms as "protection against disorder"; political opponents were taken into "protective custody"; and the media characterized Nazi terror (mass arrests, concentration camps, etc.) as "protective" (Koonz, 2003, pp. 98–102). In 2020, similarly, tyrannical measures were enacted around the world in the name of "protecting" the public against "Covid-19." In Germany, of all places, Interior Senator Andreas Geisel deemed that abrogating the people's constitutional rights to freedom of assembly, free speech, and to petition their government, was a matter of "protecting the public health," as codified under the Infection Protection Act of November 2020 (Hopkins, 2020a).

The Reichstag fire, an act of arson against the home of the German parliament in 1933, was almost certainly a false flag operation, to be blamed on communists as alleged enemies of the state (Shirer, 1991, p. 192; Klemperer,

1999, p. 5; Hett, 2014; Sutton, 2016, pp. 118–19). In the six days between the fire and the federal election on March 5, 1933, an atmosphere of terror was created as truckloads of storm troopers all over Germany rounded up victims and transported them to S.A. barracks, where many were tortured and beaten (Schirer, 1991, p. 194). In March 2020, populations around the world were terrorized through other, less obvious means, i.e. military-grade propaganda about a killer virus. The threat was grotesquely exaggerated through various means to make people fear for their lives and the lives of loved ones (Hughes, 2024, Chapter 4), and the declared state of emergency was sustained through psychological warfare (van der Pijl, 2022a, p. 25).

The imposition of authority in a climate of fear is an effective model. Erich Fromm, a Jewish psychoanalyst who left Germany after the Nazis came to power, was astounded by the millions of Germans who were "as eager to surrender their freedom as their fathers were to fight for it" (Fromm, 1942, p. 2). Ordinary Germans in 1933, without being forced, rapidly submitted to the process of *Gleichschaltung*, or self-imposed conformity (Epstein, 2015, p. 60; Gellately, 1991, p. 137). The social response to "Covid-19" was marked by a similarly astonishing level of voluntary conformity. Agamben (2021, p. 17), for instance, was astounded at how much the populace was willing to sacrifice: life conditions, social relationships, work, friendships, even political and religious convictions.

The Enabling Act was passed by a vote of 441 to 94, formally turning Germany into a dictatorship. In this way, "The Reichstag *stripped itself of its powers—a supreme act of democratic self-abnegation.* Hitler could now rule Germany free of parliamentary control" (Epstein, 2015, p. 56, my emphasis). Or, as US historian William Shirer (1991, p. 199) puts it, the German Parliament "committed suicide" in 1933, though its embalmed corpse lingered on until 1945. In 2020, similarly, the UK Parliament, like parliaments across the world, capitulated to executive power in a "most remarkable abdication" of it constitutional functions, according to former QC Lord Sumption (2020, p. 11). Although the UK Coronavirus Act grants the Government "coercive powers over citizens on a scale never previously attempted" (Sumption, 2020, p. 1), Parliament repeatedly voted—or did not even bother to vote (Steerpike, 2021)—for its renewal. For all intents and purposes, the Government was handed supreme executive power, and the UK effectively became a one-party state (Davis, 2021a). The UK's "dead parrot Parliament" (Hitchens, 2020) nevertheless lingers on, so as to maintain the facade of democracy "until the very end, even during the seizure of power" (van der Pijl, 2022a, p. 76).

Judges who had sworn an oath of allegiance to the Nazi Party strove to anticipate the will of the Führer and thereby went above and beyond what they were legally obliged to do (Müller, 1991, pp. xvii-xviii). As the practice of law became Nazified, those charged with upholding the law were, paradoxically, "complicit in its subversion" (Epstein, 2015, p. 67). We see a similar process unfolding today in the willingness of judges to uphold the constitutionality of "lockdown" measures, which represent the most egregious attack on liberal constitutionalism in history. The Irish Supreme Court, for example, ruled that such measures were constitutional (O'Faolain, 2022), while in Canada, they were ruled to be "not unconstitutional" and "justified as reasonable limits in a free and democratic society" (Ingram v. Alberta, 2023). In early 2024, Master Richard Davison of the High Court of Justice in England passed a summary judgment against investigative journalist and film maker Richard D. Hall prohibiting him from presenting evidence challenging the state account of the Manchester Arena incident of 2017, evidencing a legal system that is "neither fair nor just and serves only to protect and serve the government and other powerful interests" (Davis, 2024).

Legislating Totalitarianism

Once in power, the Nazis were able to pass law after law as they built a totalitarian state over the course of many years, as documented by independent researcher and author Simon Elmer (as in Wilson, 2022). Those who denounce comparisons between the global biosecurity state being built today and Nazi Germany, Elmer recognizes, not only fail to see that the former is not *yet* as bad as the latter proved to be, but are also blind to how totalitarian states are constructed in law. Davis (2021a) warns that, through a raft of legislation being rammed through Parliament while the population's attention is focused elsewhere, the UK is being turned into a constitutional dictatorship.

In Nazi Germany, "defense of the state" could be used as justification for breaking the law, whereby the courts let the most serious crimes go unpunished (Müller, 1991, p. 81). Under the UK Covert Human Intelligence (Criminal Conduct) Act (2021), fourteen government agencies have the mandate to commit crimes with impunity under certain circumstances—an obvious slippery slope.

The Nazi police state is notorious for its abuses: quite apart from the Gestapo, state police could attack political enemies with impunity (Epstein, 2015, p. 57). Police brutality against those protesting the "Covid-19 countermeasures" was worldwide (Broudy et al., 2022), whereas other protests did not meet with the same treatment, evidencing politicized policing (Malet, 2023). The UK Public Order Act (2023) expands police powers to deal with protests to such an extent that the United Nations High Commissioner for Human Rights calls for its repeal because it is likely to have a "profoundly chilling effect on civic freedoms" (Türk, 2023).

The Malicious Practices Act, passed on March 31, 1933, criminalized telling jokes, or making negative remarks, about the Nazi regime (Epstein, 2015, p. 67). In our own time, prominent German dissidents have been arrested and/or charged on spurious grounds, including Michael Ballweg (Beppler-Spahl, 2023), C.J. Hopkins (Hopkins, 2023a, 2023b), and Reiner Fuellmich (Harrity, 2023). The Nuremberg Public Prosecutor's Office even has a case open against Holocaust survivor Vera Sharav for speaking out against the "Covid-19 vaccination" campaign outside the Nuremberg Palace of Justice (site of the Nuremberg Trials) in August 2022 (Alschner, 2023).

So-called "asocials" in Nazi Germany, i.e., those "unwilling to adapt to the life of the community," were criminalized for "deviant, but not illegal, conduct" (Epstein, 2015, p. 87). In 2020, those who "violated community guidelines" on social media had their accounts restricted or permanently suspended. Today's "deviant, but not illegal" is what Twitter/X CEO Linda Yaccarino calls "lawful but awful" (Bergman, 2023), which is being used to render politically subversive content online largely invisible ("freedom of speech, not reach"). The UK Online Safety Act (2023) provides similar means to censor dissent: all that is required is that Ofcom (the government-approved communications regulator) label the content "harmful." The path to criminalizing dissent is clear.

One of Hitler's rhetorical strategies was to project his Jew-hatred onto his victims, who, he claimed, planned to "wage a battle for life and death" in the "final struggle" against the Third Reich (Koonz, 2003, p. 100), whereas the reality was the "Final Solution." Since 2020, the Western media has sought to frame dissidents, including "vaccine" skeptics, as far right extremists, Islamists, and terrorists (Hopkins, 2020b; Bentham, 2020; Fleet Street Fox, 2021). *Anyone* accused of undermining British institutions and values—i.e. any dissident—could be regarded as an "extremist" under UK Government proposals (Ungoed-Thomas & Townsend, 2023).

In the early years of the Third Reich, life in many ways appeared to go on as normal: "elections took place, city councils convened, and Reichstag delegates debated" (Koonz, 2003, p. 72). The Weimar Constitution was suspended but not revoked. Civil servants without Jewish ancestry or Marxist affiliations continued to work at the same offices. The Nazi dictatorship parasitically functioned "within the framework of the public culture it destroyed" (Koonz, 2003, p. 72). Although constitutional government had been done away with, most of the German population retained its belief in the "constitutional state," i.e. "a government which was subject to law" (Müller, 1991, p. 71). Similar is true today. Most of the public retains a belief in a liberal constitutionalism that is, in fact, dead and unable to offer it any meaningful protection. As in 1930s Germany, the "façade of politics as usual" masks the steady maturation of totalitarianism, with national security agencies, mass surveillance, propaganda, and the suspension of basic rights all being drastically expanded while politicians and so-called journalists appear not to notice (van der Pijl, 2022b).

Revolution from Above

National Socialism was born in reaction to the threat of revolution in the wake of the 1929 Wall Street crash and the Great Depression. Major industrialists financed Hitler, because National Socialism, in their eyes, promised to deliver against communism, socialism, and the trade unions (Shirer, 1991, p. 126). Events since 2020 have, once more, been a response to a major crisis of capitalism, only this time with a far higher degree of transnational coordination in the response. In 2019, following a decade of austerity, major protests erupted in one in five countries, involving "unprecedented political mobilization" (Wright, 2019). These uncontainable social tensions, according to van der Pijl (2022a, p. 72), were what triggered the "Covid-19" counterrevolution in 2020, the signs of revolution being too serious for the transnational ruling class to ignore.

The National Socialist project was a revolution from above—a top-down remaking of society to serve elite interests. As Hitler declared in 1934, "The German revolution will be concluded only when the entire German *Volk* has been totally created anew, reorganized and reconstructed" (cited in Koonz, 2003, p. 87). The "Great Reset," announced by World Economic Forum (WEF) director Klaus Schwab, son of Nazi industrialist Eugen Schwab, attempts the same thing on a global scale, promising to "revamp all aspects of our societies and economies, from education to social contracts and working conditions. Every country [. . .] must participate, and every industry [. . .] must be transformed" (Schwab, 2020).

The revolution from above requires that the working class remains poor and exploitable. In Nazi Germany, despite near full employment being reached in 1936, real wage levels in 1929 were not reached again until 1941. Income levels were consistently suppressed through higher goods prices, wage freezes, increased taxes, and forced savings (Epstein, 2015, pp. 106–107). Correspondingly, on a global scale, the 2020 "lockdowns" represented an historic assault on the working class. In the UK, over two million families were driven into poverty, doubling the previous number (Butler, 2020). 70,000 UK households were made homeless in the first ten months of the "pandemic" (Jayanetti, 2021). BlackRock (2019) knew *before* the "pandemic" that, "in the long run, the growth of money supply drives inflation." The inevitable high inflation resulting from Western monetary policy in 2020 (and *not* the war in Ukraine), manifesting in double-digit levels in the UK in 2022/23 (Rate Inflation, n.d.), vastly outstripping real income growth, and hitting mortgages, food, and fuel, is financially punishing all but the wealthiest.

The Nazis sought to substitute individual property rights with the principle of "*Gemeinnutz vor Eigennutz*" (communal use over personal use) (Uekötter, 2005, p. 103). The Nazi Food and Agriculture Minister, R.W. Darré, claimed that the Germanic idea of property combined the right of usufruct and inheritance in exchange for service rendered to the community, reminiscent of feudal relations (Koehl, 1972, p. 156). Fast-forward to the present, and we find a similar neo-feudalist mindset in the World Economic Forum's technocratic "own nothing and be happy" ethos. The Mises Institute notes that the WEF wants to "lead the world into a new era without property or privacy" (Mueller, 2020).

Totalitarianism demands the subordination of all individual rights and interests to "the common good." In Nazi Germany, the concept of *Volksgemeinschaft* (national community) promoted the collective over individual rights (Epstein, 2015, p. 107). As per Point 10 of the Nazi 25-Point Plan, "The activities of the individual must not clash with the general interest, but must proceed within the framework of the community and be for the general good." Correspondingly, the WEF's Schwab and Malleret

(2020, p. 87) claim that the "pandemic" forced everyone into "a philosophical debate about how to maximize the common good."

The Attack on the Middle Class

Hitler originally appealed to members of the lower middle classes who had twice been ruined—by the inflation of 1923, and by the effects of the Wall Street crash of 1929 (Huxley, 1958, p. 42). He received significant support from small- and medium-sized businesses (Turner, 1972, pp. 98–99). Yet, a fifth of such businesses disappeared under laws passed in 1937, which dissolved all corporations with capital beneath a certain threshold (Shirer, 1991, p. 262). In contrast, legislation for "compulsory cartels" was passed as early as July 15, 1933, and Big Business, deemed too big to fail, received substantial support from the state (Turner, 1972, p. 99)—not least in the form of slave labor in concentration camps, the kind of arrangement Eugen Schwab benefited from at Escher Wyss. Nazism promoted the most powerful German industrialists at the expense of all other classes (Fromm, 1942, p. 188).

Schwab and Malleret knew no later than June 2020 (and probably much earlier, given the implausibly narrow three-month window between the WHO "pandemic" declaration and the publication of their book) that small businesses would "suffer disproportionately" owing to the impact of "lockdowns" (i.e. reduced trade, closures, bankruptcies, etc.) while big businesses would get bigger (2020, p.134–135). So it proved as big businesses were deemed "essential" and allowed to stay open, while small businesses were subjected to punishing restrictions (Rectenwald, 2021).

The result was that wealth and power were transferred from the middle class to those with political power and connections (Roth, 2021). While workers lost $3.7 trillion in 2020, the billionaire class gained $3.9 trillion (Gutentag, 2021). The world's richest ten people reportedly grew half a trillion dollars richer (Newman, 2021). In September 2020, Jeff Bezos could have paid all 876,000 Amazon employees a $105,000 bonus and still have been as wealthy as he was before March 2020 (Todhunter, 2021). The United States gained 56 new billionaires in 2020 (White, 2020). By October 2021, the top 1 percent of US earners were richer than the entire middle class, defined as the middle 60 percent of US households by income (Tanzi & Dorning, 2021).

Gleichschaltung

Gleichschaltung is a term without equivalent in other languages, but can loosely be translated as "Nazification," "coordination," "integration," and "bringing into line" (Koonz, 2003, p. 72). *Gleichschaltung* is about synchronizing "virtually all areas of life" (Epstein, 2015, p. 57) and achieving "ideological coordination and uniformity in politics, culture, and private communication" (Hopkins, 2020a). It accords with Mussolini's (1932) slogan "All within the state, none outside the state, none against the state." It means that all citizens must align their speech and behavior with official narratives.

In the Third Reich, the professions were Nazified, e.g. by dismissing Jews and Communists, via the establishment of new institutions such as the Academy of German Law and the Reich Institute for the History of the new Germany, or by taking control of existing institutions (Weinreich, 1946, pp. 17–18). In 2020, similarly, the professions all fell into line with the official "Covid-19" narrative, thereby demonstrating a moral collapse of spectacular proportions. Scientists, academics, and lawyers collaborated with authoritarianism to help implement and legitimize a biosecurity state that removes human rights and civil liberties (Elmer, 2021). Media commentators called for censorship of those not toeing the official line, philosophy professors sought to justify mass internment, and human rights organizations had no objection to "vaccine passports" (Kingsnorth, 2021). Jurists allowed health dictats to form the basis of juridical norms (Agamben, 2021, p. 36). The medical profession removed licenses from dissenting doctors, threatened its members not to speak out, and abandoned medical ethics ("first do no harm") when it came to the "vaccines" (Blaylock, 2022).

The churches offered no meaningful resistance to National Socialism. In 1933, most of Germany's Protestant pastors, being part of a conservative elite, supported Hitler's nationalism, antisemitism, and anti-Marxism (Epstein, 2015, pp. 113–114). So did Germany's Catholic clergy, having abandoned its pre-1933 stance of opposition to National Socialism. The July 1933 Concordat with the Vatican saw the latter agree to ban Catholics from political activity in Germany in exchange for freedom to practice their faith. The moral failure of the churches was again evident during the "Covid-19" crisis. The Catholic Church, led by a pope named Francis, apparently forget that St. Francis embraced lepers and that visiting the sick is a work of mercy, as it followed the new countermeasures (Agamben, 2021, p. 36). Religious buildings closed their doors, zealously enforced "Covid rules" (Hookham, 2021), and even turned themselves into "vaccination" centers (spectacularly, in the case of Salisbury Cathedral). The Archbishop of Canterbury advised "to love one another—as Jesus said—get vaccinated, get boosted" (cited in Newman & Wright, 2021).

The political Left failed spectacularly to prevent the rise of National Socialism. In the last free federal election in November 1932, the KPD and SPD jointly received 1.5 million votes more than the Nazis, winning 221 of a total 584 seats, vs. 196 for the NSDAP. The Nazi share of the vote had fallen from 37 percent in July 1932 to 33 percent in November that year. Had the SPD and KPD formed a united front against fascism, they could have prevented the Nazis from coming to power. Instead, they remained enemies, and the resultant split in the labor movement at a time of deep capitalist crisis drove more and more workers into the arms of the Nazis (Wilde, 2013). Similarly, today, the Left's abject failure to oppose the global biosecurity state represents a momentous historical failure as ignominious as its failure to stop the rise of fascism a century ago (Elmer, 2022). Well-known "leftists" and "left-wing" publications had barely a word to say against the overtly fascistic measures being rolled out under the pretext of combatting a disease (Miller, 2021b, 2022). On the contrary, supposed champions of the working class were found arguing for mass unemployment, business closures, and draconian police powers (Knightly, 2020), as well as discriminatory "vaccine" mandates and "health passes" (Goldberg, 2021). Even when millions of people around the world marched against the unfolding attack on their fundamental rights, the Left doubled down on its betrayal of the working class, e.g. by following the mainstream media in portraying protestors as "far right" and "fascist" (Workers League, 2022).

The trade unions failed to provide any meaningful resistance to National Socialism. The Confederation of German Trade Unions had already separated itself from the SPD over three months before Hitler became Chancellor and by May 1, 1933, was marching under the swastika. That did not prevent its dissolution, however, after the Nazis stormed trade union offices the following day. The German Labor Front, a Nazi organization, replaced the trade unions: its purpose was not to advocate for working class Germans, but, rather, to show them how National Socialism improved their lives, e.g. through collective consumption programs such as the "people's car"—though no Volkswagen was ever manufactured for private use under the Nazis (Epstein, 2015, pp. 108, 111). During the "Covid-19" crisis, trade unions proved similarly impotent, repeatedly getting behind the official line and pressing for harmful measures. UK school and university unions, for instance, called for educational institutions to be closed and for teaching to move online in a second national lockdown ("Covid-19: PM announces four-week England lockdown," 2020). The impact on young people's mental health, the detriment to education, the predictable increase in rates of child abuse, etc. were ignored. The Met Police Federation (the closest thing to a trade union, which is not allowed for police) demanded that frontline officers be prioritized for "Covid-19 vaccination" (Saunt & Vincent, 2021). The Communication Workers Union refuses to respond to an open letter demanding that it rescind its support for "Covid-19 vaccines" in the face of extensive evidence that they are harming its members (Real Left, 2023).

University professors were among the most vocal supporters of the Nazis (Koonz, 2003, p. 194). The Jewish diarist Victor Klemperer (1999, p. 237) wrote in 1937 that "the intelligentsia and the scholars prostitute themselves." The economist Wilhelm Röpke (2008, p. 73) reflected in 1945 that academia in the Third Reich had become "a scene of prostitution that [had] stained the honourable history of German learning." The Jewish linguist Max Weinreich (1946, p. 7) notes that the worst culprits were those "of long and high standing, university professors and academy members, some of them world famous." Sadly, academia risks going down a similar path today:

> To sway the American people to accept lockdowns, professors with prestigious titles and affiliations denied scientific data about risks, effective mitigation, and biological protection. They spouted politicized opinion as if it were objective truth and demonized views counter to their preferred narrative. (Atlas, 2022)

Astonished and confused by academics' response to "Covid-19," US libertarian Jeffrey Tucker (2023) asks a pertinent question: "Why the craven deference to power? Why the silence in the face of outrage?" Most North American universities forced staff and students to take an experimental substance into their bodies, with no safety data beyond a few months, as a condition of being allowed on campus—a grotesque violation of the Nuremberg Code.

In sum, since 2020, we have witnessed the same kind of moral collapse across Western institutions as took place in Nazi Germany. The professions bend over backwards to collaborate with authoritarianism, doctors violate medical ethics, churches do not put Christian values first, the "Left" and the unions abandon the working class, academics forsake the truth, etc. Western civilization is being plunged into crisis.

Ausschaltung

The flip-side of *Gleichschaltung* is *Ausschaltung*—"switching off." In Nazi Germany, "undesirables" such as Marxists, non-"Aryans," and the disabled were "switched off," in the sense of being "banished from mainstream society" (Koonz, 2003, p. 72). This ranged from ostracization and censorship to persecution and murder. In the early days of the Third Reich, the key enforcement mechanism was through institutions, which were given an ultimatum: "*Gleichschaltung* or dissolution" (Koonz, 2003, p. 73). Officers had to belong to the Nazi Party, agendas required Nazi approval, and non-"Aryans" had to be removed, or else the organization could be closed down. So, for example, when the "Aryan Paragraph" (intended to exclude Jews from public life) entered Nazi law on April 7, 1933, stipulating that "Civil servants who are not of Aryan descent are to be retired," other organizations voluntarily followed suit by introducing an Aryan clause for membership (United States Holocaust Memorial Museum, n.d.).

In the early days of the "Covid-19" crisis, businesses and other organizations were told to "follow government guidelines." The threat of being "switched off" was palpable as those institutions deemed "non-essential" were ordered to close. In the United States, as elsewhere, the impact on unemployment was catastrophic in the short term, with the unemployment rate hitting 13.2 percent in May 2020 (by far the highest on record) (FRED, n.d.-a); US GDP levels also suffered a dramatic short-term contraction (FRED, n.d.-b). Headlines appeared in the corporate media such as "Half of world's workers 'at immediate risk of losing livelihood due to coronavirus'" (Inman, 2020). Here was a powerful disciplining device: threatening companies and workers with loss of their livelihoods lest they toe the line by becoming "Covid-compliant." There was no underlying economic weakness: US unemployment levels returned to pre-"pandemic" levels (ca. 3.6 percent) by 2022 (FRED, n.d.-a).

In the information space, there were various means of "switching people off" in Nazi Germany, from book burnings and censorship to driving dissenting news media out of business; self-censorship quickly became the norm (Koonz, 2003, p. 71). On May 10, 1933, students in nineteen university towns burned some twenty thousand books in an "Action against the Un-German Spirit" (Epstein, 2015, p. 59). The Nazi occupation of the Netherlands was accompanied by a Regulation "to protect the Dutch population from untrue news" (Delpher, n.d.). Dissenting voices were discredited as "foreign-influenced" (Koonz, 2003, p. 102).

Today, the mechanisms are more varied, but the chilling effect on free speech is the same. Scientific evidence which challenged the official "Covid-19" narrative was systematically suppressed and dissenting scientists were smeared (Bhattacharya, 2023). Medical professionals who spoke out were stripped of their license to practice, recalling the persecution of Jewish physicians in Nazi Germany (Haque et al., 2012, p. 474). As Dr. Francis Christian told a disciplinary panel at the University of Saskatchewan, "These are the types of panels that were set up in the Soviet Union and Nazi Germany [. . .] It's really disturbing that because I call for informed consent, I am not allowed to practise" (Justice Centre for Constitutional Freedoms, 2021). Big Tech companies (including payment processors) censor or shadow-ban virtually all information that contradicts official narratives. So-called "fact checkers" act as narrative enforcers and flak machines. Dissent is systematically branded "mis/disinformation" and "fake news." Those concerned with defending bodily autonomy against invasive state overreach are stigmatized as "anti-vaxxers." "Woke culture" is used to cancel and deplatform ("you cannot say that"), rather than debate. Alternative platforms, such as Parler, Telegram, and Bitchute, have either been put out of business or seem likely to be heavily censored under legislation such as the UK Online Safety Act. Anything which challenges official narratives is dismissed as foreign (typically Russian) disinformation.

Propaganda

Despite Goebbels' boasts that the press was free to report as it saw fit, it was coordinated via a press trust which "reported" stories planted by the Nazis, putting various spins on them to create the illusion that the information was not all coming from the same source (Digital Citizen, 2003). Moreover, by 2003, there was "no practical difference" between this arrangement and the "Anglo-American media and entertainment cartel." For example, just five mega-corporations own virtually all print media, film studios, and televisions and radio stations in the United States, and despite surface competition between them, they act as one when it comes to the "purpose of their cartel" (Bagdikian, 2004, pp. 3–5).

In recent years, the media cartel has become globalized. One need only look at the WEF's list of "Media, Entertainment, and Information Partners" on its website to get a flavor of this. One of those partners is Omnicom, used by the G7 to provide what Davis (2021b) calls "the approved *single version of the truth*." Another example is the disingenuously titled "Trusted News Initiative" (TNI) convened by the BBC in the summer of 2019 and described by Davis as "a global media cartel." The TNI arrogates to itself the right to determine what is true or not, and it censors dissenting voices, no matter how credentialled (Woodworth, 2022). The Global Alliance for Responsible Media (GARM), founded alongside the TNI, seeks to prevent monetization of what it subjectively determines to be "harmful" content. The result of these developments, witnessed during "Covid," was an unprecedented level of global media coordination and propaganda.

The head of the Nazi Press Division (1938–1942), Hans Fritzsche, testified in 1946 that "the German news agencies received a ten-fold increase in their budget from the Reich" (Office of United States Chief of Counsel for Prosecution of Axis Criminality, 1946, pp. 1041–1042). This was one mechanism by which the media came under the control of the Nazi state. Fritzsche called the shots: he "personally gave to the representatives of the principal German newspapers the 'daily parole of the Reich Press Chief'" and acted as "the principal conspirator directly concerned with the manipulations of the press." In 2020, the "pandemic" saw advertising revenues plunge and governments massively increase their advertising expenditure. The UK Government, for example, went from 30th on the list of UK newspaper advertisers by expenditure in 2019 to "the nation's largest advertiser across all media" in 2020 (Edward, 2021). This effectively placed the media under state control when it came to "Covid-19."

For Goebbels, the aim of propaganda was to make the people "think uniformly, react uniformly, and place themselves body and soul at the disposal of the government" (Epstein, 2015, p. 59). This could not be achieved by producing uniform propaganda, however: in fact, Goebbels complained that journalists did not rewrite his propaganda handouts thoroughly enough and that different newspapers sounded the same (Becker, 1949, p. 226). Similarly, the challenge for syndicated news media today is how to avoid the public realizing that all new items come from the same handful of agencies (AP, AFP, Reuters).

Comparing subtle persuasion to a gas, Goebbels claimed: "The best propaganda is that which, as it were, works invisibly, penetrates the whole of life without the public having any knowledge of the propagandistic initiative" (cited in Koonz, 2003, p. 13). Before Covid, this largely seemed to have been achieved. Pilger (2016), for instance, reflects: "In my career as a journalist and filmmaker, I have never known propaganda to insinuate our lives as it does now and to go unchallenged."

Since 2020, however, the propaganda has been blatant. On April 17, 2020, all UK national newspapers ran with the same "stay at home" front page messaging (expressed as "Stay" followed by an @ icon inside a house symbol), linked to an image of a rainbow. On May 14, 2020, all the same newspapers ran with the headline "Stay Alert" beneath a rainbow. In September 2020, they all ran the same front page displaying a computer-generated hand holding a smartphone, encouraging readers to download a "Covid-19" surveillance app. On December 20, 2020, they all ran with the same "Get boosted now" front page. The day envisaged by Becker (1949, p. 226), whereby "totalitarian control of information will reach the point where all newspapers handle the news in almost identical fashion," apparently had arrived.

According to Hitler's Minister for Armaments, Albert Speer, the radio and the loudspeaker were used to deprive eighty million people of independent thought, allowing the Nazi dictatorship to dominate the minds of the population (cited in Huxley, 1958, p. 38). By 1939, 70 percent of German households had a radio (mostly the cheap VE [People's Receiver] 301), and 6,000 loudspeakers in factories and public spaces meant that Nazi propaganda was near ubiquitous, although the novelty of hearing Hitler's voice soon wore off (Epstein, 2015, p. 59).

Today, the technologies are more advanced, including the television, the cinema, and, most addictively, social media (although loudspeakers were used in Ireland and the Netherlands to blare out Covid propaganda [Hugo Talks, 2021]). The goal of completely indoctrinating the population, however, remains the same. This has been particularly true since the Smith-Mundt Modernization Act (2012), whose changes to the Smith-Mundt Act (1948) removed the main legal barrier to propagandizing the US citizenry as though it were a foreign enemy. CIA influence on the media, Valentine (2017, p. 27) recognizes, amounts to "political warfare directed against the American public." It has become particularly evident since 2020 that the so-called "Fourth Estate" in fact serves as a Fifth Column, i.e. a subversive element, run by an unpatriotic transnational oligarchy, seeking to dominate public perception and opinion.

The transformation of the information space into a war zone has been evident in the UK as elsewhere. The UK Fusion Doctrine means that "strategic communications are to be considered with the same seriousness as financial or military options" (Aiken, 2018). The Government's Counter-Disinformation Unit was set up in March 2020, and the Government refuses to provide even basic details about it (Trendall, 2022). In April 2020, General Sir Nick Carter admitted that 3,000–4,000 77th Brigade personnel were involved in countering "misinformation" and "disinformation" but that 20,000 were available if necessary (Robinson, 2020). In June 2020, the 13th Signal Regiment was refounded as "the British Army's brand new cyber regiment" (Ministry of Defence, 2020). In November 2020, GCHQ was reportedly told to "take out antivaxers online" (Fisher & Smyth, 2020).

Hitler (1939, p. 148) writes that "all effective propaganda must be confined to a few [. . .] slogans [which] should be persistently repeated," a principle successfully operationalized by Goebbels (Weaver et al., 2006, p. 10). During the "Covid-19" operation, the same propaganda phrases were repeated incessantly: "flatten the curve," "new normal," "build back better," "follow the science," "trust the experts," "protect others," etc. At the end of the July 31, 2020 Downing Street press conference, the British Prime Minister turned to the Chief Medical Officer and muttered, "I think I repeated that often enough." On December 12, 2021, he used the words "booster" and "boosted" eight times each, plus "vaccination" four times in one short speech (Dodsworth, 2021).

Paraphrasing Hitler, Huxley (1958, pp. 44–5) writes that the propagandist must be systematically one-sided, never admitting the possibility of error; opponents are not to be argued with, but instead attacked, shouted down, and liquidated if necessary. Refusing to argue with opponents remains the hallmark of contemporary propaganda: dissent is labelled "dangerous" or simply "false"; dissenters are not rationally engaged or debated; instead, they are removed from public view, so as to maintain the illusion of an "inviolable, official 'reality,'" any deviation from which may incur punishment (Hopkins, 2021b).

A German philologist reflected in 1954 that Nazi propaganda kept the people continuously distracted with "continuous changes and 'crises,'" as well as the "machinations of [. . .] 'national enemies,' without and within," leaving "no time to think about these dreadful things that were growing, little by little, all around us," paving the way for the descent into barbarism (cited in Mayer, 2017, pp. 167–8). Similar is true today: Western propaganda barrages the population with crisis after crisis, enemy after enemy, e.g. terrorism, financial crisis, the "climate emergency," the threat of "pandemics," Russia/Ukraine, the specter of nuclear war, the "cost of living" crisis, Israel/Palestine, and on and on. The population does not notice the global technocratic coup gradually unfolding, or consider where it might lead and why it must therefore be put down before it is too late.

With all these similarities between Nazi and contemporary propaganda, it is little wonder that veteran propaganda specialist Mark Crispin Miller (2021a, 30:00) reflects: "I used to think it tasteless to compare our system to Nazi Germany. I no longer think so."

Health Surveillance

As early as 1926, there were calls for "health passports" containing hereditary information to be made compulsory in Germany (Ehrenreich, 2007, p. 42). "Health passports" became a reality in the Third Reich. By 1934, physicians would fill out a standardized form after every patient examination and, without the patient's knowledge, send it to the health office, where the results were transferred onto index cards and collected centrally at the Central Health Passport Archive (Aly & Roth, 2004, p. 107). The health passport contained data concerning a person's health and work suitability, and was made available to all state agencies, to aid the state's "complete control of personal life conduct" (Fahrenkrug, 1991, p. 329). Today, so-called "vaccine passports" are being pushed via initiatives such as the CommonPass, the Common Trust Network, the Vaccination Credential Initiative, the Global Health Pass Initiative, the EU Digital Covid Certificate (first envisaged in 2019, i.e. pre-"Covid" [European Commission, 2019, p. 1]), and the WHO global digital vaccine certification standards. Most of these are funded by the World Economic Forum, the Rockefeller Foundation, and/or the Bill & Melinda Gates Foundation. Their aim is to facilitate biopolitical control over the world's population.

Every health office in the Third Reich was ordered to set up centers for "genetic and racial care," which were tasked with constructing a comprehensive "genetic-biological map" of the entire Reich (Proctor, 1988, p. 135). Today, advances in genomics promise exponentially greater social control, and an attempt appears to be underway to harvest the genetic data of the population. In 2018, Schwab proposed public-private data-sharing agreements "allowing data sharing that would be illegal under normal circumstances," but which could be activated "under pre-agreed emergency circumstances (such as a pandemic)" (Schwab & Davis, 2018, p. 106). In 2020, a "pandemic" arrived as though on cue, and the Rockefeller Foundation (2020, p. 6) recommended that digital health records be used to improve Covid-19 diagnosis and treatment. The Rockefeller Foundation is behind CommonHealth, which allows people to share their electronic health record data with "health apps and partners that have demonstrated their trustworthiness" (Commons Project, 2019).

The NHS (n.d.) told patients in 2020: "your information may be used for coronavirus research purposes even if you have chosen not to share it"—a rank violation of patient confidentiality. In July 2021, the UK Government implemented what the Doctors Association UK described as an "unlawful" plan to carry out the "largest seizure of GP data in NHS history" (Mohamoud, 2021). That data, according to NHS Digital (n.d.), provides "the most reliable evidence on which to base decisions on health-care planning and delivery"—a rationale not unlike the one offered in Nazi Germany, where health data collection was officially to facilitate "planning the health of the population" (Proctor, 1988, p. 135). Since 2020, the NHS has partnered with the CIA-linked data analysis company, Palantir (Campbell, 2023).

Even before "Covid-19," companies such as Ancestry and 23andMe were harvesting genomic data from an unsuspecting public as millions of people worldwide voluntarily submitted DNA samples in exchange for information about their ancestry, failing to heed the terms and conditions regarding how their data might be used (Broze, 2021). In December 2020, the private equity giant Blackstone (2020) bought Ancestry for $4.7 billion, thus acquiring its massive database of customers' genetic information. Companies such as DnaNudge now use swab tests to extract genetic information that is used to tailor product recommendations to the customer.

Private access to the public's genetic data greatly increased during the "pandemic," with companies such as China's BGI Group selling millions of "Covid-19" test kits and genetic sequencing services worldwide (Wertheim, 2021). California-based Illumina was awarded contracts for genome sequencing worth a combined £870,000 from Public Health England (Williams, 2021). Cignpost Diagnostics, a UK Government-approved PCR test supplier, reportedly intended to sell swabs carrying customers' DNA to third parties (Stephens, 2021). Bill Gates (2020) recommends LumiraDx, which offers a rapid, non-FDA-approved test that uploads the results to a central server within fifteen minutes. All of which begs the question: "What regulatory framework and safeguards are in place to ensure that private companies carrying out PCR tests are not able to access individuals' personal genomic information? And who owns the data?" (Menage, 2020).

DNA mapping of the population has a potential military application, for a worldwide DNA database could give those in charge of it a "horrifying weapon [. . .] to target literally anyone they wanted" (Light, 2017). Designer medicine is all well and good, neurobiologist Charles Morgan (2018, 28:32) tells West Point cadets, but the flip side is that "you can engineer anything, you can engineer even a unique thing that would only kill one person in the world." The more genomic data that is harvested, the likelier genetically targeted bioweapons become.

Euthanasia

The origins of Nazi genocide can be traced back to earlier euthanasia programs (Friedlander, 1995). The Nazi extermination of Jews, Gypsies, and homosexuals during the war years was foreshadowed by the state-sanctioned sterilization and later "mercy killing" of people with disabilities (Mostert, 2002). The "life not worthy of life" concept, which found expression in the

1933 Law for the Prevention of Hereditarily Diseased Offspring, formed the basis of the "supreme duty of a national state to grant life and livelihood only to the healthy and hereditarily sound portion of the people," to quote Nazi Public Health Director Arthur Guett (cited in Ehret, 2021).

It is troubling, therefore, that euthanasia resurfaced in spring 2020, for instance, when Conservative MP Luke Evans asked Health Secretary Matt Hancock whether the NHS had enough syringe drivers, midazolam, and morphine to be able to provide a "good death" (a euphemism for euthanasia) for patients (Health and Social Care Committee, 2020). French company Accord Healthcare had just sold two years' worth of midazolam stock to UK wholesalers at the request of the NHS in March 2020 (Wickware, 2020). There was a huge spike in the prescription of midazolam hydrochloride in GP practices across NHS England in April 2020 (OpenPrescribing, n.d.).

National Institute of Clinical Excellence (NICE) guideline NG163 (published April 3, 2020) recommends: "When managing key symptoms of COVID-19 in the last hours and days of life, follow the relevant parts of NICE guideline [NG31] on care of dying adults in the last days of life (NICE, 2020). This includes pharmacological interventions and anticipatory prescribing." Concerned doctors pointed out, however, that NG31 (2015) is aimed at people likely to die imminently from advanced diseases (Ahmedzai et al., 2020). NG163, in its original formulation, thus tacitly encouraged practitioners to treat elderly people with "Covid-19" as nearing the end of life and to apply palliative care accordingly. It states: "Sedation and opioid use should not be withheld because of a fear of causing respiratory depression." Yet, according to retired neurologist Patrick Pullucino, "midazolam depresses respiration and it hastens death. It changes end of life care into euthanasia," in line with the theoretically retired Liverpool Care Pathway (cited in Adams & Bancroft, 2020).

Hancock promoted euthanasia in other ways. In November 2020, he announced travel exemptions for those seeking to travel abroad for assisted dying. In May 2021, he took the "first steps towards legalizing assisted suicide" by asking for official figures on how many people had killed themselves for medical reasons (Hope, 2021), paving the way for Baroness Meacher to campaign for the Assisted Dying Bill (Nanu, 2021). In June 2021, he resigned as Health Secretary when the midazolam revelations surfaced (video footage of his extramarital affair having been held back until then), but in August 2022, he called for a Parliamentary inquiry and free vote on assisted dying (Geissler, 2022). Canada's Medical Assistance In Dying (MAID) program, which saw 13,200 people euthanized in 2022 (a 31 percent year-on-year increase, accounting for 4.1 percent of all deaths in Canada [Hodgson, 2023]), shows that such developments are transnational.

Eugenics

Ehret (2021), in an article titled "Nazi Healthcare Revived across the Five Eyes," notes that the same organizations that promoted eugenics in Nazi Germany and North America—including the Rockefeller Foundation, the Wellcome Trust, and Engender Health (previously known as the Human Sterilization League for Human Betterment)—are implicated in mRNA "vaccine" development alongside the Galton Institute (formerly the British Eugenics Association). The Gates family could also be added to this list (Corbett, 2020). The attempt to coerce the public to take experimental "Covid-19 vaccines" follows in this tradition and belongs "firmly in the realms of a totalitarian Nazi dystopia" (Polyakova, 2021).

In Nazi Germany, the health professions were used for population control, management of dissent, and eugenics (Bell, 2023). In the "Covid-19" context, nurse educator Kevin Corbett (2021) describes the "'Nazification' of the NHS," whereby public health services were placed under a command-and-control regime, generating "an industrial-scale means for exerting mechanical and biological power over the population." This resulted in unethical practices, such as deprioritizing illnesses other than "Covid-19" for diagnosis and treatment.

Harradine (2022) identifies the seeds of a "new brand of eugenics" in NHS policy in 2020/21. "Protecting the NHS" (whose job it is to protect patients) led to hospital waiting lists increasing from just over 4 million pre-Covid to 7.7 million by September 2023 (Spectator, n.d.). This meant that large numbers of people could not get screened for illness, or get an operation, creating a ticking time bomb of health problems. Britons could not see their GP in person or obtain necessary dental care (Sumption, 2020, pp. 6–7). Five million patients were waiting for surgery in England in March 2021, the highest figure since records began (Pym, 2021). By May 2021, 10 percent of NHS patients had to wait over a year for treatment (Triggle & Jeavans, 2021). All of this looks like a eugenicist attack on the sick and the vulnerable. Blanket do-not-resuscitate orders were unethically applied in some care homes, and certain learning disability services were also targeted (Booth, 2020).

The Nazis were notorious for their grim medical experiments on human beings without their consent (Lifton, 1986, p. 269). The "Covid-19 vaccines" constitute the largest medical experiment in history. As Barack Obama put it in April 2022, "we've now, essentially, clinically tested the vaccine on billions of people worldwide" (cited in Knuffke, 2022)—the "vaccines" still being in clinical trials until 2023 when they were rolled out in 2021. The horrific results are discussed in Chapter 7.

Pseudoscientific Legitimations of "Elite" Rule

Nazi legal historian Friedrich Schaffstein claimed in his inaugural lecture in 1934: "Almost all the principles, concepts, and distinctions of our law up to now are stamped with the spirit of the Enlightenment, and they therefore require reshaping on the basis of a new kind of thought and experience" (cited in Müller, 1991, p. 71). Neither religion (the Divine Right of Kings) nor reason (the Age of Enlightenment), but, rather, biology would lie at the heart of the new social order. In place of the liberal universalism of 1789 would come "a biologically-based civil order" in which human equality was seen as illusory (Koonz, 2003, p. 205) and a bogus social Darwinism (epitomized by Herbert Spencer's "survival of the fittest" concept) would legitimize "Aryan" rule. Equality before the law contravened Nazi ideas about race hierarchy (Epstein, 2015, p. 66). Eugenics policy was intended to steer evolution in the direction of a fit, healthy, and racially pure society, able and willing to work, while the ruling class would rule in virtue of its allegedly superior breeding—a conceit by no means limited to Nazi Germany.

Transhumanism is the latest iteration of eugenics. According to military scientist Dylan Schmorrow, "We are entering an era of unprecedented human advancement in which Darwinian principles of evolution may begin to show signs of artificial self-acceleration" (cited in Coates, 2008, p. 35). Exponentially accelerating technological innovation, particularly in IT, will, according to Kurzweil (2005, pp. 20–28), lead to the reverse engineering of the human brain, whereupon age-old problems faced by humanity, including suffering and death, will finally be overcome—for some at least. Like the Eloi and the Morlocks in H. G. Wells' 1895 novel *The Time Machine*, humans will supposedly evolve into two separate species, one far superior to the other ("Human species 'may split in two,'" 2006). There will be a "small elite of upgraded superhumans" and a "mass of useless humans" who will become "an inferior caste" (Harari, 2017, pp. 355, 351). The ruling class will be determined, not by superior breeding, but by access to the most advanced technologies that will allow the limitations of human biology to be surpassed. All we are really looking at here is another pseudoscientific legitimization of the ruling class ("upgraded" humans replacing the "Aryan" race) and another attack on the inherent dignity of all humans.

The term "transhumanism" goes back to Julian Huxley (1957, p. 17). In a book co-authored with H. G. Wells, Huxley had argued for the sterilization of "defectives" who are "too stupid or shiftless or both to profit by existing birth-control methods" (Wells et al. 1934, 1470). As the first

Director-General of UNESCO, Huxley (1946, 21) was undeterred by the legacy of Nazi eugenics:

> even though it is quite true that any radical eugenic policy will be for many years politically and psychologically impossible, it will be important for UNESCO to see that the eugenic problem is examined with the greatest care and that the public mind is informed of the issues at stake so that much that is now unthinkable may at least become thinkable.

Huxley served as president of the British Eugenics Society from 1959 to 1962. The eugenics lineage of transhumanism is, thus, perfectly clear.

Nazi eugenics was premised on pseudoscience. New disciplines, such as "evolutionary racial biology," were invented and used to legitimize racial discrimination (Koonz, 2003, p. 129). When it was realized that biologists could not identify Jewish blood by physiological traits, cultural stereotypes were used instead to identify "Jewishness," with the social sciences and humanities taking over from the natural sciences in providing the "evidence" (Koonz, 2003, p. 197). Other bogus science that was taken seriously included *Ahnenerbe* (Ancestral Heritage, which involved searching for runes and old Germanic scripts in caves and elsewhere) and *Welteislehre* (Cosmic Ice Theory, a.k.a. Glacial Cosmogony, which treats ice as the basic substance of all cosmic processes) (Epstein, 2015, p. 97). The latter nonsense nevertheless "developed into an established worldview" due to "the way it was communicated" and because it found political favor (Austrian Science Fund, 2008). "Aryan physics" was promoted by two Nobel laureates (Philipp Lenard and Johannes Stark): it dismissed Einstein's theory of relativity as "Jewish physics."

Today, pseudoscience once again reigns supreme, and is known as The Science™. It manifests predominantly in the "pandemic preparedness" and "climate emergency" narratives, which form the twin basis for the attempted rollout of global technocracy (problem–reaction–solution). Because they are essential to this overarching totalitarian project, they are not allowed to be questioned. Unlike real science, The Science™ is always "settled science," and is a product of political consensus, not evidence or hypothesis testing. Skeptics are kept out of the media, they are not debated, and are instead dismissed as "conspiracy theorists"—all the hallmarks of propaganda, not science. Peer-reviewed journal articles that contradict The Science™ are simply retracted, especially if they question "vaccine" safety (Blaylock, 2022).

Hijacking Conscience

The evilest aspect of Nazi propaganda was its ability to hijack conscience through the creation of a "new moral order" founded on principles of enmity and exclusion (Westermann, 2015, p. 488). Contrary to stereotypes of blind order following and brainwashing into a state of mindless automatism, the path to the Final Solution was fundamentally paved by a rewiring of morality. Conscience no longer served to safeguard individual moral integrity against inhumane demands; instead, it became "a means of underwriting the attack by the strong against the weak" (Koonz, 2003, p. 273).

A similar attempt to subvert morality was evident in the "Covid-19" operation, where following orders ("government guidelines") was equated with virtue ("protecting others," "doing the right thing"), while noncompliance (resisting tyranny) was associated with vice ("selfishness," "irresponsibility," "putting other people's lives at risk"). The "Covid-19" moral order was systematically exploited by the authorities to turn most of society against the minority that refused to wear masks, get "vaccinated," and follow nonsensical "rules" (Hughes, 2024, Chapter 7). In some instances, the level of cruelty which ensued pointed towards "the collapse of a moral, decent, and compassionate society" (Blaylock, 2022).

Just as the Nazi press promoted an "emphasis on civic virtue" (Koonz, 2003, p. 90), UK Health Secretary Hancock claimed that it was the public's "civic duty" to follow test-and-trace instructions (Boseley & Stewart, 2020).

Tony Blair claimed that it was the public's "civic duty" to get "vaccinated" (as in Culbertson, 2021). Hancock described wearing face masks on public transport as a matter of "personal responsibility" ("Covid-19: Everyone 'has to play their part,'" 2021), and Johnson used the same phrase with respect to "social distancing" (HM Government, 2021, p. 3). In this *de facto* inversion of morality, people believed they were doing the right thing by wearing masks, cheering on "lockdowns," etc., even though their actions caused profound harm, and they all too easily relinquished personal responsibility by claiming to be following government guidelines (Harradine, 2020).

Ecopolitics

Until war preparations took center stage in the late 1930s, the Nazis led the world in ecopolitics (Brüggemeier et al., 2005; Imort, 2005, p. 58). They introduced a raft of ecological legislation in 1933 at national, regional, and local levels that led to reforestation programs, Europe's first nature preserves, and massive government support for organic farming and renewable energy (Staudenmaier, 2011, pp. 29–38). Today, politics is, once more, being subordinated to environmental concerns, only this time at a global level via Agenda 21/Agenda 2030, "sustainable development," renewable energy, rewilding programs, calls for a "Net Zero" economy, ESG (Environmental, Social, and Governance) ratings, and so on.

According to Botany professor Ernst Lehmann in 1934, "Humankind alone is no longer the focus of thought, but rather life as a whole," such that "striving toward connectedness with the totality of life, with nature itself [. . .] is the deepest meaning and the true essence of National Socialist thought" (cited in Staudenmaier, 2011, p. 13). Today, such thinking, shorn of the Nazi connotations, goes by the name of "ecocentrism," which resists "anthropocentrism" by paying attention to "the larger web of life, made up of nested ecological communities at multiple levels of aggregation" (Eckersley, 2007, p. 251). Contrary to Genesis 1:26, human beings are to be treated as part of nature, rather than as having dominion over it.

The Nazis' ecological achievements were not all they were cracked up to be, and were largely abandoned with the onset of World War II:

> swamp drainage and dam-construction programs devastated local ecosystems. The autobahn, Prora, and other large-scale building programs destroyed natural landscapes and animal habitats. Rearmament increased air pollution and factory waste. Industrial demand led to the relaxation of strict forestry laws. The military ruined landscapes with shooting ranges and drill fields. In the end, most historians agree, the Nazis caused more ecological harm than good. (Epstein, 2015, pp. 112–113)

Today, similar warnings have been voiced regarding the environmental damage wrought by wind turbines (Liu & Barlow, 2017; Frick et al., 2017), mining for lithium for electric car batteries (Hantanasirisakul & Sawangphruk, 2023), taking fleets of private jets to attend climate change conferences (Roberts et al., 2023), etc. There is something obviously bogus about the "green" agenda.

Young people proved particularly susceptible to Nazi ecopolitics, as reflected in the strong attraction of the *Wandervogel* movement to the NSDAP (Staudenmaier, 2011, p. 34). In that regard, it is probably no accident that the Nordic Greta Thunberg, who was just fifteen when she was catapulted to notoriety, was chosen as the face of the current environmental movement. Yet, if there is anything we should learn from Nazi ecologism, it is that a naive ecopolitics mystifies the social and class relations behind it, while imbuing power structures with a "naturally ordained" status (Staudenmaier, 2011, p. 42). The dangers of this are discussed in Chapter 7.

Historical Discontinuities

Notwithstanding the continuities between National Socialism and the emergent totalitarianism of the present, there are also some important differences. Most obviously, the phenomenon we are dealing with today is global, not national. It refers not to a specific country or set of countries, but, rather, to a "decentralized network of governments, global corporations, banks, think tanks, media conglomerates, global health authorities, non-governmental governing entities, and other unaccountable persons and entities" (Hopkins, 2023c). It does not go under traditional names, such as "fascism" and "National Socialism," but, rather, cloaks itself in the garb of "biosecurity," "Net Zero," "stakeholder capitalism," etc. (Elmer, 2022). It is not based on ethnocentrism and racism, but, rather, encourages migration and racial diversity. Whereas the Nazis promoted deurbanization to "ameliorate the population's alienation from the land, thus binding them more closely to the Fatherland" (Lekan, 2005, p. 85), Agenda 2030 is about moving people off the land and swelling smart cities (Koire, 2011, p. 16; Wood, 2018, p. 129).

Whereas the Nazis promoted idealized gender roles—"muscle-rippled workers, and warrior soldiers," married to women who would bear many children, serve their husband, etc. (Epstein, 2015, p. 75–76), conventional gender roles today are under attack through, *inter alia*, the trans agenda and attempts to redefine the term "woman." Whereas the Nazis were determined to raise birth rates (Epstein, 2015, p. 77), the global fertility rate (number of children per woman) has halved since 1968 (United Nations, 2022a) and is now at or below the 2.1 replacement rate in all regions apart from Africa (United Nations, 2022b). Whereas the Nazis were determined to increase the general health of the "Aryan" population (Epstein, 2015, p. 75), today there appears to be a concerted attack on the health of populations, duplicitously waged under the banner of "public health" (Hughes, 2024, Chapter 1).

Conclusion

The parallels between developments in the global political economy in the 2020s and the early political economy of Nazi Germany are extensive and alarming. There are far too many parallels, across all areas of life, for this to be a "coincidence" (and those enumerated above had to be cut short for reasons of space). Despite the differences between the two eras, the same fundamental logic is present: "totalitarianism is totalitarianism [. . .] The historical context and costumes change, but its ruthless trajectory remains the same" (Hopkins, 2021a). If that trajectory is allowed to continue, civilization is in jeopardy. How did we reach such a perilous situation?

CHAPTER 3

WALL STREET AND THE
RISE OF HITLER

The Nazis could never have come to power, built up their industry, or gone to war were it not for the backing of Wall Street. The Anglo-American ruling class promoted the rise of Hitler, lured by the potential of fascism to crush the working class. Loans by US investment banks to assist with German reparations payments led, through the Dawes and Young Plans, to the creation of the Bank for International Settlements (BIS), which quickly fell under Nazi control despite its transnational board membership. Sullivan & Cromwell provided the legal channels for US investment banks to acquire clandestine control over major German corporations, acquire key patents, and launder money through both the BIS and the Vatican Bank. The Harrimans, George Herbert Walker, and his son-in-law, Prescott Bush, were linked to the Hamburg-America Line, Union Banking Corporation, Silesian-American Corporation, and Brown Brothers Harriman, all of which were intimately involved with Nazi Germany. Other US corporations with close ties to Nazi Germany include Ford, General Motors (du Pont), Chase National Bank (Rockefeller), Standard Oil of New Jersey (Rockefeller), International Telephone and Telegraph Corporation (Morgan), IBM, and American I.G. Chemical Corporation. Notwithstanding some high-profile seizures made under the Trading with the Enemy Act in 1942, most of this collaboration was achieved with the blessing of the US political system.

Wall Street Interest in Germany

Wall Street first began to take an interest in Germany after World War I. The punitive reparations payments demanded by the Versailles treaty afforded an opportunity to make loans to Germany in return for the acquisition of German stock, which, in the case of high-tech industries, particularly those involving chemical processes, was "priceless," despite the collapsing Germany currency, and thus the Rockefellers, J.P. Morgan, and the Du Ponts all became heavily invested in Germany during the interwar years (Loftus, 2011, p. 17).

Despite strict antitrust legislation such as the Sherman Antitrust Act (1890) and the Clayton Antitrust Act (1914), the Webb-Pomerene Act (1918) legalized monopolistic and cartel practices by US export businesses, provided that such practices only applied to trade outside the United States and did not impact upon domestic trade and competition. This incentivized the early US multinationals to seek opportunities abroad, especially in Germany, where cartels were actively encouraged as a means of rebuilding industrial might after defeat in World War I (Aarons & Loftus, 1998, p. 291). By 1932, the Webb-Pomerene Act had come to be applied far beyond its original scope and served as a "most satisfactory vehicle for 'lawfully' violating the Sherman law" (Fournier, 1932, p. 18). This facilitated the rise of "corporate socialism" both at home and abroad (Sutton, 2016, pp. 50, 121).

Wall Street did not act alone. Rather, in the post-World War I era, Anglo-American power, focused on both the City of London and Wall Street, coordinated its designs for the world via the Royal Institute of International Affairs (Chatham House, founded 1920) and the Council on Foreign Relations (1921). Montagu Norman, Governor of the Bank of England, was a "rabid supporter of Hitler" (Higham, 2007, p. 5), who helped to maneuver Hitler and the Nazis into power, as did Henry Ford and the major Wall Street actors (Sutton, 2016). Edward, Duke of Windsor, was later involved in an intrigue to return to the throne as the Nazi King of England in the event of German victory in World War II (Higham, 2007, pp. 179–181; Loftus, 2011, p. 9). Such were the pro-Nazi sympathies of leading sections of the Anglo-American ruling class.

The reason for those pro-Nazi sympathies was the potential of National Socialism to cripple working class resistance to capitalist rule. Prominent German industrialists and financiers, lured by Hitler's promise to destroy the trade unions and the political left, covertly financed the Nazi Party, e.g. Alfried Krupp, Günther Quandt, Hugo Stinnes, Fritz Thyssen, Albert Vögler, and Kurt Baron von Schröder. But note: those industrialists were "predominantly directors of cartels with *American* associations, ownership, participation, or some form of subsidiary connection" (Sutton, 2016, p. 101, my emphasis). For example, whereas German General Electric (AEG) and Osram (with Gerard Swope and Owen D. Young holding influential positions in both) financed Hitler, Siemens, which was without American directors, did not (Sutton, 2016, p. 59).

It was specifically Wall Street investment bankers, plus Henry Ford— and not "the vast bulk of independent American industrialists"—which enabled the build-up of Nazi industry:

General Motors, Ford, General Electric, DuPont and the handful of US companies intimately involved with the development of Nazi Germany were—except for the Ford Motor Company—controlled by the Wall Street elite—the J.P. Morgan firm, the Rockefeller Chase Bank and to a lesser extent the Warburg Manhattan bank. (Sutton, 2016, pp. 31, 59)

For example, the two largest tank producers in Nazi Germany, Opel and Ford A.G., were subsidiaries of US corporations controlled, respectively, by J.P. Morgan and Ford. The roles of specific US financiers, families, and corporations are explored in more depth below.

The Dawes Plan, the Young Plan, and the Bank for International Settlements

The Dawes Plan of 1924, hatched in response to the occupation of the Ruhr by France and Belgium in 1923, was ostensibly intended to help Germany with reparations payments. It was structured to reduce payments as the German economy improved, with the final amount remaining undetermined. Wall Street loaned gold to Germany with which to make reparations payments to France and Britain, which then recycled the gold to repay their war loans to the United States (Aarons & Loftus, 1998, pp. 291–292). J.P. Morgan floated a $200 million loan on the US market, which was quickly oversubscribed. Approximately 70 percent of the money that went to rebuild the German economy after World War I came from Wall Street.

Yet, the loans extended to Germany under the Dawes Plan were hardly benign. They were used to "create and consolidate the gigantic chemical and steel combinations of I.G. Farben and Vereinigte Stahlwerke," cartels which not only sponsored Hitler but also staged war games exercises in 1935–6 and supplied the key war materials used in World War II (including synthetic gasoline, 95 percent of explosives, and Zyklon B) (Sutton, 2016, pp. 23–4, 31). Roughly 75 percent of this loan money came from just three US investment banks: Dillon, Read & Co.; Harris, Forbes & Co.; and National City Company, which in turn reaped most of the profits (Sutton, 2016, p. 29).

The Young Plan (1929), named after GE chairman Owen D. Young (appointed to the board of trustees of the Rockefeller Foundation in 1928, when negotiations began), aimed to broker a final settlement to German reparations payments. The Bank for International Settlements, a joint creation of the world's central banks, was supposedly established for this purpose in 1930 (BIS, n.d.), the same year that France agreed to withdraw troops from occupied Rhineland. One of the BIS architects was Reichsbank President Hjalmar Horace Greeley Schacht, whose early years were spent in Brooklyn and who had powerful Wall Street connections in later life. Yet, the BIS quickly proved to serve the opposite function, funneling Anglo-American funds into Hitler's coffers and helping to finance the Nazi war machine (Higham, 2007, p. 2).

In the context of the Great Depression, German reparations payments fell to around one eighth of previous levels via the Hoover Moratorium (1931) and Lausanne Agreement (1932), and the Nazis refused to pay any more. Yet the Bank for International Settlements persisted, essentially as "an instrument of Hitler" (Higham, 2007, p. 7), with full support from the United States and Britain. Despite Britain having declared war on Nazi Germany, Montagu Norman and Sir Otto Niemeyer of the Bank of England were still on the BIS board in May 1941, and the American, Thomas H. McKittrick, was its chairman. These men sat alongside I.G. Farben head, Hermann Schmitz, the head of Cologne's J.H. Stein Bank, Kurt Baron von Schröder, Reichsbank President Walther Funk, and Reichsbank Vice-president Emil Puhl. Washington State Congressman John M. Coffee angrily objected in 1944: "The Nazi government has 85 million Swiss gold francs on deposit in the BIS. The majority of the board is made up of Nazi officials. Yet American money is being deposited in the Bank" (cited in Higham, 2007, p. 11).

Sullivan & Cromwell

The law firm, Sullivan & Cromwell, which originally advised John Pierpont Morgan during the creation of Edison General Electric in 1882 and invented the concept of a holding company to avoid antitrust laws, had "extensive business dealings with numerous German companies and banks that had supported the Third Reich" (Trento, 2001, p. 25). The columnist Drew Pearson listed the firm's German clients who had contributed money to the Nazis, describing John Foster Dulles (a partner in the firm along with his brother Allen) as the linchpin of "the banking circles that rescued Adolf Hitler from the financial depths and set up his Nazi party as a going concern" (cited in Kinzer, 2014, p. 51). Sullivan & Cromwell floated the first US bonds issued by Krupp A.G., extended I.G. Farben's reach as part of an international nickel cartel, and helped to block Canadian restrictions on steel exports to German arms manufacturers.

Sullivan & Cromwell expertise in disguising foreign investments and protecting clients from the Trading with the Enemy Act made the firm attractive to some of the largest US investment houses, including Dillon, Read & Co. and Brown Brothers, Harriman (Aarons & Loftus, 1998, pp. 293–294). Following the Wall Street crash of 1929, Sullivan & Cromwell clients invested heavily in the German economy (as did British corporations, such as Imperial Chemicals). The total US gold investment in Germany in the early 1930s was ten times greater than the entire value of the gold stolen by the Nazis during World War II (Aarons & Loftus, 1998, p. 292).

In return, Wall Street investors acquired effective control over major German corporations, as well as patent rights to advanced technologies at below market value. This was all cunningly concealed through the machinations of Sullivan & Cromwell:

> The Americans secretly owned the stock in certain Swiss banks, including a significant share in the Bank of International Settlements, as well as undetermined interests in several others such as Credit Suisse and Union Bank. These institutions were also represented by Sullivan & Cromwell at key points before World War II. The Swiss banks, in turn, owned significant stock interests in several of the leading German banks (again represented by Sullivan & Cromwell), which in turn owned the stock of major German corporations, such as I.G. Farben (also represented by Sullivan & Cromwell), which in turn owned the valuable patent rights and processes so desperately desired by the American investors, such as

the Rockefellers (represented, inevitably, by Sullivan & Cromwell). (Aarons & Loftus, 1998, pp. 292–293)

Although Hitler immediately moved to ban foreign ownership of German companies, the Swiss Bank Secrecy Act of 1933, plus US lawyers on the boards of German banks and corporations, enabled Wall Street to conceal its influence.

In 1934, Switzerland became the Dulles brothers' base of operations, and Allen Dulles later ran the Office of Strategic Services (1942–1945) from Bern. He also sat on the board of Schröder Bank (controlled by Sullivan & Cromwell clients though nominally owned by a German banking family), which handled its transactions through the Bank for International Settlements, headquartered in Basel, whose director, McKittrick, was Dulles' personal client (Aarons & Loftus, 1998, p. 296). Sullivan & Cromwell clients laundered nine billion francs through the BIS on the eve of Operation Torch (the Allied invasion of French North Africa) in November 1942.

Sullivan & Cromwell also became entangled with the Vatican Bank, which enabled its clients to launder profits "under the watchful eyes of both the Nazis and their own governments," and in return the Vatican needed the Dulles brothers to protect its investments in Nazi Germany (Aarons & Loftus, 1998, p. 295).

Harriman and Bush

The McCormack-Dickstein Committee (1934/35) found that the shipping company, Hamburg-America Line, owned by W. Averell Harriman, had provided free passage to Germany to US journalists willing to write favorably about Hitler's rise to power, while bringing fascist sympathizers into the United States. The president of W.A. Harriman & Co. was George Herbert Walker, whose son-in-law, Prescott Bush (the father and grandfather of two future US presidents), sat on the board of directors. Joseph Kennedy, the US Ambassador to the United Kingdom between 1938 and 1940, bought stock in Nazi companies through Bush (Loftus, 2011, p. 13). Bush and E. Roland Harriman (both members of the Skull & Bones secret society) were also directors (and Bush the vice-president) of Union Banking Corporation (UBC). UBC was a subsidiary of the Rotterdam-based Bank voor Handel en Scheepvaart, which was used by Hitler-financier Fritz Thyssen to pay for the conversion of Barlow Palace in Munich into the Brown House, the headquarters of the Nazi Party (Aris & Campbell, 2004). UBC's assets, like those of Hamburg-America Line, were seized by the US government in 1942 under the 1917 Trading with the Enemy Act.

Bush also sat on the board of the Silesian-American Corporation (SAC), another company to be seized in 1942 under the Trading with the Enemy Act. SAC was managed by the Harrimans and controlled valuable coal and zinc mines in Silesia, where the Auschwitz concentration camp was located (Loftus, 2011, p. 19). According to Loftus, Auschwitz was originally planned as a "profit center for Wall Street," the site having been chosen for its access to the Vistula (allowing for raw materials to be barged in from Russia), its proximity to huge coal deposits, and its use of slave labor.

Bush was also a partner in the investment bank, Brown Brothers Harriman (BBH, established 1931), which, like UBC, acted as a US base for the Hitler-supporting (until 1938/39) industrialist Fritz Thyssen. The Harriman papers in the Library of Congress show that Bush was a director of several companies involved with Thyssen. By the late 1930s, BBH and UBC had sent "millions of dollars of gold, fuel, steel, coal and US treasury bonds to Germany," aiding Hitler's war preparations (Aris & Campbell, 2004). BBH had so many connections to the Nazis that, postwar, it became "the only bank in New York State history ever to obtain permission to shred its wartime and prewar files," with two of its Nazi investment clients, Nelson Rockefeller and Averell Harriman, having become Governors of New York (Loftus, 2011, p. 17). When UBC was liquidated in 1951, the Bush family received $1.5 million from the proceeds, which, in Loftus' (2000, 29:42) view, is "where the Bush family fortune came from: It came from the Third

Reich" and was, moreover, "blood money" based on Thyssen's exploitation of slave labor.

Ford

Henry Ford financed Hitler from the early 1920s on, and Hitler lifted sections of Ford's book *The International Jew* verbatim in *Mein Kampf.* Hitler awarded Ford the Grand Cross of the German Eagle, a Nazi decoration for distinguished foreigners, in 1938, and kept a portrait of Ford on prominent display in his office (Sutton, 2016, pp. 92–93).

Ford manufactured vehicles for the US Army *and* the Wehrmacht during World War II, profiting from both sides. Ford A.G. plants, like those of German General Electric, were neither seized by the Nazis, nor targeted for bombing by the Allies during World War II—so important was Ford's support deemed by both sides. The Nazis made promises to certain US corporate leaders that their properties would not be damaged in the event of German victory in the war, making the war a win-win scenario for those businessmen (Higham, 2007, p. xvi). At its plant in Cologne, Ford made use of slave labor, typically involving those deported from Eastern Europe, as well as Jewish prisoners (Reginbogin, 2009, p. 138). Through his son, Edsel, Ford collaborated with the Nazis in Occupied France, and when the RAF bombed the Poissy plant, the Vichy government paid for all damages (Higham, 2007, pp. 158–159). Another branch of Ford was set up in Vichy Algiers to build trucks and armored cars for Rommel's Afrika Korps.

Ford's anti-Semitism was not exceptional among the Anglo-American ruling class: the Roosevelt administration, for example, refused to change its immigration policy to admit Jewish refugees fleeing the Holocaust, much as the British Foreign Office in 1943 confidentially revealed to the State Department its fear that if requests to Germany to release Jews were "pressed too much that that is exactly what might happen" (cited in Aarons & Loftus, 1998, p. 14). The United States Air Force rejected requests to bomb the railway tracks leading to Auschwitz, which were deemed "non-military" targets.

Du Pont/General Motors

General Motors (GM) was controlled by the du Pont family of Delaware, known for its pro-fascist politics. Irénée du Pont was "obsessed with Hitler's principles," including eugenics, racial purity, and antisemitism (Higham, 2007, p. 162). He not only conspired in the Business Plot to topple Roosevelt and bring fascism to the United States, but he and his brothers Pierre and Lammot were also the primary funders of the anti-Semitic, anti-black American Liberty League (1934–1940). GM president Alfred P. Sloan and Du Pont vice president John Jacob Raskob also funded the Liberty League. The du Ponts additionally helped to turn Clark's Crusaders, whose 1.25 million members in 1933 had originally been organized to fight prohibition, into a body used to combat militant labor (James Warburg was also a supporter). In 1936, Irénée du Pont used GM money to finance the Black Legion, a 75,000-strong terrorist organization used to dissuade automobile workers from unionizing. Like the Nazi Death's Head Units, its members wore skull and crossbones insignia. They fire-bombed union meetings, murdered union leaders, and persecuted Jews and communists (Higham, 2007, p. 165).

General Motors invested $30 million into I.G. Farben plants between 1932 and 1939, knowing that 0.5 percent of the salary roll went to the Nazis (Higham, 2007, p. 162). In 1938, GM's James D. Mooney was, like Henry Ford, awarded the Grand Cross of the German Eagle. Together with Ford, GM controlled over 70 percent of the German automobile market in 1939, and both companies retooled for war production on behalf of the Wehrmacht (Reginbogin, 2009, pp. 179–181). Hitler's chief architect, Albert Speer, reflected in 1977 that the invasion of Poland would have been impossible without the synthetic fuel technology provided by GM. Like Ford, GM profited from both sides during the war: according to a 1974 US Government subcommittee report, "GM's plants in Germany built thousands of aircraft propulsion systems for the Luftwaffe at the same time that its American plants produced aircraft engines for the US Army Air Corps" (cited in Reginbogin, 2009, p. 179). GM was, like Ford, protected from seizure during World War II, and, again like Ford, it handled repairs and modifications to German army vehicles in "neutral" Switzerland (Higham, 2007, pp. 175–176).

Rockefeller/Chase National Bank

The Rockefellers' Chase National Bank (later Chase Manhattan) was the most powerful financial institution in the United States at the time of Pearl Harbor, and had close ties to fascism (Higham, 2007, pp. 20–22). For example, Vice-president Joseph L. Larkin managed both the Franco account and the Reichsbank account.

A separate organization, Schröder, Rockefeller, and Company (a partnership with Schröder Bank of New York), was described by *Time* in 1936 as "the economic booster of the Rome-Berlin Axis." Its partners included Avery Rockefeller (nephew of John D. Rockefeller) and Kurt Baron von Schröder of the BIS and the Gestapo; the Dulles brothers of Sullivan & Cromwell were its lawyers. Winthrop Aldrich (John D. Rockefeller's brother-in-law) and the Schröders financed Germany's expanding war economy to the tune of $25 million just before the outbreak of World War II and provided a detailed record to the Reichstag of 10,000 Nazi sympathizers in the United States.

Between 1936 and 1941, Chase acted as a conduit by which the Nazi government incentivized Nazis living in the United States to return to Germany by buying marks with dollars at a heavily discounted rate (4.10 Reichsmarks per dollar vs. the market exchange rate of 2.48) (Reginbogin, 2009, p. 183). The "Remigrant Mark" program was largely funded through confiscated Jewish property and was used to help acquire dollars with which to pay for US goods.

Once the war began, Chase handled the account of the German embassy in Paris, as well as Otto Abetz, the ambassador. Millions of francs were used to finance the military government and the Gestapo High Command,

Nazi propaganda, campaigns of terror against civilians, and the terrorist Mouvement Synarchique Revolutionnaire, which was used to flush out and exterminate resistance cells (Higham, 2007, p. 27). Among other sources, the Paris Chase received large amounts of money from the Banco Aleman Transatlantico, through which most Nazi businesses in South America handled their affairs. The Morgan Bank also stayed open in Paris throughout the war, and British banks, too, made large profits there during the Occupation (Higham, 2007, p. 29).

Rockefeller/Standard Oil

The Rockefeller-owned Standard Oil of New Jersey was the largest petroleum corporation in the world in 1941. Its chairman, Walter C. Teagle, became a director of American I.G. Chemical Corp., a subsidiary of I.G. Farben, along with Edsel Ford and William E. Weiss, chairman of Sterling Products (Higham, 2007, p. 32–36). Teagle partnered with I.G. Farben in the production of tetraethyl lead, used in aviation gasoline, without which the German and Japanese air forces could not have flown. He also built a refinery in Hamburg that provided 15,000 tons of aviation gasoline a week for the Nazis.

Standard Oil subsidiaries distributed pro-Nazi propaganda all over the world, while in the United States, Teagle and Hermann Schmitz paid P.R. man Ivy Lee to distribute inflammatory Nazi propaganda and provide intelligence on the American response to German armament (Higham, 2007, pp. 39, 34).

By 1939, Standard Oil had contracted with Hitler to provide certain kinds of synthetic rubber needed for planes, tanks, and armored vehicles, while the United States, which was dangerously short of such rubber, would receive nothing—an arrangement that persisted beyond Pearl Harbor (Higham, 2007, pp. 36, 49–50; Reginbogin, 2009, p. 179). Rubber was not the only essential war material whose production Standard deliberately skewed in favor of the Nazis. The same also went for acetic acid, synthetic ammonia (needed for explosives), and paraflow (needed for airplane lubrication at high altitudes). In conjunction with I.G. Farben, Standard Oil also developed the hydrogenation process required to produce synthetic gasoline for the Wehrmacht: German output rose from 300,000 tons in 1934 to 5.5 million tons in 1944 (Reginbogin, 2009, p. 180–181). For over a decade, the Rockefeller company "aided the Nazi war machine while refusing to aid the United States," and without this assistance, "the Wehrmacht could not have gone to war in 1939" (Sutton, 2016, p. 75).

William Stamps Farish, the company president, initially manned Standard Oil tankers with Nazi crews, before re-registering the entire fleet as Panamanian to avoid seizure by the British Navy (Higham, 2007, pp. 36–39). James V. Forrestal, the erstwhile Under Secretary of the Navy (and Vice-president of General Aniline and Film) granted Farish's vessels immunity under the Panamanian flag. Farish's tankers transported oil to Tenerife, where they syphoned oil to German tankers for shipment to Hamburg, as well as fueling U-boats. Farish also managed to send large amounts of petroleum to Berlin via the Trans-Siberian Railroad, and to Vichy North Africa. Despite his flagrant disregard for Lend-Lease and good neighbor policies, Farish remained on the War Petroleum Board.

Remarkably, all of this was going on while Nelson Rockefeller was Coordinator of Inter-American Affairs (1940–1944), in which role he helped to prepare the Proclaimed List of enemy-associated corporations with which it was illegal to trade in time of European war (Higham, 2007, pp. 39–40, 54, 59). However, an amendment to the 1917 Trading with the Enemy Act, made in December 1941, meant that such trade was still legal, provided authorization was obtained from the Secretary of the Treasury, pursuant to Executive Order 8389. So, in August 1942, Standard's West India Oil Company shipped to the Nazi-associated Cia Argentinia Comercial de Pesqueria in Buenos Aries on Treasury licenses. In August 1943, a Standard subsidiary was allowed to trade with Proclaimed List entities in Caracas, Venezuela, that were shipping oil to fascist Spain via refineries in Aruba.

Gasoline, sulphate of ammonia, and cotton were all shipped to Spain in large quantities in 1943, despite US shortages in those commodities.

ITT

The American International Telephone and Telegraph Corporation (ITT) was set up by Sosthenes Behn in 1920. In 1923, ITT acquired the Spanish telephone monopoly, Compania Telefonica de Espana. With Morgan partners Arthur M. Anderson and Russell Leffingwell joining on its parent board, ITT became "a Morgan-controlled company" and acquired what would become known as the International Standard Electric group of manufacturing plants (Sutton, 2016, p. 78). Behn and ITT's German representative Henry Mann met with Hitler in August 1933. Through Himmler's Circle of Friends—the innermost core of Nazism—they made contact with Kurt Baron von Schröder, who provided access to the profitable German armaments industry, including Focke-Wolfe aircraft used by the Luftwaffe, in which ITT bought a 25 percent stake through its subsidiary, C. Lorenz AG of Berlin (Sutton, 2016, p. 123).

Following Pearl Harbor, the Nazi postmaster general, Wilhelm Ohnesorg, opposed ITT's German subsidiaries continuing to function under New York management in time of war, but this obstacle was overcome when Behn substantially increased ITT payments to the Gestapo through the Circle of Friends. Thereafter, ITT supplied the Nazis with a wide range of electronic and communications equipment, without which "it would have been impossible for the German air force to kill American and British troops, for the German army to fight the Allies in Africa, Italy, France, and Germany, for England to have been bombed, or for Allied ships to have been attacked at sea" (Higham, 2007, p. 99).

IBM

Using the punch card technology invented by US Census Bureau employee Herman Hollerith in the 1880s, International Business Machines (IBM) enabled the Nazis to "automate and accelerate all six phases of the twelve-year Holocaust," i.e., identification, exclusion, confiscation, ghettoization, deportation, and extermination (Black, 2009, p. 130).

In terms of identification, a 1933 national census in Germany was used to collect detailed data on the population using the Hollerith system. The resultant IBM data records were steadily updated with information from church baptism records, historical records of conversion from Judaism to Christianity, genealogical records, birth and death notices, information from eugenics agencies, etc. to determine who was Jewish and who was not. "Where did Hitler get the names?" bewildered Jews asked. "Answer: IBM" (Black, 2009, p. 132). This information was used to expel Jews from their professions and to confiscate their assets, a straightforward task given that IBM also serviced nearly all financial institutions and tax authorities.

The next step was ghettoization, where bespoke IBM machines were used to calculate precisely which Jews, living at which addresses, would be relocated to which ghetto buildings. The persecution was highly systematic. Hollerith systems were used to calculate "the exact number of trains running the exact number of needed boxcars [. . .] for the exact number of ghetto Jews to be deported to the concentration camps" (Black, 2009, p. 134). Hollerith codes were assigned to each of the major camps: Auschwitz 001, Buchenwald 002, Dachau 003, etc. In the case of Auschwitz, a five-digit Hollerith number was tattooed onto inmates' arms, at least until the mass killing ramped up. IBM machinery was used to manage the flow of millions of prisoners through the camps; without it, mass extermination could not have been organized (Black, 2009, p. 154). To conceal evidence of mass murder, Himmler ordered all Hollerith cards at concentration camps to be destroyed at the end of the war.

The president of IBM during this period was Thomas J. Watson, who personally received 5 percent of every transaction with the Third Reich (after tax and dividends) (Black, 2009, p. 134). Hitler bestowed upon Watson the Merit Cross of the German Eagle with Star, the highest medal of honor for a foreigner. Watson was the first to receive the award, in 1937, before Henry Ford and GM's James Mooney.

American I. G.

American I.G. Chemical Corporation, founded in 1929, was a wholly owned subsidiary of I.G. Chemie in Switzerland, which in turn was controlled by the colossal industrial trust, I.G. Farben, formed out of six German chemical companies in 1925. I.G. Farben's joint chairman, Hermann Schmitz, became president of American I.G. and sat on the board alongside five other Farben executives (including his nephew, Max Ilgner), as well as Edsel Ford (president of the Ford Motor Company), Walter Teagle (president of Standard Oil of New Jersey), Charles Mitchell (chairman of the National City Bank), and Paul Warburg (a founder of the US Federal Reserve System). The directors sponsored Hitler's rise to power (Sutton, 2016, p. 34). I.G. Farben was instrumental in Göring's Four-Year Plan to make Germany militarily self-sufficient by 1940, it was largely responsible for building Auschwitz, and it manufactured the Zyklon B that was used there (Aarons & Loftus, 1998, 293; Higham, 2007, p. 131). Much as Ford installations in Nazi Germany were not bombed during the war, so it emerged that Commanding General of the US Army Air Forces, Henry H. Arnold, "had protected I.G. and [. . .] that the installations and communications systems of Auschwitz had not been destroyed" (Higham, 2007, p. 213). American I.G. became General Aniline and Film Corporation in 1939 and was seized by the US Government in February 1942, under the Trading with the Enemy Act.

SKF

Sweden's SKF controlled 80 percent of ball bearing production in Europe during World War II; 60 percent of its worldwide production of ball bearings went to Nazi Germany. Without them, the Luftwaffe could not have flown, the Wehrmacht's tanks and armored vehicles could not have operated, and nor could the vehicles supplied by Ford (Higham, 2007, pp. 116–122). Meanwhile, SKF ball bearings manufactured in the United States were, despite massive demand for them there, shipped on Panamanian-registered vessels to Nazi-associated firms in Latin America, and the profits were funneled back to Sweden through National City Bank of New York. When Germany began to run short of ball bearings in 1943, SKF's American director, Hugo von Rosen, arranged for more to be shipped from Rio and Buenos Aires via Sweden, Spain, Portugal, and Switzerland. Remarkably, Britain and Russia allowed this because, they, too, were reliant on SKF for ball bearings.

US Government Complicity

Notwithstanding some high-profile seizures made under the Trading with the Enemy Act in 1942 (principally relating to Bush/Harriman enterprises), the US political system proved remarkably permissive towards US corporations that traded with the enemy in time of war:

> ITT was allowed to continue its relations with the Axis and Japan until 1945 [. . .] No attempt was made to prevent Ford from retaining its interests for the Germans in Occupied France, nor were the Chase Bank or the Morgan Bank expressly forbidden to keep open their branches in occupied Paris. (Higham, 2007, p. xvi)

The US Treasury allowed SKF to pose as a US-owned corporation despite its strong support for the Nazis. General Aniline and Film collaborated with the German Secret Service and I.G. Farben's political intelligence unit (NW 7), which the Senate and the House must have tacitly approved. GM in Sweden imported Nazi products, such as Freon, with permission from the State Department (Higham, 2007, pp. 121, 135, 176).

In September 1947, Judge Charles Clark declared: "Standard Oil can be considered an enemy national [sic] in view of its relationship with I.G.

Farben after the United States and Germany had become active enemies" (cited in Higham, 2007, p. 62). Nevertheless, when Petroleum Administrator and Coordinator for National Defense and War, Harold Ickes, sought to hold Standard Oil accountable in 1941, the company thwarted him by bringing pressure on the State Department. When Thurman Arnold, head of the Antitrust Division of the Department of Justice, accused Standard of acting against US interests in 1942, company president Farish replied that Standard was providing most of the fuel to the US military—tacit black-mail—and the matter went nowhere (Higham, 2007, pp. 43–45).

Roosevelt made no attempt to punish any of the key US actors respon-sible for aiding Nazi Germany for treason. Perhaps he had learned from the House committee investigating the treasonous 1933 conspiracy to depose him, which declined to summon the du Ponts and ended up as farce (Higham, 2007, p. 164).

Conclusion

The above connections between US corporations and Nazi Germany are not intended to be exhaustive and could easily be extended. Hollywood, for instance, did not make a single anti-Nazi film until 1940 for fear of losing access to the German market (Urwand, 2013). Subsidiaries of the Eastman Kodak company traded with Nazi Germany long after the United States entered World War II, and Kodak used slave labor in its Stuttgart and Berlin-Kopenick plants (Friedman, 2001).

The key point is that the complex web of financial and business inter-connections above demonstrates beyond reasonable doubt that Wall Street (as well as elements of the British ruling class) was profoundly sympathetic to Hitler and the project of National Socialism. It also confirms the accuracy of Marxist analysis from the 1930s that fascism (the default term before Arendt distinguished between it and totalitarianism) represents "a tool in the hands of finance capital" (Trotsky, 1977, p. 173), indeed nothing less than "an open terroristic dictatorship of the [. . .] most imperialistic elements of finance capital" (Georgi Dimitrov, cited in Marcon, 2021, p. 55). The defeat of Nazi Germany did not change the attractiveness of totalitarianism to Anglo-American finance capital.

CHAPTER 4

THE POSTWAR ERA

The Nuremberg Trials delivered a victor's justice that saw the true architects of World War II go largely unpunished, if not later rewarded. The Bank for International Settlements, which was implicated in Nazi crimes against humanity, survived despite calls for it to be liquidated at Bretton Woods. The Vatican, in league with Swiss banks to protect its investments in Nazi Germany, helped to smuggle Nazis and Nazi treasure out of Germany after the war. Denazification was an abject failure: former Nazis quickly returned to leading positions in German society and industry, as well as in international organizations, especially NATO. Corporate control over German society was not disrupted in any meaningful way, despite the apparent dismantlement of I.G. Farben. The United States actively recruited ex-Nazis, many of whom had committed crimes against humanity, to serve in its fight against communism. It also recruited Unit 731 personnel, who, like the Nazis, had conducted gruesome medical experiments on human beings, initiating decades of covert US military experimentation on various civilian populations. Such experiments also formed the basis of early CIA mind control programs.

Justice the US Way

At the Nuremberg Trials, many senior Nazis and their industrialist backers evaded justice. Of an estimated 150,000 war crimes committed by the

Nazis during WWII, fewer than 50,000 received even minimal punishment (Loftus, 2011, p. 174). Following the trial of twenty-one leading Nazis by the International Military Tribunal between November 20, 1945, and October 1, 1946, the twelve subsequent Nuremberg Trials, also held in the Palace of Justice, were conducted by US military courts and so represented an exclusively US rendering of justice.

Some very senior figures who were found guilty at Nuremberg were released a few years later, owing largely to the influence of former Wall Street lawyer and US High Commissioner of Germany, John J. McCloy. Nazi Agriculture Minister Richard Walter Darré (the architect of "blood and soil" agrarian policies) served only three years of a seven-year sentence and was released in 1950. So-called "war economy leaders," including Hermann Schmitz, Alfried Krupp, and Friedrich Flick, were found guilty of using slave labor (among other things) but were freed in the early 1950s; Flick went on to become the richest man in the Federal Republic. I.G. Farben's Max Ilgner was freed in the same year he was sentenced (1948), and by 1955, he was the chairman of a Swiss chemical company. Twenty-three I.G. Farben directors were tried for war crimes in 1947/1948 and thirteen were convicted, yet by 1951 all had been released from prison early. Whereas most *Einsatzgruppen* commanders were sentenced to death at Nuremberg, Franz Alfred Six was handed a twenty-year prison sentence; he, too, was released early in 1952 and went to work for the Gehlen Organisation (Breitman, 2001).

In an apt description of the emergent transnational deep state (see Chapter 5), the DoJ's James Stewart Martin explains the failure to achieve meaningful justice with respect to Nazi crimes as follows:

> The forces that stopped us had operated from the United States but had not operated in the open. We were not stopped by a law of Congress, by an Executive Order of the President, or even by a change of policy approved by the President [. . .] in short, what-ever it was that had stopped us was not "the government." But it

clearly had command of channels through which the government normally operates. (Martin, 1950, p. 264)

No American was tried at Nuremberg, despite the role of Wall Street and Ford in facilitating the rise of Hitler, building Nazi industry, and enabling and prolonging the war. Sutton (2016, p. 48) wryly speculates that the true purpose of this victor's justice was to divert attention away from US involvement in the rise of Nazism.

Nor was justice forthcoming through the US domestic legal system. On April 17, 1945, for example, the Chase National Bank of New York was placed on trial in federal court on charges of having violated the Trading with the Enemy Act, yet was acquitted just nineteen days later, its wartime connections with the enemy having neither been made public nor subjected to Senate or Congressional investigation (Higham, 2007, p. 30). No US or British corporate officer went to jail for doing business with the Nazis, and the reason why Nazi financial crimes investigations kept getting closed down is that the money originally came from Wall Street and the City of London (Loftus, 2011, pp. 4–5, 12).

Far from being punished, US Nazi collaborators were actively rewarded. Albert Bertrand, for example, the collaborationist head of the Chase bank in Vichy France, was appointed to the board of the Chase bank in Paris (Higham, 2007, p. 31). ITT's Sosthenes Behn, in February 1946, was awarded the Medal of Merit, the nation's highest award to a civilian, and he later received millions of dollars in compensation for war damage to his German plants in 1944 (Higham, 2007, p. 115). Ford and GM also received reparations for damage to their German plants caused by Allied bombing. SKF Nazi connections in the United States were "forgiven, forgotten, and—more importantly—unexposed" (Higham, 2007, p. 126).

Those who did seek to investigate US corporate Nazi connections, such as Harry Dexter White and Lauchlin Currie, were smeared by the House Un-American Activities Committee as communist agents in 1948. White died of a heart attack that year, and Currie's US citizenship was revoked in 1956 (Higham, 2007, p. 223).

The Bank for International Settlements

It is written into the Bank for International Settlements' charter that it "should be immune from seizure, closure, or censure, whether or not its owners were at war" (Higham, 2007, p. 2)—a power scarcely imaginable for any other entity. The BIS, thus, seamlessly continued operations during World War II, despite Anglo-American representatives sitting alongside Nazis on its board. The Nazi directors included I.G. Farben CEO Hermann Schmitz, Kurt Baron von Schröder, "a dedicated leader of the Death's Head Brigade" (the SS organization responsible for administering concentration camps [Higham, 2007, p. 132]), Emil Puhl, who was in charge of processing dental gold looted from the mouths of concentration camp victims, and Walther Funk, referred to at the Nuremberg trials as "the Banker of Gold Teeth." All four men were convicted of crimes against humanity.

Although the Bretton Woods conference in 1944 recommended that the BIS be liquidated at the "earliest possible moment" (Department of State, 1944, p. 13), this did not occur. Instead, the BIS was allowed to survive despite its complicity in the crimes of the Third Reich. In 1948, the Bretton Woods recommendation was reversed, and the BIS handed over a meagre $4 million (of a suspected $378 million) in looted gold to the Allies (Higham, 2007, p. 18).

Had an investigation into the Bank's records during the war years taken place, the Nazi-US connection would certainly have been exposed. Yet, there was no interest in the BIS. At Nuremberg, for instance, former Reichsbank President Hjalmar Schacht was not asked about the BIS or its American president, Thomas H. McKittrick, who was rewarded by the Rockefellers with a post as vice-president of the Chase National Bank (Higham, 2007, pp. 18–19, 210).

The Role of the Vatican

Whatever the Holy See's true attitude towards Nazism, the Vatican is known to have invested part of its wealth in Nazi Germany via Swiss banks (Aarons & Loftus, 1998, pp. xv-xvii). When the Nazis were defeated in 1945, the Vatican was keen to help smuggle Nazi treasure—which included billions of dollars' worth of gold, currency, gems, artworks, jewelry, and other valuables pillaged from conquered nations—back out of the country. Much of that treasure has never been recovered and is suspected to lie in the vaults of the Vatican Bank. Some of it made its way, via the Nazi diaspora which the Vatican helped to facilitate, to Latin America (whence an estimated 30,000 fugitive Nazis escaped), in particular Argentina (Aarons & Loftus, 1998, p. 88). A tiny cabal of senior Catholic Church officials, including Bishop Alois Hudal, Father Krunoslav Draganović, and Pope Pius XII, appears to have been responsible for establishing the "ratlines" that allowed prominent Nazis and Nazi collaborators, including accused war criminals and mass murderers, to escape, in part with the help of with Western intelligence (Aarons & Loftus, 1998, pp. xiii, 114, 119; Loftus, 2011, p. 61). A black market in forged Red Cross documents, plus Vatican relief and welfare agencies, were used to obtain Allied travel passes (Aarons & Loftus, 1998, p. 42).

Although the Swiss Nazi gold scandal in the mid-1990s pointed the finger at Swiss banks for continuing to hold Nazi gold (some of it stolen from those who perished in the Holocaust) and profiting from the interest, this distracted from a much bigger scandal, namely, that the Vatican Bank, which enjoys diplomatic immunity and therefore cannot be audited, laundered most stolen Nazi money from Switzerland. The "ugliest secret of World War II," according to Aarons & Loftus (1998, p. xv, cf. 289), was "the bloody circle of Western money laundered through Switzerland to the Third Reich, then out through the Vatican Bank to South America, and then finally back to the original owners in Germany." This latter stage was accomplished, among other means, through the World Commerce Corporation (1947–1962), an OSS outgrowth used to launder money internationally.

The Failures of Denazification

After World War II, Wall Street controlled the appointment of officials responsible for denazifying and governing the Federal Republic. The Allied Control Council, headed by General Lucius Clay, included Louis Douglas, director of Morgan-controlled General Motors, and William Draper, a partner in Dillon, Read & Co., among others (Sutton, 2016, p. 158). Draper claimed that purging Nazis would hold back German economic development, and he refused to denazify any German financial institution (Higham, 2007, p. 219).

Some former Nazis went on to assume very powerful positions. Hermann Abs, for example, who had been the most powerful commercial banker in the Third Reich, was arrested in 1946, but was quickly freed by the British and went on to become an adviser to Chancellor Adenauer. Hans Josef Globke wrote a legal annotation on the Nuremberg Race Laws in 1936 that did not express any objection to discrimination against Jews; he was responsible in 1938 for the Name Change Ordinance, which forced Jewish men to take the middle name Israel and Jewish women Sara for easier identification; and in 1941, he authored a statute that stripped Jews in occupied territories of their statehood and possessions. Yet, as Chief of Staff of the German Chancellery (1953–1963), he went on to become one of the most powerful men in West Germany. Nazi propagandist Eberhard Taubert, who worked on the script for the anti-Semitic film *The Eternal Jew* and was responsible for the law requiring Jews to wear the yellow star, became an adviser to Defense Minister Franz Josef Strauß (1956–1962).

Where global governance was concerned, denazification was fundamentally irrelevant and systematically avoided. Prince Bernhard of the Netherlands, who served in the SS in the early 1930s before joining I.G. Farben, co-founded the Bilderberg Group in 1954. Walter Hallstein, who served as First Lieutenant in the German Army and whose name was proposed by the University of Frankfurt in 1944 as a potential National Socialist Leadership Officer (charged with teaching Nazi ideology to soldiers), was appointed the first president of the EEC (now EU) Commission (1958–1967). Kurt Kiesinger, who headed the radio propaganda section of the Nazi foreign ministry for part of World War II, attended the 1957 Bilderberg conference and later became West German Chancellor (1967–1971). Kurt Waldheim, a former intelligence officer in the Wehrmacht, became UN Secretary General (1972–1981) and President of Austria (1986–1992).

NATO proved particularly accommodating of ex-Nazis. Hans Speidel, who was Rommel's Chief of Staff, played a key role in German rearmament and integration into NATO, and served as NATO Commander of the Allied Land Forces Central Europe (1957–1963). Adolf Heusinger, once Hitler's Chief of the General Staff of the Army, became Inspector General of the Bundeswehr (1957–1961) and Chairman of the NATO Military Committee (1961–1964). Nazi U-Boat commander Friedrich Guggenberger, who was awarded the Knight's Cross for sinking 17 Allied ships, served as Deputy Chief of Staff in NATO Armed Forces North (1968–1972). Luftwaffe pilot Johannes Steinhoff received the Knight's Cross from Hitler; he was also awarded the Order of Merit of the Federal Republic of Germany for his work in rebuilding the West German air force within NATO, where he held a series of senior positions from 1960 on and was appointed Chairman of the NATO Military Committee (1971–1974).

The position of NATO Commander in Chief of Allied Forces Central Europe (Brunssum) was continuously filled by ex-Nazis between 1968 and 1983. These were: Johann von Kielmansegg (1967–1968), who was General Staff officer to the High Command of the Wehrmacht (1942–44); Jürgen Bennecke (1968–1973), who received both the silver and gold versions of the German Cross for his service in the 100th Jäger Division; Ernst Ferber (1973–1975), who joined the Army High Command in 1943 (and later the Gehlen Organization, 1945–1951); Karl Schnell (1975–77), who was First General Staff officer of the LXXVI Panzer Corps and received the Knight's Cross in 1944; Franz-Joseph Schulze (1977–79), who received the Knight's Cross in 1944 as Chief of the Third Battery of Flak Storm Regiment 241;

and Ferdinand Maria von Senger und Etterlin (1979–1983), who fought in the Battle of Stalingrad and was awarded the German Cross in 1944.

The Failure of Decartelization

After 1945, corporate control of German society was not disrupted in any meaningful sense. Stedman (1950, p. 443) reflects:

> Nazi Germany presented an extreme case of monopoly control, domination of the economy by a few powerful industrialists and financiers, and the use of cartel agreements and other restrictive business practices to hold the German economy in thrall and to extend German control into foreign areas. The extent to which these evil practices participated in bringing about World War II is well known. It was thought, and rightly, that these practices had to be eliminated if there was to be any hope of permanent and satisfactory world peace. It was to the elimination of these evils that the decartelization program was directed.

Yet, Stedman adds, at no point was there any genuine enthusiasm for that program among the authorities. Notwithstanding the Decartelization Branch established in January 1946 under the command of James Stewart Martin, for example, and with the I.G. Farben leadership awaiting trial at Nuremberg, all fifty-five I.G. plants located within the US zone continued operations and were prioritized in assignments of transport and energy resources (Heinelt, n.d.). Some I.G Farben units after 1945 produced "more than ever before in their history" (Stedman, 1950, p. 451).

The blame for I.G. Farben's resilience to decartelization has been pinned variously on William Draper, who "blocked plans to have an I.G. poison gas plant dismantled," General Patton for "sabotag[ing] the Potsdam Agreement calling for a destruction of I.G.," according to J.S. Martin (Higham, 2007, pp. 213, 218), and John Foster Dulles, a board member of I.G. Farben and legal counsel to the US agency responsible for seizing German assets (Aarons & Loftus, 1998, p. 293). Pointing the finger at individuals is less helpful, however, than identifying the class interests that protect corporate power.

In 1952, virtually all I.G. Farben assets and activities were returned to the original constituent companies (including Bayer and BASF), leaving I.G. Farben itself as a shell company for all intents and purposes, even though it continued to trade for over half a century more, almost as a reminder of a Nazi past that refused to disappear. Whereas the 1948 currency reform issued 1 Deutsche Mark (DM) for every 10 Reichsmarks (RM), every 1,000 RM of I.G. Farben stock was redeemable by shareholders for 915 DM, meaning that, despite everything, I.G. Farben stock was valued over nine times higher than the national currency. In effect, J.S. Martin realised, I.G. Farben was "simply being split into components and allowed to continue with several of [former CEO Hermann] Schmitz's minor executives continuing in higher positions" (Higham, 2007, p. 218). The I.G. Liquidation Conclusion Law (1955) annulled previous legislation forbidding "renewed mergers among the successor companies and [preventing] former I.G. executives convicted in the Nuremberg trial from assuming leading roles in the successor companies" (Wollheim Memorial, n.d.). Thus, the door was deliberately left open to a repeat of the past.

Recruiting Former Nazis

Not only was there a failure to deliver justice to many former Nazis for war crimes and crimes against humanity, but after the war, the West actively facilitated extensive emigration of ex-Nazis to the United States, Britain, Australia, and especially Canada (Loftus, 2011, p. 174). The identities of those ex-Nazis remained concealed for decades, until they had either died or become too old to be prosecuted for anything more than immigration fraud (Aarons & Loftus, 1998, p. xv). For example, Otto von Bolschwing was brought to the United States by the CIA in 1954, and the CIA hid his close ties to Adolf Eichmann following the latter's capture in Argentina in 1960; von Bolschwing was allowed to live freely until prosecutors discovered his wartime role and revoked his US citizenship in 1981, and he died a year later at the age of seventy-two (Lichtblau, 2014).

Not only ex-Nazis, but also collaborators and war criminals from Nazi puppet regimes in Eastern Europe were "systematically imported" by the US State Department between 1948 and 1950, allegedly without President Truman's knowledge and against Congressional intent to ban the immigration of fascists, but with legal support from the DoJ (Loftus, 2011, pp. 166–169, 2). This was done mainly through the Office of Policy Coordination (see Chapter 5), which, Loftus (2011, p. 30) alleges, "recruited Nazi war criminals, hid the Nazi files inside the unwitting CIA, and then destroyed the CIA's ability to retrieve the information by removing the index." (On the other hand, Loftus goes to such great lengths to exonerate the CIA in his book, whose first edition "the CIA rather liked" [2011, p. 21], that we must recognize the possibility that the book is a limited hangout.) Henry Kissinger oversaw the intelligence file room containing records of Nazi recruitment, although there is no evidence that he was personally responsible for recruiting Nazis (Loftus, 2011, p. 11).

The Gehlen Organization, established under Western auspices in June 1946 and headed by former Nazi intelligence chief Reinhard Gehlen, offered an important channel for the recruitment of ex-Nazis; it evolved into the West German Federal Intelligence Service in 1956. Over 100 former Gestapo and SS officers were recruited by the CIA through the Gehlen Organization (Feinstein, 2005). Names included Alois Brunner, who sent over 100,000 Jews to ghettos and concentration camps, Franz Alfred Six, who led a death squad unit in the Soviet Union, Emil Augsburg, who planned SS executions of Jews in occupied Poland, Karl Silberbauer, who captured Anne Frank, Klaus Barbie, the so-called "Butcher of Lyon," Otto von Bolschwing, who instigated the 1941 Bucharest pogrom, and Otto Skorzeny, who was acquitted of alleged war crimes at Nuremberg.

Former death squad commander Friedrich Buchardt worked for MI6 and the CIA after World War II, and his history of the Nazi occupation of Eastern Europe was plagiarized by Stanford's Alexander Dallin as *Russia Under German Rule* (Loftus, 2011, p. 143). Franz Halder, the Nazi Chief of General Staff of the Army High Command, was responsible for the Barbarossa Decree allowing German soldiers to execute Soviet citizens for any reason without fear of prosecution; instead of being tried at Nuremberg, he became lead consultant for the US Army Historical Division and was allowed to rewrite history, such that the Wehrmacht was free from blame for the War of Annihilation in the East (Reif, 2023a). This was in line with Chancellor Adenauer's claim that Waffen-SS were soldiers like any other (cf. Hausser, 1966)—a myth graphically exposed in the *War of Annihiliation: Crimes of the Wehrmacht* exhibition (curated by Hannes Heer) in the mid-1990s.

The United States actively recruited over 1,600 former Nazi scientists, engineers, and technicians through Operation PAPERCLIP (1945–1959), the Western counterpoint to Operation Osoaviakhim. PAPERCLIP was approved in principle by the Joint Chiefs of Staff on July 6, 1945, without President Truman's knowledge of it; more than a year passed before the president gave his approval. Those recruited included nuclear scientists as well as V-1 and V-2 rocket experts such as Wernher von Braun (former SS, awarded the Knight's Cross, appointed director of NASA's Marshall Space Flight Center in 1960), Georg Rickhey (accused of helping to hang twelve slave laborers from a crane, received the Knight's Cross, later worked at Wright-Patterson Air Force Base), and Arthur Rudolph (accused of committing atrocities at the Nuremberg Trials but later given US citizenship and a major role in the US missile program [Simpson, 1988, p. xiii]). They also included scientists who had conducted medical experiments on concentration camp inmates, such as Walter Schreiber, while the Nuremberg Code of 1947 was being drawn up.

I.G. Farben's Otto Ambros jointly developed the nerve agent sarin in 1938, as well as synthetic rubber, which was produced using slave labor at Auschwitz under his direction. Having been found guilty of mass murder at Nuremberg in 1948, Ambros was released in early 1951. "Angel of Death" Joseph Mengele almost certainly experimented with sarin on Auschwitz inmates and, according to Loftus (2011, p. 68), bought his freedom (he managed to flee to Argentina) by selling the test records to British intelligence. Nazi doctors were brought to Fort Detrick to advise on the use of sarin and to explain the results of experiments with mescaline on human subjects at the Dachau concentration camp (Gross, 2019).

Kurt Blome, who led the way in Nazi biological warfare research (including experimentation on concentration camp inmates), was tried on charges of euthanasia and experimenting on human beings at the 1947 Doctors' Trial at Nuremberg but was acquitted and hired a few years later by the US Army Chemical Corps to conduct a new round of biological weapons research (Simpson, 1988, p. xiii).

Experimenting on Human Beings

Unit 731 of the Japanese Imperial Army performed lethal human experiments during the Second Sino-Japanese War, leaving no survivors. Those experiments included vivisection, injecting victims with venereal diseases disguised as vaccinations, using live human targets to test grenades and flamethrowers, electrocution, injection with animal blood, exposure to lethal levels of x-ray radiation, and rape and forced pregnancy. Unit 731 also developed biological warfare methods, including the release of plague-infected fleas over China, injecting wells with typhoid and paratyphoid, and injecting prisoners with various diseases including bubonic plague, cholera, smallpox, and botulism. War criminals from Unit 731, such as Shito Ishii, were granted secret immunity by the United States in exchange for their "expertise." This amnesty, first revealed by John Powell in a 1981 *Bulletin of Atomic Scientists* article, was not formally conceded by the US government until 1999 and the relevant documentation was not published until 2017 (see Kaye 2017). All subsequent US biowarfare research must be seen in this context (cf. van der Pijl 2022, Chapter 5).

The postwar US national security apparatus, from the outset, had no compunction about experimenting on US citizens without their informed consent. For example, the US Navy's Project CHATTER (1947) involved administering *Anabasis aphylla*, scopolamine, and mescaline to test subjects to determine their speech-inducing properties (United States Senate Select Committee on Intelligence, 1977, p. 67). Operation Seaspray (September 20–27, 1950) saw the US Navy spray *Bacillus globigii* and *Serratia marcescens* along the coast in San Francisco, ostensibly to assess the vulnerability of the local population to such attacks; eleven people were hospitalized and one died (Bentley, 2019). In 1951, *Aspergillus fumigatus*, a fungal spore known to cause lethal infections, was dispersed among the mostly African-American workforce at the Norfolk Naval Supply Center in Virginia (Cole, 1994).

The Nazi germ warfare scientists who came to the United States dropped poison ticks from planes to test their capacity to spread rare diseases, most notably on the Plum Island artillery range off the coast of Connecticut during the early 1950s (Loftus, 2011, p. 68). The Lyme disease outbreak in the United States has been attributed to this. North Korea alleges that the United States dropped canisters full of infected insects during the Korean War (Ryall, 2010). Biological warfare techniques pioneered by Unit 731 are known to have been used by the United States during the Korean War in 1952, including "anthrax, plague, and cholera, disseminated by over a dozen different devices or methods" (Kaye, 2018). Operation Big Itch (1954) established that rat fleas, which spread bubonic plague, can be loaded into munitions (Department of the Army, 2009).

In 1949, the Army's Chemical Corps circulated harmless bacteria through the Pentagon's air conditioning systems to explore what a bio-weapon attack might look like (Bentley, 2019). In the mid-1950s, and again a decade later, the US Army used motorized blowers to spray cadmium sulfide (known to cause lung cancer) over poor areas of St. Louis and Minneapolis, chosen for their resemblance to target cities in the Soviet Union ("Secret Cold War tests in St. Louis cause worry," 2012; Salter, 2012; Bentley, 2019). The Pentagon's Project 112 (1962–1974) saw a large increase in bioweapons funding and testing. The Army released microorganisms at Washington National Airport in 1965, and in June 1966 it smashed light-bulbs full of bacteria on New York City subway tracks and monitored the bacteria spread while people went about their business (Cole, 1994; Loria, 2015). Between 1949 and 1969, the Pentagon conducted 239 secret open-air germ warfare experiments on a public serving as "unknowing guinea pigs," ostensibly to learn more about how to wage and defend against bio-logical warfare (Wilson, 1977). The US Government Accountability Office (2008) estimates that the DoD since 1945 has exposed tens of thousands of military personnel and civilians to chemical or biological substances.

The situation was scarcely different in Britain. From 1940 to 1979, in over a hundred covert experiments carried out by government scientists at Porton Down, allegedly harmless chemicals and micro-organisms were released "over vast swaths of the population without the public being told," supposedly to test Britain's vulnerability to Russian germ warfare (Barnett, 2002). In 1956, bacteria were released on the London Underground at lunchtime along the Northern Line between Colliers Wood and Tooting Broadway. Between 1955 and 1963, planes flew from north-east to south-west England spraying the population with large quantities of zinc cad-mium sulfide, regarded as a chemical weapon by the Allies in World War II. Between 1961 and 1968, a military ship anchored off the Dorset coast sprayed bacteria including *E.coli* and *bacillus globigii* (which mimics anthrax) over a ten-mile radius; a million people were exposed. The DICE trials in south Dorset (1971–1975) involved the US and UK militaries spraying the population with "massive quantities of *serratia marcescens* bacteria, with an anthrax simulant and phenol" (Barnett, 2002).

There was also extensive usage of human beings as guinea pigs to test the effects of nuclear radiation, not least using the inhabitants of the Marshall

Islands (Pilger, 2016; Takeuchi, 2021). The *Atomic Veterans Newsletter* published the following statement:

> We were the victims of radiation experiments, too. They exposed over 200,000 of us in over 200 atmospheric atomic and hydrogen bomb tests between 1945–1962. They deliberately bombed us with nuclear weapons and exposed us to deadly radioactivity to see how it would affect us and our equipment in nuclear warfare on land, sea, and air. They didn't need our informed consent because we were under military discipline. They devalued our lives too! They made us sterile! They crippled and killed our children! They made widows out of wives! Then denied repeatedly and publicly that there was ever any danger! (cited in Thomas, 2011, p. 44)

In the United States, between April 1945 and July 1947, eighteen test subjects were injected with plutonium, uranium, polonium, and americium (Atomic Heritage Foundation, 2017). President Clinton apologized in 1995 for thousands of human radiation experiments conducted by the US government between 1944 and 1974 ("Human Radiation Experiments Report," 1995).

CIA Mind Control Programs

Project BLUEBIRD (1950) involved the use of polygraphs, drugs, and hypnotism for "offensive uses of unconventional interrogation techniques," such as were applied to captured North Koreans in October 1950 (United States Senate Select Committee on Intelligence, 1977, p. 68). BLUEBIRD was renamed ARTICHOKE on 20, August 1951, and "Artichoke work" became code for medical torture, including "dosing unwilling patients with potent drugs, subjecting them to extremes of temperature and sound, strapping them to electroshock machines, and other forms of abuse" (Kinzer, 2019, p. 59). A CIA memo on ARTICHOKE cited by Kinzer additionally mentions exposure to gases and aerosols, use of "bacteria, plant cultures, fungi, poisons of various types," and "a great many psychological techniques," including exploitation of phobias and manipulation of the physical environment. The aim of ARTICHOKE, according to a 1952 CIA memo cited by Krishnan (2016, p. 21), was to "get control of an individual to the point where he will do our bidding against his will and even against fundamental laws of nature, such as self-preservation." ARTICHOKE was, thus, a crime against Creation.

In 1952, the CIA enlisted the help of the Army's Special Operations Division at Fort Detrick in order to develop and test biological weapons for use against humans. This project was known as MKNAOMI and included, among other things, "methods and systems for carrying out a covert attack against crops and causing severe crop loss" (United States Senate Select Committee on Intelligence, 1977, p. 69). The tactics used in North Korea in 1952 and 1953 (see above) are consistent with this.

Allen Dulles took over as the Director of Central Intelligence on February 26, 1953, and fifteen days later authorized MKULTRA. MKULTRA was "essentially a continuation of work that began in Japanese and Nazi concentration camps," and it involved the same vivisectionists and torturers who had worked in Japan and in Nazi concentration camps (Gross, 2019). MKULTRA yielded the *KUBARK [CIA] Manual* (1963), intended as a guide to "interrogation" (torture). To break down a prisoner, the *Manual* claims, it is necessary to apply "a kind of psychological shock or paralysis. It is caused by a traumatic or sub-traumatic experience which explodes, as it were, the world that is familiar to the subject as well as his image of himself within that world" (CIA, 1963, p. 66). Trauma-based mind control traces back to MKULTRA (Hughes, 2024, Chapter 3), as does what Klein (2007) calls the "shock doctrine," i.e. shock techniques applied to entire societies (cf. Hughes, 2024, Chapter 2).

Descendants of Nazis in Positions of Power Today

Descendants of former Nazis remain influential in today's world. Eugen Schwab was the managing director of Escher Wyss, which was granted special status by the Nazis (permitting slave labor). His son, Klaus, founded the World Economic Forum in 1973 and praises his father for "assuming many functions in the public life in post-war Germany," a slap in the face to West Germans of his age who in the 1960s protested against the continuation of ex-Nazis in positions of power (Schwab, 2021, p. 255). Schwab Jr. openly boasted at Harvard's John F. Kennedy School of Government in 2017 that his Young Global Leaders have "penetrated the cabinets" of multiple countries. But it is not only politics that has been infiltrated by the WEF. Former Young Global Leaders occupy leading positions in investment banks, Big Tech, the mainstream media, think tanks, and beyond, and have been "in the middle of everything covid" (Engdahl, 2022; Swiss Policy Research, 2021).

Günther Quandt was a German industrialist and Nazi Party member whose former wife went on to marry Joseph Goebbels in 1931 with Adolf Hitler as best man at a property owned by Quant himself; Goebbels later adopted Quandt's son Harald (Richter, 2017). In 1937, Hitler named Quandt a war economy leader (*Wehrwirtschaftsführer*), which enabled him to make extensive use of slave labor, and in 1943, with support from SS, the Quandts set up a "company-owned concentration camp" in Hanover where workers were told upon arrival that they would not live longer than six months on account of exposure to poisonous gases (Bode & Fehlau, 2008). Quant's daughter-in-law, Johanna, was, on her mother's side, the granddaughter of Max Rubner, who directed the Institute for Hygiene at Friedrich Wilhelm University, later associated with Nazi eugenics experiments. It is, therefore, of note that Johanna Quandt gave €40 million to the Charité Foundation between 2014 and 2022 for the establishment of the Berlin Institute for Health Research, to which Christian Drosten was appointed in 2017. Her daughter, Susanne Klatten (Germany's richest woman) attended the 2017 Bilderberg meeting with Jens Spahn, the Young Global Leader who in 2018 was appointed German health minister. Klatten also owns Entrust (chosen by the UK government to produce vaccine passports), linking her to the "Covid-19" biodigital surveillance agenda. Other "Nazi billionaire" families remaining influential today include Flick, von Finck, Porsche-Piëch, and Oetker (de Jong, 2022).

Michael Chomiak was a Ukrainian Nazi collaborator (Pugliese, 2017); his granddaughter, Chrystia Freeland, sits on the WEF board of trustees and is the Minister of Finance and Deputy Prime Minister of Canada. In 2022, not long after announcing that she would freeze the bank accounts of Canadian truckers and their supporters, she tweeted a picture of herself holding a red and black flag associated with the Bandera movement in Ukraine (later deleted without comment and a new photograph minus the scarf was posted). Stepan Bandera led a militia that fought alongside the Nazis in World War II, and the anti-Russian Azov battalion, established during the 2014 Western-backed coup in Ukraine, openly displayed Nazi insignia until this became politically sensitive in June 2022. In September 2023, the Canadian Parliament gave a standing ovation to former Waffen-SS member Yaroslav Hunka (Blumenthal, 2023).

Ursula von der Leyen, President of the European Commission since 2019, is the daughter of Ernst Albrecht, who was the aide of ex-Nazi Hans von der Groeben in his role as European Commissioner for Competition in the Hallstein Commission (Hallstein being another ex-Nazi). As President of Lower Saxony (1978–1990), Albrecht stands accused of complicity in a false flag operation (the Celle Hole scandal of 1978), which was blamed on the Red Army Faction (Reif, 2023b), in keeping with the Gladio model of the time (see Chapter 5). That very same year, the Red Army Faction allegedly threatened to kidnap Ursula, who enrolled at the LSE under the name of Rose Ladson, after another branch of her family, the Ladsons of South Carolina—historical slave owners and plantationists. She is also a distant relative of Joachim von der Leyen, who served as a Nazi district governor in Galicia (1942–1944). An unlikely choice for German Defense Minister (2013–2019), Ursula von der Leyen presided over a scandal which exposed neo-Nazi sympathies in the ranks of the Bundeswehr; she also joined the WEF Board of Trustees in 2016.

Conclusion

Contrary to received wisdom that the Nazis were vanquished in 1945, the truth is that only 199 defendants were tried at Nuremberg, of whom only 161 were convicted, with 37 being sentenced to death (Holocaust Encyclopedia, n.d.). The Bank for International Settlements survived despite aiding Hitler in numerous ways. The Vatican's role in helping Nazis to escape is still not widely understood. Global governance was indifferent to denazification. Corporate control over German society persisted. The United States and its allies actively recruited former Nazis, including the most depraved, to serve their Cold War agendas, and almost immediately they began experimenting on their own populations without informed consent, most horrifyingly in the early CIA mind control programs. Troublingly, descendants of former Nazis remain highly influential in today's world.

CHAPTER 5

THE DEEP STATE

The US national security state, established by the National Security Act of 1947, was a Wall Street creation, with fascist sympathizer George Kennan at the heart of instituting its political warfare arm through the State Department. A bewildering array of blandly named alphabet agencies were formed and dissolved within the space of a few years, ultimately seeing covert operations fall under the purview of the CIA. A "dual/deep state" power structure was established, providing the outward-facing aspect of the "invisible government" identified in the first half of the twentieth century. Its primary purpose was to facilitate the criminal political violence necessary to expand capitalist accumulation. From the outset, the deep state was transnational and in part coordinated under NATO, as per evidence relating to so-called "stay behind" armies. As new knowledge about the transnational deep state comes to light, conventional Cold War narratives need to be reappraised, including the very idea of a "Cold War." Stalinist parties facilitated the stabilization of capitalism in the West after 1945 in exchange for Moscow's dominion over Eastern Europe. Despite early Cold War attempts to portray the Soviet Union as an implacable existential threat, Wall Street and the Kremlin had enjoyed a mutually beneficial partnership ever since the end of World War I. During the Cold War, the United States and the Soviet Union partnered to suppress international class conflict.

Wall Street, Kennan, and the Birth of the US National Security State

In July 1947, the National Security Act was signed into law by President Truman, ostensibly aimed at improving coordination between military and intelligence agencies. It provided for, among other things, a National Military Establishment to be headed by the Secretary of Defense, a National Security Council (NSC), and the Central Intelligence Agency (CIA). The latter would replace the Office of Strategic Service (OSS, 1942–1945), run during the war as an equivalent of MI6. It was the brainchild of Allen Dulles, who formed an advisory group of six men, five of whom (including William H. Jackson and Frank Wisner) were Wall Street investment bankers or lawyers (Scott, 2017, p. 14). A blueprint for the National Security Act was provided by Ferdinand Eberstadt (erstwhile vice-president of the War Production Board), who, like his long-time collaborator James Forrestal, was a former Dillon, Read & Co. investment banker. Forrestal was appointed the first US Defense Secretary in September 1947. The creation of the CIA was lobbied for by former Wall Street lawyers and OSS directors William Donovan and Allen Dulles (who later became Director of Central Intelligence). According to future CIA executive director A. B. "Buzzy" Krongard, "the whole OSS was really nothing but Wall Street bankers and lawyers" (cited in Ahmed, 2012, p. 65). 1949 legislation meant that it enjoyed "maximum secrecy" of budget, the Director of Central Intelligence being required merely to certify that the money had been spent appropriately, rather than having to account publicly for specific expenditures (Karalekas, 1977, p. 40).

In its first session in December 1947, the NSC approved the creation of an undercover unit, the Special Procedures Group (SPG), which became operational in March 1948 under the leadership of Frank Wisner. Before the war, Wisner had worked at Carter, Ledyard and Milburn, Franklin Roosevelt's old law firm. After the war, Wisner was the architect of the Bloodstone program, through which scores of Nazi collaborationist leaders entered the United States to be trained for political warfare (including sabotage and assassination) in Eastern Europe (Simpson, 2014, p. 100). Giving the lie to the Truman doctrine of "free institutions, representative government, [and] free elections" (as per Truman's address to Congress on March 12, 1947), the first act of the SPG was to subvert the Italian election of April 1948.

As part of the 1947 national security shake-up, George Kennan was appointed at Forrestal's recommendation as the inaugural Director of Policy Planning at the State Department. In 1938, Kennan had proposed an authoritarian form of government in the United States, calling for suffrage to be withdrawn from "bewildered" and "ignorant" women, immigrants, and African Americans (Miscamble, 1993, p. 17; Costigliola, 1997, p. 128). Professing admiration for Austria's fascist Schuschnigg regime, he claimed that "if malicious despotism had greater possibilities for evil than democracy, benevolent despotism had greater possibilities for good" (cited in Botts, 2006, p. 844). After the war, he had the 1938 document removed from his papers in Princeton's Seeley G. Mudd Manuscript Library. In 1947–8, Kennan was the architect of the Reverse Course in Japan, maintaining the *zaibatsu* and "reinstating the prewar political class with its Class A war criminals, as was not possible in Germany"; the US occupation, he remarked, could "dispense with bromides about democratization" (Anderson, 2017, p. 60). Kennan claimed he "prefer[red] to remain ignorant" of Nazi war crimes; rather than purging Nazis from postwar German governments, it would be better, he claimed, to hold "the present ruling class of Germany [. . .] strictly to its task and teach it the lessons we wish it to learn" (Simpson, 2014, pp. 88–89). Kennan personally intervened to obtain high-level security clearance for Gustav Hilger, who had served in Nazi foreign minister von Ribbentrop's personal secretariat and played a role in the Holocaust, taking his advice on East-West policy (Simpson, 2014, p. 116). In Latin America, Kennan advocated "harsh measures of repression," even though this "would not stand the test of American concepts of democratic procedures" (cited in Anderson, 2017, p. 86).

While publicly advocating "containment," Kennan authored an important memo dated 4 May 1948 proposing that the State Department establish a directorate of political warfare operations capable of rivalling those of Britain and the Soviet Union (Kennan, 1948). Such operations may be overt, involving political alliances, economic measures such as the Marshall Plan, and propaganda. Or they may be covert, involving "clandestine support of 'friendly' foreign elements, 'black' psychological warfare and even encouragement of underground resistance in hostile states" (Kennan, 1948). All covert operations, Kennan recommends, should be run under cover of the NSC, headed by a single individual answerable to the Secretary of State.

NSC directive 10/2 (June 18, 1948) provides for the establishment of an Office of Special Projects (OSP) within the CIA with powers to engage in covert activities relating to propaganda, economic warfare, preventive direct action (including sabotage, anti-sabotage, demolition, and evacuation measures), subversion against hostile states (including assistance to underground resistance movements, guerrillas, and refugee liberation groups), and support of indigenous anticommunist elements in "threatened countries of the free world" (Office of the Historian, n.d.).

Although NSC 10/2 states that covert operations "shall not include armed conflict by recognized military forces, espionage, counter-espionage, and cover and deception for military operations," Kennan and Charles Thayer secretly pushed for the restoration of the Vlasov Army, an anti-Communist émigré campaign created by the SS for use against the USSR, which could work together with US military specialists as a part of a new school for anti-Communist guerrilla warfare training (Simpson, 2014, p. 8)—not dissimilar from the School of the Americas, founded in 1946.

The Office of Special Projects replaced the Special Procedures Group, inheriting its resources, and was renamed the Office of Policy Coordination (OPC) to deflect attention from its covert activities before becoming operational in September 1948. It was headed by Wisner, Kennan's second choice behind Allen Dulles (now CFR President, 1946–1950), who declined the position in the mistaken expectation of becoming CIA Director following a Republican victory in the 1948 election. According to Loftus (2011, p. 61), the Ford, Carnegie, and Rockefeller foundations acted as money launderers for the OPC.

In August 1952, the OPC was merged with the Office of Special Operations, the 1946 successor to the Strategic Services Unit, which replaced the Office of Strategic Services in 1945. The resultant entity, the Directorate of Plans, was placed under CIA control, meaning that the DCI finally had management authority and was not simply providing the budget and personnel (Karalekas, 1977, p. 36). It was led by Wisner, who replaced Allen Dulles as Deputy Director of Plans (a post created in January 1951 to try to ameliorate tensions between the OPC and OSO). Dulles was simultaneously promoted to Deputy Director of the CIA.

The Korean War saw the number of OPC personnel treble between 1950 and 1951 and resulted in the CIA growing six times its original size by 1953, helping to establish the CIA's jurisdiction in the Far East (Karalekas, 1977, pp. 36–40). One might be forgiven for seeing the unnecessary prolongation of the Korean War as a means of growing CIA power and influence, rather than as a legitimate response to an alleged threat. By the end of that war, "the basic paramilitary capability" of the CIA was put in place, including aircraft, amphibious craft, and experienced personnel, and for the next twenty-five years, paramilitary activities were "the major CIA covert activity in the Far East" (Karalekas, 1977, p. 36). In effect, Wall Street had developed its own private military apparatus.

The Dual/Deep State

The above genealogy of alphabet agencies, with Kennan as the red thread, charts the emergence of what Hans Morgenthau, in a 1955 study, calls the "dual state" (Morgenthau, 1962). Morgenthau was concerned, at the height of the Second Red Scare, that certain officers in the State Department no longer reported to the Secretary of State and the President, but rather to Senator McCarthy. Confounding the later neorealist stereotype of the state as a unified rational actor, Morgenthau posited both a "regular state hierarchy" and a "security hierarchy" in the United States. Whereas the regular state hierarchy is visible and obeys the rule of law, the security hierarchy is invisible and de facto "monitors and controls the former," exercising veto power over it via the ability to impose emergency measures in the name of security (Tunander, 2016, pp. 171, 186).

The logic of the veto function goes back to Nazi Germany. A common misconception is that totalitarianism relies on a tightly regimented top-down command-and-control structure. Despite the *Führerprinzip*, which encouraged such a structure, the bureaucratic reality in the Third Reich was altogether different: far from creating a streamlined bureaucracy, Hitler "left most of the old structure standing and added to it a proliferation of new state and party agencies, allowing lines of authority to become confused and areas of competency to overlap" (Turner, 1972, p. 151). Thus, the Third Reich had "a vast and sprawling bureaucracy," full of institutional rivalries, contradictions, and infighting (Shirer, 1990, p. 276). Hannah Arendt pointed to "the peculiar 'shapelessness'" of totalitarian government, while Hans Mommsen claimed that the Nazi regime displayed "an unparalleled institutional anarchy" (cited in Uekötter 2005, pp. 102–3). The way it functioned was not that agreement was required on all issues, but, rather, that the regime exercised veto power on fundamental issues. In this way, Nazi officials had considerable leeway to act without the Führer's explicit endorsement, yet nothing could happen against his declared will (Uekötter 2005, p. 102). In that sense, Hitler remained "supreme political arbiter" (Turner, 1972, p. 181).

The US security hierarchy of the mid-twentieth century can, in the first instance, be seen as the outward-facing aspect of the "invisible government" identified by multiple authors previously. These include the Progressive Party in its 1912 platform; New York City mayor John Hylan's

"Invisible Government" article of 1922, which points the finger at an "oligarchy of big business," headed by "the Rockefeller-Standard Oil interests, certain powerful industrial magnates, and a small group of banking houses [. . .]" (Hylan, 1922, pp. 659–61, 714–16); and Bernays' (1928, p. 1) claim that those who exercise a "conscious and intelligent manipulation of the organized habits and opinions of the masses [. . .] manipulate this unseen mechanism of society constitute an invisible government which is the true ruling power of our country."

Together, the invisible government and the security hierarchy form "a new deep apparatus"—sometimes referred to as the deep state (Scott, 2017)—by which private actors "leverage the state into instrumentalizing or facilitating the criminal political violence necessary to sustain and expand [capitalist] accumulation" (Ahmed, 2012, p. 63). The deep state amounts to a high-level conspiracy between key elements of Wall Street, intelligence and other government agencies, the military-industrial complex, the police, multinational corporations, think tanks, foundations, the media, and academia. Regardless of which government is nominally in charge, the deep state subverts democracy and the rule of law to make sure that ruling class agendas are continuously advanced. Although there are tensions and power struggles between different groups and institutions of the deep state, ultimately those different class fractions tend to coalesce and unite around certain fundamental control paradigms and policies for their mutual class benefit. The deep state makes its most significant interventions in the form of "deep events," i.e. events which profoundly transform the trajectory of politics and society yet whose provenance is ambiguous, e.g. the JFK assassination, 9/11, and "Covid-19" (cf. Scott, 2017, Chapter 9).

The CIA, in Marcus' (1974, pp. 8–13) view, "represents the base of a kind of dual power, an illegal, parallel government" that is "more a conspiracy against the USA itself than the USSR." By 1974, the CIA had encroached "on every branch of government and enormous sectors of private institutions," with presidential power unable to restrain it. Little has changed since then:

> The CIA is the most corrupting influence in the United States. It corrupted the Customs Bureau the same way it corrupted the DEA. It corrupts the State Department and the military. It has infiltrated civil organizations and the media to make sure that none of its illegal operations are exposed. (Valentine, 2017, p. 52)

Increasingly from the mid-to-late 1960s on, counterinsurgency techniques previously reserved for non-Western populations also came to be applied to Western populations in the form of low intensity operations (Hughes, 2024, Chapter 2). In this context, the CIA appears as a "US financier-promoted Anglo-American insurgency-counter-insurgency project" (Marcus, 1974, p. 13). Its primary purpose is not to protect the public, but, rather, to control it by whatever means necessary.

The Transnationalization of the Deep State

The emergence of the United States as the dominant imperialist power after 1945 led to the creation of a "US-dominated transnational *deep system* which transfigured, and continues to attempt to manipulate, the trajectories of local and regional politics" (Ahmed, 2012, p. 63). Scott (2017, p. 30) points to the emergence of a "supranational deep state."

This began with the Five Eyes surveillance network, which is conventionally understood as an Anglophone signals intelligence alliance based on the UKUSA Agreement of 1946 (whose origins, in turn, lie in an informal agreement relating to the Atlantic Charter of 1941). The 1946 treaty was soon expanded, however, to include Canada (1948), Norway (1952), and Denmark (1954), plus West Germany, Australia, and New Zealand (1955) (Norton-Taylor, 2010). Thus, the "Five Eyes" label is in fact misleading, notwithstanding the formal declaration by Britain and the United States in 1955 that only Canada, Australia, and New Zealand would be regarded as "UKUSA-collaborating Commonwealth countries" (cited in Norton-Taylor, 2010). The transnational surveillance system had already integrated several Western European partners and was being run by the US with the UK as junior partner. Other "vassal states," including France, South Korea, and Japan, were also drawn into the network, alongside Israel, for the benefit of the Atlantic ruling class (van der Pijl, 2022, p. 73).

There are two levels of power operative in the deep system, one visible, the other hidden, based on "the *Grossraum* divide between the hierarchy of the nation-state and the security hierarchy of the protecting power or Reich" (Tunander, 2016, p. 186). *Grossraum* is a concept found in the writings of Nazi jurist Carl Schmitt and translates as "Grand Area," a concept central to Council on Foreign Relations planning documents of 1944 for postwar international order, expressible as "a core region, which could always be extended to include more countries" (Shoup & Minter, 1977, p. 138). In that postwar order,

> US intelligence and security forces would always be present in the local states to guarantee the security of the *Grossraum*. In other words, the US security hierarchy would intervene if "necessary" as a veto force or an "emergency power," or what Carl Schmitt called the sovereign. It might intervene to influence the nation-state hierarchy or with operations able to manipulate policies of this hierarchy or, in the final analysis, veto its decisions by replacing its leaders. (Tunander, 2016, p. 186)

According to Tunander, this dual structure is present in all NATO states, indicating that NATO is not just a formal alliance of sovereign states but also "something of an informal US 'super-state'" (2016, p. 185).

The evidence demonstrating the existence of a transnational deep state has been historically slow to emerge, precisely because that system was intended to remain hidden. Nevertheless, it was graphically exposed in 1990, when revelations emerged that the Italian military intelligence agency SIFAR had, since the late 1940s, collaborated with the CIA to establish a secret army in Italy code-named "Gladio" ("sword"). According to Davis (2018), it is unclear whether any organization other than the CIA or MI6 was able to authorize Gladio operations. Ostensibly coordinated by NATO, the Gladio secret army was part of a clandestine international network theoretically intended to provide resistance in the event of a Soviet invasion of Western Europe (Ganser, 2005, p. 88). Every Italian Prime Minister had known about Operation Gladio, and one of them, Francesco Cossiga (1978–1979) even claimed to be "proud of the fact that we have kept the secret for 45 years" (cited in Ganser, 2005, p. 88).

In Germany, of all countries, around 2,000 former SS and Wehrmacht officers, with the support of ex-Nazi military leaders such as Albert Schenz, Hans Speidel, and Adolf Heusinger, formed a secret paramilitary army in 1949 (in the absence of a West German army), with as many as 40,000 recruits waiting to be activated in the event of a Soviet invasion (Peck, 2019). Given the many continuities between the Nazi military and NATO, not least involving Speidel and Heusinger (see Chapter 4), it seems likely that this was part of the same transnational NATO exercise as Gladio.

In a memo of 4 May 1948, Kennan proposes the establishment of a directorate of political warfare operations by the State Department and recommends four specific policies, one of which remains redacted (Kennan, 1948). Could it be that the redacted policy refers to stay-behind armies? Kennan himself (1985, p. 214) would later acknowledge his own role in setting up "clandestine defensive operations" in the late 1940s. According to Ahmed (2012, p. 67), the stay-behind armies were established via close collaboration between the Office of Political Coordination (established on Kennan's initiative) and the Special Operations branch of MI6 on White House orders.

The purpose of the Gladio stay-behind armies changed over time. Following working class revolts in East Germany (1953) and Hungary

(1956), Kennan (1957) claimed in his fourth Reith lecture that the primary danger posed by the USSR was not, in fact, a military invasion of Western Europe, but, rather, political subversion from within by local communist organizations directed by the Kremlin. This theme was echoed in a 1959 Italian Armed Forces report, which saw the danger as originating, not in Soviet military invasion, but rather in domestic communist groups (see Davis, 2018). Kennan recommended that "paramilitary forces" be deployed as "the core of a civil resistance movement on any territory that might be overwhelmed by the enemy." However, the "enemy" here does not really mean Soviet communism. It means the working class, veiled by the misimpression that it is really the Soviet Union that is being fought, for "as long as the capitalist ruling class was not strong enough to roll back the Left working class, these [NATO] forces had to be kept in reserve for an emergency" (van der Pijl, 2020).

In the same year, 1957, the operational command of Gladio was transferred from NATO's Clandestine Planning Committee to the Allied Clandestine Committee, which was overseen by the US Supreme Allied Commander in Europe who reported directly to the Pentagon (Davis, 2018). Then, in 1963, that same command post was taken by General Lyman Lemnitzer who in 1962 had approved Operation Northwoods, a plan for a series of false flag attacks to be blamed on Cuba for the purpose of provoking war. Though NATO has repeatedly denied freedom of information requests on the subject, it seems reasonable to mark this period (1957–1963) as one in which the Gladio operation morphed from a supposedly defensive military operation in the event of Soviet occupation into an offensive operation against the working class, involving false flag terrorism.

The Gladio program became a de facto conduit for state-sponsored terrorism in the post-1968 era, committing numerous acts of terrorism that were blamed on the Red Brigades, including the kidnap and murder of ex-prime minister Aldo Moro and five of his staff in 1978, as well as the bombing of the Bologna Centrale railway station in 1980, which killed eighty-five people and wounded over two hundred. False flag operations used to incriminate communists can be traced to the Reichstag fire of 1933 (Hett, 2014; Sutton, 2016, pp. 118–19).

Vincenzo Vinciguerra, a neo-fascist convicted of killing three Italian police officers in a car bombing in 1972 with C4 explosive taken from a Gladio arms dump, testified during his trial in 1984, "there existed a real live structure, occult and hidden, with the capacity of giving a strategic direction to the outrages" (cited in Ganser, 2005, pp. 88–89). A secret network composed of both military figures and civilians, Vinciguerra claimed, had infiltrated the state, operating parallel to the armed forces, and was tasked with "preventing a slip to the left in the political balance of the country," which it achieved with help from intelligence services. Similarly, the former head of Italian counterintelligence, General Giandelio Maletti, testified in the trial of right-wing extremists accused of involvement in the 1969 massacre in Milan's Piazza Fontana that the CIA wanted "an Italian nationalism capable of halting what it saw as a slide to the left, and, for this purpose, it may have made use of right-wing terrorism" (cited in Ganser, 2005, p. 91).

In a passage that presciently unmasks the underlying logic of twenty-first century governance, Vinciguerra testified:

You had to attack civilians, the people, women, children, innocent people, unknown people far removed from any political game. The reason was quite simple. They were supposed to force these people, the Italian public, to turn to the State to ask for greater security. This was precisely the role of the right in Italy. It placed itself at the service of the State which created a strategy aptly called the "Strategy of Tension" in so far as they had to get ordinary people to accept that at any moment over a period of 30 years, from 1960 to the mid eighties, a State of emergency could be declared. So, people would willingly trade part of their freedom for the security of being able to walk the streets, go on trains or enter a bank. This is the political logic behind all the bombings. They remain unpunished because the state cannot condemn itself. (cited in Davis, 2018)

The same logic of trading freedom for security based on false flag terrorism was evident in the "War on Terror," just as it is in the building of the "Covid-19" biosecurity state. The Italian experience perhaps explains why one of the most perspicacious critics of both security paradigms has been the Italian philosopher, Giorgio Agamben.

The Strategy of Tension, in which repeated acts of terrorism were used, in Schmittian vein, to impose authority in a climate of terror, was not limited to Italy. The "stay-behind" networks were also responsible for terrorist attacks that were officially blamed on communists in Spain, Germany, France, Turkey, and Greece (Ahmed, 2012, p. 68). In Turkey, they followed the 1961 US Army Field Manual 31–15: Operations Against Irregular Forces (Davis, 2018). The inescapable conclusion, for Davis, is that Western intelligence agencies and security services orchestrated "terrible crimes committed against civilians throughout Europe and beyond."

Most remarkable about the Italian Strategy of Tension is that it left "at most only one or two government officials actually aware of the existence of the program" (Ahmed, 2012, p. 68). Elected politicians and government officials remained both blind and without operational command, evidencing "another form of government, hidden from both the public and many within the political establishment, that was operating beyond the rule of law, without democratic oversight or control. A 'Deep State'" (Davis, 2018). Davis continues that those responsible, including "many committed Nazis and neo-fascists," had formed a parallel European government and could harness state resources seemingly without constraint in pursuit of their aims. Meanwhile, the public, which was being targeted by such operations, was also paying for them and was the last to know about them.

One can only speculate on the extent to which the serial killer phenomenon since the 1970s, plus the rise of school shootings in the United States since the 1990s, serve a similar "strategy of tension" function, assuming individuals can be programmed to carry out such heinous acts. Evidence from the CIA's Project BLUEBIRD indicates that it is possible to hypnotize victims into unknowingly committing murder and planting bombs, however, it is unknown whether such techniques have been deployed in actual covert operations (Ross, 2006, Chapter 4). Similar research was continued in MKULTRA Subproject 136, begun in August 1961 (Ross, 2006, p. 66), and there is no obvious reason to think it would stop until the CIA had perfected the techniques for creating a Manchurian candidate.

The Postwar Stabilization of Capitalism

It behooves scholars of the Cold War, in light of emergent knowledge regarding the transnational deep state working on behalf of finance capital, to reappraise conventional Cold War narratives. In particular, it seems important to question whether the "Cold War," a term invented by George Orwell (1945) and dramatized by Walter Lippmann (1987), was ever anything more than propaganda.

At the end of World War II, the legitimacy of Western capitalism, which had led to the Great Depression, the rise of fascism, and two world wars, hung by a thread. The situation throughout Europe was a political powder keg: living conditions were poor, anti-capitalist sentiment was widespread, and sections of the bourgeoisie had to answer for their collaboration with the Nazis. The balance of class forces in the world was precarious (Adereth, 1984, p. 131). Bourgeois rule, as its ideologues knew, was anything but secure: Western Europe and Japan had been massively destabilized by the war, the Soviet Union had emerged with great prestige for its primary role in defeating the Nazis, the world communist movement was largely unified under Stalin, and communist parties threatened to come to power in several countries (Kennan, 1987, pp. 886–887).

Communist parties won a significant share of the vote in postwar elections: 19 percent in Italy, 24 percent in Finland, 26 percent in France (Steil,

2018, p. 19). French Communist Party (PCF) membership rose from half a million in June 1945 to 750,000 in December that year (Adereth, 1984, p. 131). Similarly in Italy, hundreds of thousands joined the Party in 1945 and the revolutionary Left seemed destined to take control (Ginsborg, 2003, p. 45; Steil, 2018, p. 19). The Italian ruling class emerged from the war in trepidation, believing that "only indefinite Allied occupation would save them from social revolution" (Ginsborg, 2003, p. 73).

US intelligence paid special attention to defeating communism in France and Italy. In France, the working class was esteemed for its contribution to the Resistance (Adereth, 1984, p. 131). To suppress the French working class, the power of the Communist Party over the labor movement had to be broken. This was achieved, in part, through promotion of the General Confederation of Labor (CGT), which supported a Popular Front, styled itself as the defender of small business, and prohibited strikes in plants and ports under its control (Wall, 1991, pp. 96–7). Meanwhile, the PCF pursued the "French road to socialism," which, though differing from Moscow over certain policies (such as the internationalization of the Ruhr), followed the Stalinist model of "socialism in one country," putting off the question of revolution and calling on the workers to work harder in the name of national unity and democratic reformism (Adereth, 1984, p. 141, 144). Both the CGT and the PCF were following principles previously laid down by the Communist International (Comintern, the Moscow-led international organization for world communism) and both thereby worked to *suppress* revolutionary impulses.

In Italy, Communist Party leader Palmiro Togliatti played a similarly decisive role in dampening revolutionary impulses. Already during the war, for Togliatti, the key communist aim was liberating Italy, not socialist revolution, and at the war's end (again following Comintern principles laid down at the Seventh Congress of July 1935), Togliatti promoted national unity, progressive democracy, and a Popular Front (Ginsborg, 2003, p. 43). His role was, thus, to ensure that the revolutionary impulses that were simmering within the Party were contained during a potentially explosive situation (Agarossi & Zaslavsky, 2011, p. 95). As a result of his policies, "the most powerful weapon in the hands of the left," i.e. working-class militancy, was discarded (Ginsborg, 2003, p. 83).

The key lesson here is that the post-1945 stabilization of capitalism, at a time when revolution was a realistic prospect, was politically enabled by Western European Stalinist parties and organizations. Capitalism had overcome none of its fundamental contradictions, yet it was able to rely on Stalinism to diffuse revolutionary impulses. In return for the disciplining of the international working class, the establishment of Communist regimes in Eastern Europe was an acceptable price to pay.

Conjuring an Existential Threat

The former Dillon, Read & Co. banker turned Secretary of the Navy, James Forrestal, solicited George Kennan's "long telegram" from Moscow in response to the USSR's refusal to join the World Bank and IMF in February 1946. He then distributed the telegram within official circles, whence it was leaked to *Time* magazine and made the subject of a full-page article that included some suggestive cartography showing communism spreading to "infect" other countries (McCauley, 2016, p. 89). In December 1946, Forrestal invited Kennan to produce another paper, which was published anonymously in *Foreign Affairs* in July 1947 under the title, "The Sources of Soviet Conduct" and introduced the idea of "containment." Thus originated the image of the Soviet Union as an implacable foe, an existential threat (as it proved to be for Nazi Germany), "a political force committed fanatically to the belief that with [the] US there can be no permanent *modus vivendi*" (Kennan, 1946, p. 14).

Paul Nitze, the former vice-president of Dillon, Read & Co., who married the daughter of a Standard Oil financier, succeeded Kennan as director of the State Department's Policy Planning Staff. Nitze had significant input into NSC-68 (1950), which warns darkly of "the Kremlin's design for world domination" and its threat to "civilization itself" and advocates for "roll-back" in place of "containment." NSC-68 failed to explain why Moscow would risk everything by invading Western Europe; it ignored a CIA finding that the Soviets did not have the strength and resources to do so successfully; and it vastly overestimated the size of the Soviet nuclear arsenal (Braithwaite, 2018, p. 147). It did, however, provide the pretext for US imperialism globally, aimed at "upholding capitalist social relations, be they politically liberal or otherwise" (Colás, 2012, p. 42).

Nazi ideology was based on the idea of existential threat, epitomized in Carl Schmitt's (1996) friend-enemy distinction. A similar logic applies to the existential threat allegedly posed to the United States by the Soviet Union, as evidenced by Senator Arthur Vandenberg's 1947 recommendation to "scare hell out of the American people" (his nephew, Hoyt Vandenberg, was CIA Director at the time), the "Doomsday clock" (1947), the apocalyptic rhetoric of NSC-68 (1950), the contagion metaphor for communism, the 1952 "duck and cover" film used to terrorize school children, graphic accounts of the potential effects of a nuclear attack on the United States in the *Wall Street Journal* and *Reader's Digest*, and Kissinger's (1957, Chapter 3) description of the effects of a ten megaton nuclear weapon detonated in New York.

Wall Street–Soviet Relations

In reality, the Soviet Union offered nothing like the threat painted by Nitze and his Wall Street collaborators. From the beginning, the Bolshevik Revolution was infiltrated by Wall Street interests, many of which even shared a common address (120 Broadway), e.g. the Bankers Club, individual directors of the Federal Reserve Bank of New York, the American International Corporation, and the first Bolshevik ambassador to the United States, Ludwig Martens. US-Russian relations were henceforth dominated by "Morgan and allied financial interests, particularly the Rockefeller family," with a view to opening up new markets and taking control of a centrally planned economy by financing state-approved oligopolies (Sutton, 1981, p. 127).

In the 1920s and 1930s, the Soviet Union "persistently wooed the United States," much as Tsarist Russia had made a series of overtures to the United States between 1905 and 1912 (Williams, 1992, p. 70) and much as Wall Street had supported the Bolshevik Revolution—not for any ideological reason, but because it saw the possibility for opening up new markets for investment (Sutton, 1981). Even as the United States participated in the Allied intervention against the Bolsheviks during the Russian Civil War, the Harrimans began illegal gold shipments to Lenin and the Bolshevik Party, probably because of the Bolsheviks' promise to continue the Tsarist policy of condoning cartels—Russia being rich in raw materials such as magnesium and iron ore (Loftus, 2011, pp. 18–19).

In 1922, Kennan's great uncle (also called George Kennan) published a biography of Averell Harriman's father, the "railroad tzar," E.H. Harriman (Kennan, 2011). Kennan must, therefore, have known, when writing the "long telegram" as deputy US ambassador to Russia under Averell Harriman, that the Kremlin had enjoyed close ties with the Harriman family for over two decades and was intent on preserving good relations. For example, even when the Harrimans' manganese mining concession in the Soviet Union was withdrawn as a result of Stalin's quest to reduce dependence on foreign investment, Moscow agreed to repay Harriman $3.45 million of the original $4 million investment *plus* 7 percent annual interest on both the remainder and an additional $1 million loan between 1931 and 1943, an agreement that was dutifully honored even during the peak of World War II, resulting in a substantial profit for Harriman (Pechatnov, 2003, p. 2). Harriman, in turn, was a key architect of US support for the Soviet Union during the war, to weaken Nazi Germany.

In 1943, Stalin disbanded the Comintern as a sign of goodwill to Western allies, thereby "spreading among the masses the illusion that equality and fraternity between nations were compatible with the survival of the principal imperialist state" (Claudin, 1975, p. 30). In October 1944, Churchill's infamous "percentage note" at the Fourth Moscow Conference proposed significant influence for Stalin in eastern Europe (90 percent in Romania, 75 percent in Bulgaria, 50 percent in Hungary and Yugoslavia, but only 10 percent in Greece). Stalin immediately acquiesced by drawing a tick on the note and passing it back to Churchill. The unspoken premise was that Stalin would not interfere with the postwar stabilization of capitalism in Western Europe in exchange for control of Eastern Europe. In December 1944, US Assistant Secretary of State Dean Acheson, a former Standard Oil lawyer, wrote in a memo from Greece: "The peoples of the liberated countries [i.e. from Nazi rule] are the most combustible material in the world. They are violent and restless"; he warned that "agitation and unrest" could lead to "the overthrow of governments" (cited in Steil, 2018, pp. 18–19). Yet, when the communist revolt in Greece arrived two years later, Stalin refused to send aid, resulting in the Tito-Stalin split of June 1948.

Like the declining European empires, the Soviet Union was heavily reliant on US financial support after World War II. As Sanchez-Sibony (2014, p. 295) explains, "the Soviet leadership not only welcomed, but pursued American credit" and indeed expected it as a moral right after having suffered by far the highest number of fatalities to defeat the Nazis. US Ambassador Harriman offered $1 billion of credits to Moscow before the Yalta conference (February 1945), an amount that was eventually agreed upon in 1946, but only after a prolonged period of tension following Stalin's failed insistence on $6 billion (Sanchez-Sibony, 2014, p. 296). Stalin courted Roosevelt at Yalta, deferring to him as the formal "host" for the conference, staging plenary sessions in the American accommodation at the Livadia Palace, and allowing Roosevelt to sit centrally in group photographs. At Yalta as previously at Tehran, Stalin offered significant commercial incentives for US firms engaging in business deals with the USSR; every effort was made to "buy into the very system of financial and commercial exchange that could guarantee the quick recovery of the USSR" (Sanchez-Sibony, 2014, pp. 295–6). These are not the actions of an empire bent on world domination but rather of a regime seeking accommodation with Western capitalism.

Strategically, Stalin and his successors may have welcomed the US troop presence in West Germany after World War II because it served as "one of the more reliable guarantees against German revanchism" (Judt, 2007, p. 243). This would explain, for example, why Stalin accepted a larger French presence in the occupation of Germany once he heard at Yalta that Roosevelt would only commit US troops in Europe for two years—hardly the action of a fanatic salivating at the prospect of subverting a defenseless Europe (Sanchez-Sibony, 2014, p. 295, n. 18). Stalin also made no attempt to challenge US aerial supremacy during the Korean War despite having signed off on plans for Korean unification with Chairman Mao (Craig & Logevall, 2012, p. 115). In general, the Soviet Union proved surprisingly willing to compromise with the West; it was, as Arendt observed in 1951, "quite capable of interrupting every existing class struggle with a sudden alliance with capitalism without undermining the reliability of [communist] cadres or committing treason against their belief in class struggle" (Arendt, 1962, pp. 38–67).

The Cold War and Transnational Class Relations

The "Cold War" was never about "deterring" the Soviet Union; rather, it amounted to "a vast transitional program of political economic rehabilitation of the imperial system to subvert de-colonization and impose global capitalist discipline against anti-imperialist resistance" (Ahmed, 2012, p. 70). Meanwhile, at home, the Second Red Scare in the 1950s, based on alleged fifth column communism in the United States, was a strategy to create public hysteria and, with it, increased social control. To the extent that communist sympathizers and fellow travelers had taken root in the United States since the 1930s, even this owed, in part, to "the power of the international financial coterie," which backed all sides; Tom Lamont, for example, a partner in the Morgan firm, sponsored "almost a score of extreme

Left organizations, including the Communist Party itself" (Quigley, 1966, p. 687).

In *The Civil War in France* (1871), Marx describes how the French and German ruling classes, which had just been at war with one another, put aside their differences and joined forces to put down the Paris Commune (Epp, 2017). Similar proved true again in response to working class uprisings in the 1950s. The East German uprising of 1953 was not only crushed by Soviet tanks, but Britain, France, and the United States made sure it did not spread by constructing a "wall of police and military might" to prevent West Berlin workers from marching to join their counterparts in the East (Glaberman & Faber, 2002, pp. 171–2). When Soviet tanks rolled into Hungary in 1956 to crush the workers' uprising, the Eisenhower administration protested vehemently, but did not intervene militarily, exposing liberation as a sham (Wilford, 2008, p. 49). Radio Free Europe and the Voice of America never again called on Eastern Europeans to revolt (Glaberman & Faber 2002, p. 173). The Soviet Union and the West were united in their determination to keep the international working class in check.

Working class lives, regardless of nationality, are expendable to a transnational ruling class that cares only about power and profit. Sutton (1972, p. 13), for instance, argues that the 100,000 US lives lost in Korea and Vietnam owed, in part, to the availability of US technology to the enemy. In 1950, the North Korean army crossed the border into South Korea in Soviet T-34 tanks fitted with US Christie suspensions; its artillery tractors were direct copies of Caterpillar tractors; some of its trucks were manufactured by Ford; and the North Korean Air Force featured planes built in plants with US Lend-Lease equipment, which were replaced by MiG-15s powered by copies of Rolls Royce engines sold to the Soviets in 1947 (Sutton, 1972, p. 42). During the Vietnam War, Ford manufactured the vehicles used by the North Vietnamese to carry weapons and munitions for use against US forces (Sutton, 2016, p. 90). Similar technology transfers continue today (Corbett, 2019).

Samuel Huntington admitted in a 1981 roundtable event that the "Cold War" was a cover story used to legitimize US imperialism: "You may have to sell [intervention in another country] in such a way as to create the misimpression that it is the Soviet Union that you are fighting. That is what the United States has been doing ever since the Truman Doctrine" (cited in Hoffmann et al. 1981, p. 14). The true guiding principle of US foreign policy, according to Chomsky (2012), is "the right to dominate," though this is typically disguised as "defense" (for example, the US War Department was rebranded as the Department of Defense in the late 1940s). The "Russian threat," Chomsky adds, is routinely invoked, even when the Russians are "nowhere in sight." Devoid of new ideas, the "Russian threat" continues to be invoked today, even though the 2022 Russian invasion of Ukraine was provoked by relentless expansion eastwards by NATO (Mearsheimer, 2014).

Conclusion

The US national security state was put in place, not to protect the citizenry but rather the interests of Wall Street, with Kennan's fascist sympathies as the guiding motif. Once this is understood, it should come as no surprise that power quickly ended up consolidated in a single agency, the CIA, itself the product of Wall Street. The covert power structure—the deep state— was always already transnational, on account of the globalizing tendencies of capitalism, whose perpetuation it was charged with ensuring through criminal political violence. The NATO "stay behind" armies offer the best evidence of this. The "Cold War" was not fundamentally about defeating the implacable "Soviet menace," as Western propaganda would have it. Rather, it involved collaboration with the Soviet Union to facilitate the stabilization and expansion of Western capitalism while keeping the international working class in check.

CHAPTER 6

INTELLIGENCE CRIME

The history of US foreign policy since the birth of the CIA has been a tale of near continuous violations of international law and war crimes, operating under cover of propaganda and psychological warfare. This has included terror tactics, death squads, assassination of political opponents, and mass murder of civilians, tactics also used by the Nazis. It has also included what de Lint (2021, p. 210) calls "intelligence crime," i.e. crimes by dark actors" in the highest echelons of power who furtively manipulate national security apparatuses to advance their agendas, inflicting near unimaginable harm on others if necessary. False flag terrorism is a classic example of intelligence crime, and, considering the United States' known history of planning and engaging in false flag terrorism, not to mention NATO's Operation Gladio, it would be intellectually and morally unpardonable to neglect the possibility that "9/11" was a false flag operation intended to legitimize imperialist wars and increased repression of domestic populations. "9/11" initiated a globalized Strategy of Tension in the twenty-first century, based on the Italian version of the 1970s and 1980s. The increasing failure of that paradigm to contain socially progressive movements in the years leading up to the "Covid-19 pandemic," however, meant that the paradigm had to be changed—to biosecurity—in 2020, and the massive psychological warfare operation waged under the banner of "Covid-19" was intended to facilitate that transition (Hughes, 2024).

Intelligence Crime

The transnational deep state—the Wall Street-led "security hierarchy" operating above and beyond democratic politics—has always been willing to resort to any means to achieve its objectives. Although many different institutions are involved, including other intelligence agencies, the belly of the beast is undoubtedly the CIA, described by Valentine (2007, pp. 31–39) as "a criminal conspiracy on behalf of wealthy capitalists," "the organized crime branch of the US government," and "a criminal organization that is corrupting governments and societies around the world. It's murdering civilians who haven't done anything wrong." The ties between the CIA, the mafia, and transnational drug trafficking are well known (Scott, 2003; Webb 2022a, 2022b). The history of US foreign policy since the birth of the CIA has been a tale of near continuous violations of international law and war crimes, operating under cover of propaganda and psychological warfare in the name of "national security" and a range of exceptionalist myths (Blum, 2006; Chomsky, 2007; Hughes, 2015).

De Lint's (2021, p. 210) concept of "intelligence crime" refers to crime committed by "dark actors" in the highest echelons of power who furtively manipulate national security apparatuses to advance agendas that benefit themselves while, if required, inflicting near unimaginable harm on others. "Type 2 intelligence crime" refers specifically to "actors or assets empowered or enabled by intelligence agencies" and counts "among the most prolific and deadly types of crime in recent modern history" (de Lint, 2021, p. 59). Such crimes may in certain instances be committed on a scale almost defying comprehension ("apex crimes," such as 9/11), yet they remain "invisible" (because of propaganda), unpunished (because the perpetrators stand above the law), and under-analyzed by academics (who form part of the power structure) (Lint, 2021; cf. Hughes, 2022b; Woodworth & Griffin, 2022). De Lint (2021, pp. 59–60) lists a range of intelligence crimes involving the CIA that have cost millions of lives and destroyed entire societies, from Indonesia and Vietnam to Chile, Guatemala, and Rwanda.

Repeatedly violating the principles of territorial integrity and political independence enshrined in Article 2.4 of the UN Charter (1945), President Eisenhower authorized 104 covert operations on four continents in eight years, focused mainly on postcolonial countries, followed by President Kennedy, who authorized 163 covert operations in only three years (McCoy, 2015). Results included coups against Mohammad Mosaddegh in Iran in 1953 (over moves to nationalize Iranian oil) and Jacobo Árbenz in Guatemala in 1954 (following lobbying by the United Fruit Company), the assassination of Patrice Lumumba in the Republic of the Congo in 1961, the Bay of Pigs fiasco followed by Operation Mongoose in Cuba, and electoral inference in Italy, the Philippines, Lebanon, South Vietnam, Indonesia, British Guyana, Japan, Nepal, Laos, Brazil, and the Dominican Republic (Blum, 2006, Chapter 18). Such operations were used to force open markets and establish client regimes facilitating Western capital penetration and labor dispossession (Ahmed, 2012, pp. 70–1). They demonstrated that the United States was indeed exceptional, if only for its selective ability to exempt itself from the rule of international law, an application of the Schmittian principle of sovereign exceptionality at the international level (McCoy, 2015; Schmitt, 2005, p. 31).

The Korean War was one long exercise enabling the CIA and the Pentagon to test out various forms of weaponry on a helpless population (cf. Karalekas, 1977, p. 36). Although it was dragged out for three years, the war was won within weeks: as early as September 1950, the US Air Force complained in communiqués that there was nothing left to destroy, having given villages "saturation treatment" with napalm to dislodge a few soldiers (Stone, 1952, pp. 256–9). More bomb tonnage was dropped on North Korea than in the entire Pacific theatre of World War II, killing 10–15 percent of the population, a figure close to the proportion of Soviet citizens killed in World War II (Armstrong, 2009, p. 1). Biological warfare was deployed against North Korea in 1952 (Kaye, 2018). President Eisenhower was keen to use nuclear weapons, even if there were no good tactical targets (Hanania, 2017, p. 50).

Having devastated every major urban and industrial region of North Korea by 1953, USAF then destroyed five reservoirs, "flooding thousands of acres of farmland, inundating whole towns and laying waste to the essential food source for millions of North Koreans"—a war crime committed only two years after the Genocide Convention came into force (Armstrong, 2009, p. 2). The Nazi High Commissioner in the Netherlands, Arthur Seyss-Inquart, was one of only thirty-seven Nazis to be sentenced to death at Nuremberg for his role in the bombing of dikes, which caused "widespread flooding of agricultural land and led to most of the population being forced to survive on less than 900 calories a day" (Kolko, 1972, p. 139). By destroying dams in North Korea, Kolko notes, the US Government followed the Nazi precedent in under a decade, fully aware of the humanitarian and political implications, and it later did the same in Vietnam—"a war crime of the first magnitude."

McCoy (2015) describes a "'reverse wave' in the global trend towards democracy from 1958 to 1975," as coups (mostly US-sponsored) took place in over three dozen countries, a quarter of the total at that time. For Latin America, special training in torture, murder, and political repression of leftist movements was provided by the School of the Americas, a US Army center at Fort Benning, Georgia. Graduates included Leopoldo Galtieri, president during the Argentine Dirty War (1976–1983), Roberto D'Aubuisson, who trained death squads in El Salvador before becoming president, and Panamanian dictator and drug trafficker Manuel Noriega. Thus were the methods of Hitler's SS allowed to continue during the Cold War. "Forced disappearances" were modeled on Hitler's 1941 "Night and Fog" operation, in which resistance fighters in Nazi-occupied countries were made to "vanish into the night and fog" (Klein, 2007, p. 91)—it being known that many ex-Nazis found refuge in Chile and Argentina. General Augusto Pinochet was installed by the 1973 CIA coup in Chile, whereupon neoliberal experiments in economic shock therapy began, based on principles derived from CIA torture techniques (Klein, 2007, p. 9). The torture and interrogation techniques applied throughout Latin America came from the CIA's 1963 *KUBARK Counter-intelligence Interrogation Handbook* (McCoy, 2007, p. 50). In Nicaragua, the US-trained National Guard massacred the population "with a brutality a nation usually reserves for its enemy," in the words of the NSC's Robert Pastor, killing around 40,000 people (cited in Chomsky, 2006, p. 251). The CIA facilitated the trade of cocaine from the Contras in Nicaragua (deployed to crush the 1979 Sandinista revolution) to gangs in Los Angeles, fueling a crack cocaine epidemic (Scott & Marshall, 1998, pp. 23–50).

Many Southeast Asian governments also became US-backed military dictatorships, including Indonesia, the Philippines, South Korea, South Vietnam, Taiwan, and Thailand. As Samuel Huntington wrote in 1965, this was borne of fear of revolution: "the social forces unleashed by modernization" entail the "*vulnerability of a traditional regime to revolution*" (1965, p. 422, emphasis in original). The means deployed to counter the threat of revolution were brutal: the Taylor-Staley strategic hamlet program in South Vietnam, for instance, resulted in 13 million people being forcibly relocated to 12,000 "fortified villages, surrounded by barbed wire fences and ditches fortified with bamboo spikes" (Schlesinger Jr., 2002, p. 549). The 1965 coup in Indonesia, orchestrated to prevent the world's third largest communist party from coming to power, killed hundreds of thousands (possibly rising to over two million over several years) when the CIA leaked the names and details of party members (van der Pijl 2014, p. 174). Operation Phoenix (1968–1972) was a covert CIA program of torture and assassination that led to the deaths of an estimated 20,000 Vietnamese citizens and the imprisonment of thousands more (Cavanagh, 1980; Oren, 2002, p. 149). Critics described it as "the most indiscriminate and massive program of political murder since the Nazi death camps of World War II," but the release of the Pentagon Papers in 1971 deflected attention (Butz et al., 1974, p. 6; Valentine, 2017, pp. 29–34). Carpet bombing of Vietnam, Cambodia, and Laos, involving napalm and Agent Orange, caused untold loss of life and environmental damage, and produced generations of birth defects. US arms to Indonesia in 1975 resulted in "near-genocidal levels" of atrocities in 1978 (Chomsky, 2008, p. 312).

There are many more examples of US/UK-sponsored violations of international law and war crimes, far too many to recount here. Obvious examples include:

- $3 billion a year to Israel despite routine brutality against the Palestinians, reaching news levels in Gaza since October 2023.
- Training and support for the Rwandan Patriotic Front whose death squads in 1994 resembled "the mobile units [*Einsatzgruppen*] of the Third Reich" (Rever, 2018, p. 229).
- Supplying large amounts of arms to Turkey in the mid-1990s to help crush Kurdish resistance, "leaving tens of thousands killed, 2–3 million refugees, and 3,500 villages destroyed (seven times Kosovo under NATO bombing)" (Chomsky, 2008, p. 306).
- "Genocidal" sanctions (to quote successive UN humanitarian coordinators, Denis Halliday and Hans von Sponeck) estimated to have killed over a million Iraqis, including half a million children (Media Lens, 2004).
- Backing of the Kagame-Museveni invasion and mass killings in Zaire/Democratic Republic of Congo, which led to the largest loss of life in a single conflict since World War II (Herman & Peterson, 2014), but also further access (after Rwanda) to coltan, needed to manufacture mobile phones and personal computers, as well as 60 percent of world's known cobalt supply, needed for lithium-ion batteries (30 percent of which is mined by hand by child laborers) (Sanderson, 2019). Lest any doubt remain as to the role

of Kagame, he appeared (otherwise inexplicably) alongside Bill Gates as part of a panel at Davos 2022 on "Preparing for the Next Pandemic."

- Massive destruction of civilian infrastructure during the "ethical" Kosovo War: "Anyone scrutinizing the unpublished list of targets hit by NATO," Pilger (2000, p. 135) notes, "is left in little doubt that a deliberate terror campaign is being waged against the civilian population of Yugoslavia."
- "Preventive war" in the 2002 US National Security Strategy (first used by Hitler to invade Norway) to justify the invasion of Iraq; torture at Guantánamo Bay, in extraordinary renditions, and at Abu Ghraib prison; the Nisour Square massacre by Blackwater's hired guns and the crimes shown in Wikileaks' "Collateral Murder" video (both 2007).
- The destruction of Libya and regime change under the guise of R2P following Colonel Gaddafi's proposal of an African reserve currency and alternatives to the World Bank and IMF (Brown, 2016).
- Endless attempts at subversion in the "dirty war" against Syria (Anderson, 2016) and against Iran.
- Support for Saudi Arabia while 377,000 civilians (according to UN estimates) lost their lives in Yemen by the start of 2022 ("Yemen: Why is the war there getting more violent?," 2023), etc. etc.

False Flag Terrorism

Another way of thinking about intelligence crime is through the known history of false flag terrorism, i.e. staged attacks used as the pretext for war. The sinking of the USS *Maine*, for instance, provided the pretext for the Spanish–American War of 1898 and the conquest of various Pacific islands (Anderson, 2016, pp. v–vi). Kennan dropped a hint in 1951 when he attributed the origins of the Spanish–American War to "a very able and very quiet intrigue by a few strategically placed persons in Washington, an intrigue which received absolution, forgiveness, and a sort of public blessing by virtue of war hysteria" (cited in Stone, 1952, p. 345).

Then came the sinking of the *Lusitania* in 1915—"a horror device to generate a public backlash to draw the United States into war with Germany," which Sutton blames on "Morgan interests, in concert with Winston Churchill" (2016, p. 175). A 2008 dive to the sunken "passenger ship" confirmed that it was carrying "more than 4 million .303 rifle bullets and tons of munitions—shells, powder, fuses and gun cotton" (David, 2015). It was effectively a disguised military vessel. According to "Colonel" E.M. House, the British Foreign Secretary, Edward Grey, and King George V discussed the sinking of the *Lusitania* before it took place (Corbett, 2018). The German embassy in Washington gave fair warning before the *Lusitania* set sail that "vessels flying the flag of Great Britain, or any of her allies, are liable to destruction" in waters adjacent to Great Britain. When the German torpedo hit, 1,198 people, including 128 US citizens, lost their lives.

The 1930s confirmed the far right coloration of false flag attacks. In 1931, imperial Japan sabotaged a railway line that it operated in the Chinese province of Manchuria, blamed the incident on Chinese nationalists, and launched a full-scale invasion, occupying Manchuria and installing a puppet regime there (Felton, 2009, pp. 22–23). Operation Himmler in 1939 involved a series of false flag events, the most famous being the Gleiwitz incident, the day after which Germany invaded Poland (Maddox, 2015, pp. 86–87).

Operation Northwoods, approved by the Joint Chiefs of Staff in 1962, contained proposals for all manner of false flag attacks to be blamed on Fidel Castro and used as the pretext for invading Cuba (Scott, 2017, p. 94). These included sinking a US Navy ship in Guantánamo Bay, sinking boats carrying Cuban refugees, staging terrorist attacks in Miami and Washington, DC, and making it appear as though Cuba had blown up a US passenger plane by replacing the plane with a drone in mid-flight and secretly disembarking the passengers.

The Gulf of Tonkin incident in 1964 was cynically invoked by President Johnson as the reason to launch air strikes against North Vietnam, which in subsequent years led to mass loss of life on both sides; however, it is known never to have occurred (Moise, 1996). Johnson was vice president under John F. Kennedy, who had planned to withdraw troops from Vietnam. Kennedy's apparent assassination in 1963 was instead followed two days later by an escalation of the US commitment in Vietnam, likely internalizing the coup pattern already established by the CIA and putting the deep state firmly in charge of the US political system, with the "visible political establishment" becoming "regulated by forces operating outside the constitutional process" (Scott, 1996, p. 312). As Scott (2017) argues, the institutional structures and actors involved in US deep politics can be traced through to the present.

In light of the above evidence regarding intelligence crime and false flag operations, only the willfully blind, the irrationally fearful, and the intensely propagandized will refuse to recognize the possibility, if not the high likelihood, that the terrorist attacks of September 11, 2001, were a false flag operation conducted by transnational deep state actors in order to legitimize imperialist wars plus vastly expanded social control at home (Hughes, 2020). The fact that my widely read article on the subject from February 2020 (over 23,100 views at the publisher's paid access website alone as of February 2024) remains unchallenged after four years, despite the initial howls of outrage (see Hayward, 2020; Hughes, 2021), while academia's silence regarding the events of 9/11 continues, reflects diabolically on the profession and provides strong evidence of the complicity of academia in covering up deep state criminality. Even in rare cases where academics do allude to my article, they "refrain from citing that particular paper [so as] not to legitimize conspiracy-promoting content through a citation" (Urman et al., 2022). Here, none of the voluminous evidence which my article presents is considered; instead, the CIA's most effective thought-terminating cliché (DeHaven-Smith, 2013, p. 25) is trotted out, and academia's disciplined silence regarding the events of 9/11 is maintained.

The Global Strategy of Tension in the Twenty-First Century

The strategy of tension has been central to keeping the global population in check since 9/11. Not just Italy, but societies everywhere were propagandized into believing that terrorist attacks were an ever-present possibility despite all evidence to the contrary (Mueller & Stewart, 2016). That propaganda legitimized repeated US wars of aggression, the destabilization of the North Africa and Middle East region, and the deprivation of civil liberties at home, including arbitrary detention, increased surveillance, and torture. The trigger event was 9/11 itself, the absurd official explanation for which is indefensible (Griffin, 2005; Wood, 2011; Davidsson, 2013; Griffin & Woodworth, 2018; Hughes, 2020, 2021). The so-called "War on Terror" not only spread terrorism throughout many regions of the world but also terrorized entire populations into living in fear of terrorist attacks (Chomsky, 2007, p. 211; Amnesty International, 2013). As de Lint (2021, p. 8) recognizes, the whole thing was "stoked and inflamed arguably more from within than from without by authorities who are dependent on the controlled production of 'unease'" to maintain their rule. Official enemies of the United States went along with the "War on Terror" narrative, because it meant that they, too, could invoke the terror threat as a pretext for authoritarianism—and because, ultimately, a global form of dictatorship is the only hope for the ruling classes of all countries to maintain control over a massive, growing, and increasingly restless global population (cf. van der Pijl, 2022, p. 36; Hughes, 2024, Chapter 1).

There are evidence-based reasons, studiously ignored by "critical terrorism studies," to question the provenance of many of the terrorist attacks that have taken place since 9/11. For example, the censored documentaries *7/7 Ripple Effect*, *The Boston Unbombing*, and *Manchester: The Night of the*

Bang provide extensive material evidence that calls into question the official accounts of the July 7, 2005, bombings in London, the 2013 Boston Marathon attack, and the Manchester Arena incident of May 2017. Anyone who dismisses these documentaries using thought-terminating clichés such as "dangerous conspiracy theory"—without engaging honestly with the evidence they bring to light—may be either too propagandized to think straight or part of the propaganda campaign to censor or dissuade critical discussion and dialogue around politically sensitive topics.

The case of France is particularly interesting when it comes to terrorism. The Charlie Hebdo attack (January 2015) followed days after President Hollande spoke out against sanctions on Russia over Ukraine; the socialist majority in parliament had also recently voted in favor of recognizing an independent state of Palestine. Weighing the evidence, van der Pijl (2022, p. 64) regards the Charlie Hebdo attack as a possible "false flag operation intended to force Hollande to change course and instill fear in French society." This was followed on November 13, 2015, by coordinated terrorist attacks at the Stade de France stadium, at cafés and restaurants in Paris, and at the Bataclan theatre. Then came the Nice truck attack (July 2016), the Normandy church attack (July 2016), the Louvre knife attack (February 2017), the Champs Elysees attack (April 2017), and the Strasbourg attack (December 2018). The upshot of these attacks was the introduction of a state of emergency, renewed multiple times since, which has seen 10,000 troops deployed on French streets under the *Sentinelle* anti-terrorism operation. Although it is hard if not impossible to establish the extent to which deep state actors were behind individual attacks, the end result is exactly in line with Vinciguerra's 1984 testimony in the previous chapter, i.e. a permanent state of emergency.

Nor was France alone in experiencing an uptick in the rate of terrorist attacks in the pre-Covid era, as social tensions deepened. Attacks in other Western states included the Brussels bombings (March 2016), the Berlin Christmas market truck attack (December 2016), the Westminster

Bridge attack (March 2017), the Stockholm truck attack (April 2017), the Manchester Arena incident (May 2017), the London Bridge attack (June 2017), the Finsbury Park Mosque attack (June 2017), the Barcelona attack (August 2017), the Las Vegas shooting (October 2017), the Christchurch mass shootings, and the London bridge stabbings of 2019. These attacks account for around half of all "major terrorist incidents" identified by Wikipedia since 2015, with most of the rest occurring in Iraq, Syria, and Afghanistan, all key areas of US interference.

If intended to quell social unrest by moving societies ever further in the direction of police states, the effort failed, as conspicuously expressed by the rise of the Yellow Vests in France in 2018, as well as mass uprisings in Chile and India, and major protests in one in five countries in 2019 (van der Pijl 2022, 54–58). This, for van der Pijl, is one key reason why the "Covid-emergency brake" was pulled in early 2020. Indeed, it is conspicuous that once the deep state control paradigm switched from the perpetual "War on Terror" to biosecurity, major terrorist attacks in the West virtually ceased. Are terrorists afraid of the virus, or were those attacks mostly planned and executed by deep state operatives?

"Covid-19" and Intelligence Crime

The so-called "Covid-19 pandemic" bears all the hallmarks of intelligence crime. For example, the psychological warfare operation of 2020–2021 (Hughes, 2024) was clearly modelled on what Klein (2007, p. 8) calls the "shock doctrine," which traces back to MKULTRA experiments and seeks to generate "moments of collective trauma to engage in radical social and economic engineering." During such moments, democratic practices are suspended, allowing for "iron-fisted leadership" (Klein, 2007, p. 11) in line with the Schmittian state of exception. Klein (2007, p. 21) continues: "Only a great rupture—a flood, a war, a terrorist attack—can generate the kind of vast, clean canvases" desired by social engineers, i.e. moments in which the public finds itself "psychologically unmoored" and "malleable." The "Great

Reset," like 9/11, is modeled on this kind of "great rupture," with the attendant psychological warfare involving the same techniques of isolation, defamiliarization, depatterning, disruption of behavioral patterns, etc. (Hughes, 2024, Chapter 2). Schwab and Malleret (2020, pp. 100, 102), for instance, encourage decision-makers to "take advantage of the shock inflicted by the pandemic" to implement radical, long-lasting, systemic change.

Or take the issue of face masks, which were mandated in public spaces in most countries in 2020 in the absence of policy-grade scientific evidence for doing so (Hughes, 2024, Chapter 4). We cannot ignore the fact that inmates at Guantánamo Bay were made to wear blue surgical face masks (Amnesty International, 2020):

Detainees upon arrival at Camp X-Ray at Guantanamo Bay Naval Base, February 12, 2002. *Photo courtesy of: Everett Collection (HISL024 EC272)*

Guantánamo Bay is a torture facility. MKULTRA experiments found that psychological torture is far more effective than physical torture: in particular, a combination of sensory deprivation and self-inflicted pain are the most effective methods, as practiced at Abu Ghraib prison in 2003 (McCoy, 2007, pp. 8, 41). Other photographs of Guantánamo Bay inmates from 2002 show them wearing blackout goggles, gloves, thick caps, and industrial earmuffs, (i.e. sensory deprivation) as well as face masks (Dyer 2002; cf. "Open letter from former Guantánamo prisoners," 2013; Rosenberg, 2021). Despite the inmates' abject condition, there appears to be no reason, from the photographs, why they cannot reach up and remove the face mask, other than fear of the consequences. This is the self-inflicted pain. Mask wearing is known to lead to "psychological and physical deterioration as well as multiple symptoms described [as] Mask-Induced Exhaustion Syndrome" (Kisielinski et al., 2021). So it was with the social pressure to wear the mask during "Covid-19," which essentially induced mask wearers to self-harm. It was an advanced, highly effective form of psychological warfare aimed at breaking down public resistance to multiple nefarious agendas all being enacted at once (Hughes, 2024, Chapter 3).

Numerous psychological warfare techniques deployed as part of the "Covid-19" operation are exposed in Hughes (2024), including trauma-based mind control, use of fear and threat, cognitive attack, weaponized deception, and techniques for turning society against itself. The transnationally coordinated war against humanity is not just psychological, however. Rather, following the pattern of intelligence crime, it has resulted in crimes against humanity on an almost unimaginable scale. The "lockdowns," for example, left behind a "legacy of harm for hundreds of millions of people in the years ahead" owing to:

> a rise in non-Covid excess mortality, mental health deterioration, child abuse and domestic violence, widening global inequality, food insecurity, lost educational opportunities, unhealthy lifestyle behaviours, social polarization, soaring debt, democratic backsliding and declining human rights. (Bardosh, 2023)

There is clear evidence of democide (Rancourt, 2020; Rancourt et al., 2021), state-sponsored euthanasia, and experimentation on human beings that is consistent with eugenics (Hughes et al., 2022). Patterns of sadism and cruelty were deliberately instigated, from locking elderly people up in care homes and not allowing relatives to visit (Health Advisory & Recovery Team, 2022), to forcing children to wear masks in schools all day, to persecuting those not complying with tyranny (Hughes, 2024, Chapter 7).

A reported 5.55 billion people (Holder, 2023) have been injected with dangerous experimental substances containing a devil's brew of undisclosed ingredients, violating the principle of informed consent and, therefore, constituting a global crime against humanity (Hughes, 2022c). Huge numbers of people, including previously fit and healthy people, have suffered serious adverse reactions to those injections, including severe disability and death, as per Yellow Card (MHRA, n.d.-a) and VAERS data (OpenVAERS, n.d., with most deaths accruing towards the time of injection), which probably only account for 1–10 percent of the total (Ross et al., 2010; MHRA, 2019). "Died suddenly" and "vaccine genocide" trend routinely on social media, and highly distressing videos are all over the internet of people suffering horrific adverse reactions to the "vaccine" and/or collapsing and dying in public. The "vaccine" rollout to children and young people was premised wholly on corruption and not science, as I warned *before* the rollout reached five- to eleven-year-olds in Britain (Hughes, 2022a), and since then, children, young adults, and athletes have been collapsing and having heart attacks at an historically unprecedented rate (Dowd, 2022).

Conclusion

According to Scott (2017, 30), a former Turkish president and prime minister once remarked that the Turkish deep state was "the real state, and the public state was only a 'spare state,' not the real one." This is now true also of Western "liberal democracies." While most citizens, including nearly all academics, remain oblivious of the "deep state" and the full extent of its operations, contemporary social reality is fundamentally determined by "deep state" operations. Most people genuinely believe they have just survived a "pandemic"—which just so happens to necessitate a restructuring of the global political economy in the interests of the transnational ruling class—and many will vehemently defend that proposition (see the "Cognitive Dissonance" section in Hughes, 2024, Chapter 6). The reality, however, is that those people are the victims of the largest psychological warfare operation in history, which ranges all the way from military-grade propaganda to psychological torture techniques. It is little wonder that the powers that be now want to censor the internet. For once the reality of what is going on is widely understood, it seems inevitable that Wall Street's long "century of enslavement" (Corbett, 2014) will finally be brought to an end.

CHAPTER 7

WHERE IT LEADS

It takes years to build a totalitarian state, at either the national or the transnational level, meaning that we live in an interregnum, like Germans in the 1930s who still imagined they were living in a civilized society and had no idea what was coming. If we draw the proper lessons of the Nazi past, however, we can infer full well what is coming if the global technocratic coup is not put down. We can expect the global centralization of political power in a New World Order. Slavery will return in a biodigital guise. All of society will be transformed into a giant biodigital camp in which the state will exercise direct control over human bodies. There will be judicial murder and legalized brutality. A global land grab will result in the creation of "smart" human settlement zones. Natural asset companies will privatize nature/the global commons. Centralized control over the global economy will be established in the name of "net zero." Control of the food supply will be lost to a class which in the past has demonstrated its willingness to starve tens of millions of people to death. Human beings, treated no differently from trees or cattle, will be bred or culled as required. Disastrous eugenics experiments will be conducted in the name of "humanity," probably involving genetic engineering and synthetic biology, with the complicity of the medical profession. Euthanasia will become normalized. Dissidents will suffer escalating persecution before being systematically murdered in the name of morality.

Building a Totalitarian State

The building of a totalitarian state, at either the national or the transnational level, does not take place overnight. Rather, it takes years to put in place the necessary legislation and to condition the population psychologically. It should be remembered that some of the worst discriminatory legislation against Jews did not appear until 1938, five years into the Third Reich. As of the publication of this book in 2024, the totalitarian biosecurity state is four years in incubation. It took six and a half years after the Nazis came to power for World War II to break out. The worst atrocities, including the Holocaust and the War of Annihilation in the East, did not begin until eight years into the Nazi era. The Auschwitz complex "was not built overnight" and was, rather, "a major construction project that lasted years and was never completed" (Yad Vashem, n.d.). "It might take us ten or twelve years to get there," Hopkins (2020) argues, but totalitarianism has an inevitable historical trajectory if those behind it are not defeated.

Holocaust survivor Vera Sharav (2022) notes that the Holocaust did not begin in the gas chambers, but was, rather, preceded by nine years of incremental restrictions on personal freedom, the suspension of legal and civil rights, and hate-mongering propaganda. Elmer (as in Wilson, 2022a) summarizes the incremental construction of totalitarianism in law in Nazi Germany. A repentant ex-Nazi recounted in 1954 that the descent to the Holocaust took place in hundreds of small (sometimes imperceptible) steps, each rendering the next less shocking, and "unless one understood what the whole thing was in principle, [. . .] one no more saw it developing from day to day than a farmer in his field sees the corn growing. One day it is over his head" (cited in Mayer, 2017, pp. 168–170).

The difference this time, however, is that knowledge of the Nazi past allows us to see *exactly* what the "whole thing" is in principle—i.e. deliberately orchestrated totalitarianism to preserve the rule of the transnational ruling class—and *exactly* where the whole process of "small steps" leads. If another Holocaust is to be averted, Sharav (2022) claims, the ominous

parallels between 1930s Germany and the present must be clearly identified and understood. That having been done (see Chapter 2), action must
now be taken to stop the advance of global technocratic totalitarianism.
Otherwise, history teaches where it will lead. "We will go down," Zimbardo
(2005, p. 152) warns, "if we do not learn from the lessons of the past to
oppose tyranny at its first signs." If left unopposed, Rectenwald (2021)
warns, the "Great Reset" will "leave a lot of destruction in its wake," which
is "all the more reason to oppose it now and with all our might." The rest of
this chapter explains, based on the lessons of the Nazi past, what lies ahead
if the global technocratic coup is not swiftly and decisively put down.

The New (World) Order

The Nazis' New Order in Europe

Goebbels declared in April 1939 that "Europe in its entirety is adopt-
ing a new order and a new orientation under the intellectual leadership
of National Socialist Germany and Fascist Italy" (cited in Martin, 2016,
p. 112). That same month, senior financial figures in the US, Britain, and
Germany agreed a massive US gold loan that would underpin the New
Order, the loan being made through the lawless Bank for International
Settlements (Higham, 2007, pp. 168–169). The aim was a negotiated peace
with Germany that would "bar any reorganization of Europe along liberal
lines," helping to facilitate "a world fascist state without war" (Higham,
2007, pp. xiv, 211, 96). GM vice-president Graeme K. Howard penned
America and a New World Order (1940)—the earliest reference to a "New
World Order" that I know of—which seeks to appease Hitler.

Following the Nazi occupation of France in June 1940, the "New
Order" in Europe (*Neuordnung Europas*) appeared close to realization.
With Britain seemingly close to defeat, with Ford refusing to build aircraft
engines for the RAF and instead supplying the Wehrmacht with five-ton
military trucks (Higham, 2007, p. 156), with Operation Barbarossa not yet

having been launched, and with the United States not yet having entered the war, it appeared to some that Nazi Germany could emerge in a position to "dictate the New Order that would define the peace" (Martin, 2016, p. 1). Even after the United States entered the war, a Bank for International Settlements report dated September 7, 1942, anticipated an imminent peace in Germany's favor, underwritten by US gold to stabilize currencies (Higham, 2007, p. 10). The British MP George Strauss (Labour) realized that "some form of collaboration between the Nazis and the Allies still exists and that appeasement still lives in time of war" (cited in Higham, 2007, p. 10).

World Government

Although the Nazis' New Order in Europe never materialized, the idea of a New World Order began to take root, not explicitly by that name, but, rather, via the idea of world government. Aldous Huxley's *Brave New World* (1932), for instance, prominently features the World State, a unified government that administers the entire planet. Huxley's brother Julian, as UNESCO's first director, stressed the need for "world political unity," recommending that its education program be used to familiarize all peoples with "the implications of the transfer of full sovereignty from separate nations to a world organisation" (Huxley, 1946, p. 13). The advent of nuclear weapons was used to make the case for a world state as the alleged alternative to omnicidal nuclear war (Morgenthau, 1948, p. 391). In 1952, Bertrand Russell warned that the unprecedented level of destruction that a thermonuclear war would bring necessitated global "unification under a single government" (Russell, 2016, p. 24). However, realists also saw the key obstacle to a world government, namely, that it does not arise organically from the "social tissue" of all communities (Niebuhr, 1949) and that "a world community must antedate a world state," hence the role of UNESCO and UN specialized agencies (Morgenthau, 1948, pp. 406–407).

With neither the United States nor the Soviet Union willing to cede sovereignty to a world government, Niebuhr (1949, pp. 382–384) understood that the most likely outcome would be, not a constitutional world state, but, rather, the imposition of imperialism because of the "preponderance of power" in the West. So it proved during the Cold War and beyond, as the United States dictated the terms of its "rules-based international order" while violating them at will (see Chapter 6).

From 1968 onwards, however, in response to acute social crises on both sides of the "Iron Curtain," efforts intensified to manufacture the global consciousness necessary for world community, based on alleged problems such as global overpopulation, environmental damage, and the need for "sustainable" growth (Hughes, 2024, Chapter 6). Thus, even as the United States became the world's "sole superpower" at the end of the Cold War, the world government project was already well underway. The ruling classes have long known that their rule can only be sustained—and worldwide revolution precluded—through a totalitarian world state.

The New World Order

Ever since President Bush Sr.'s "New World Order" speech in September 1990 ("Bush 'Out of these troubled times . . . a New World Order," 1990), followed by Senator Joe Biden's (1992) *Wall Street Journal* article titled "How I learned to love the New World Order," the "New World Order" concept has come increasingly into the open, linked at first to the United States' "unipolar moment," later to global governance networks (Slaughter, 2004) and multipolarity. George Soros, interviewed by Chrystia Freeland for the *Financial Times* in 2009, claimed: "You really need to bring China into the creation of a new world order [. . .] They have to own it the same way as, let's say, the United States owns the Washington consensus [. . .]" (Transcript: George Soros Interview, 2009). It does not matter to the transnational ruling class which state, or group of states, dominates the New World Order: all that matters is that such an order exists.

During the "Covid-19" era, the "New World Order" was blatantly propagated. *Forbes*, for instance, asked in May 2020: "Are we ready to embrace a New World Order?" (Jones, 2020). The Mayor of Chicago, Lori Lightfoot, subverting the US Pledge of Allegiance, claimed that agency heads should be those "pledging allegiance to the New World Order and good governance" (Dowling, 2021). New South Wales chief health officer, Kerry Chant, claimed in 2021: "We will be looking at what contact tracing looks like in the New World Order" ("Australian public health chief says Covid contact tracing is part of 'New World Order,'" 2021). President Biden, in March 2022, claimed that major inflection points in the world economy occur every three or four generations and that "Now is a time when things are shifting, there's going to be a New World Order out there" (cited in Davis, 2022). The World Government Summit in March 2022 ran a session titled "Are we ready for a New World Order?" (Kempe, 2022), and in June 2023, Klaus Schwab ended a WEF session with Henry Kissinger by remarking, "What a wonderful opportunity to conclude our week here with such concrete proposals and ideas of how we can really create, I would say, a New World Order" ("Klaus Schwab wants to create a 'New World Order,'" 2023). The totalitarian dream of a New World Order threatens to become reality.

The Centralization of Political Power

The *sine qua non* of totalitarianism is centralization of political power. In Nazi Germany, the Law for the Reconstruction of the Reich, issued in January 1934, abolished German federalism by transferring the sovereignty of the states to the Reich (Epstein, 2015, p. 59). This put an end to state parliaments, and new Reich governors of each state were installed (apart from Prussia, which Hitler retained direct control over through Göring). They were directly answerable to the Interior Minister, Wilhelm Frick, who declared that Germany had been "converted from a federal to a unitary state," in which the imperial government could not be challenged by lower levels of political authority (cited in Epstein, 2015, p. 59).

Today, power is being centralized at the global level, and it is nation states that are ceding sovereignty, as was evident in the transnationally coordinated response to "Covid-19," in which most states acted in lockstep to harm and oppress their populations while their leaders slavishly mouthed the same slogan, "build back better," indicating their allegiance to a supranational network rather than to the citizens they are meant to serve. Davis' (2021c) "global public-private partnership" offers a useful visualization of that network, with governments acting as mere enforcers of policies formulated and distributed at higher levels. The WHO Pandemic Treaty and amendments to the 2005 International Health Regulations threaten to open the door to a global health dictatorship able to decree compulsory "lockdowns," "vaccinations," and the centralization of health data surveillance tied to a globally interoperable digital passport and ID system (Kheriaty, 2022; Knightly, 2022). This global project may be far more expansive than the nationalist fascism of eighty years ago, Bell (2023) notes, but "the similarities in the structure and the corporate-authoritarian model for decision-making have clear echoes." The architecture of a totalitarian world state is starting to materialize.

Slavery

In May 1940, the Nazi Minister of Agriculture, Richard Walther Darré, declared the Nazis' ambition to enslave two continents by the autumn, creating a "new aristocracy of German masters." Lest the term "slave" be interpreted metaphorically, Darré cautions, it is literally intended to refer to "a modern form of medieval slavery which we must and will introduce [. . .] to fulfil our great tasks" ("Secret Nazi Speech," 1940, pp. 43–44). Today, it has not escaped critics' attention that the "Fourth Industrial Revolution" implies a new form of slavery, i.e. "a form of feudalism with the technocratic gatekeepers overseeing the masses dispossessed of their natural human rights to reproduce freely, to speak, to own property, and to preserve their personal bodily integrity" (Broudy, 2021, p. 111).

The Nazis saw the work-shy and so-called "asocials" (beggars, alcoholics, drug addicts, prostitutes, gypsies, homosexuals, pacifists) as taking from the public purse, belying Nazi law and order, and undermining the image of a strong and healthy "Aryan" population (Epstein, 2015, p. 87). From 1937 on, many ended up in concentration camps, where they were tagged with an inverted black triangle, used for slave labor, and often worked to death (or exterminated in other ways). Today, WEF ideologue Harari (2020) speaks of the "new useless class," rendered economically redundant by new technologies, and "separated by an ever-growing gap from the ever more powerful elite." What is to be done with such people? "A sober assessment of the [WEF] plans," according to the Mises Institute, must conclude that there will be "no place for the average person" and that they will be "put away along with the 'unemployable,' 'feeble minded,' and 'ill bred'" (Mueller, 2020). The final solution to the "useless class" is to cull it.

Accelerating technological advancement, supposedly (but only because equitable wealth redistribution is never considered), will not only necessitate mass economic redundancy, but the wealthiest in society will be able to "upgrade" themselves and eventually merge with artificial intelligence (Kurzweil, 2005). Eventually, transhumanists argue, a new, technologically enhanced species will emerge, vastly superior to *homo sapiens* in evolutionary terms ("Human Species may 'split in two,'" 2006). A cull then becomes inevitable: "You want to know how super-intelligent cyborgs might treat ordinary flesh-and-blood humans? Better start by investigating how humans treat their less intelligent animal cousins" (Harari, 2017, p. 67). Boris Johnson used his 2019 speech at the UN to warn of AI in terms of "pink eyed terminators sent back from the future to cull the human race" (Prime Minister's Office, 2019).

Culling the "useless class" is not the only option. Biodigital technologies create new means of exploitation. McDowell (2020) asks "how life can be made profitable for transnational global capital interests once the poor have no buying power and are drowning in debt"? The solution she anticipates is "human capital bond markets," in which everyone is "tagged and trackable for 'impact.'" Should the Internet of Bodies become real, human beings could be reduced to mere commodities on which to speculate. One version of this sees the emergence of "portfolios of [. . .] poor people" as a new asset class (McDowell, 2020), their performance in the (slave) labor market presumably determining their "share price."

Microsoft patent WO/2020/060606 (awarded March 26, 2020) is for a device that will "award cryptocurrency to the user whose body activity data is verified" via a "mining process" (Abramson et al., 2020). Human bodies thereby become part of the financial system, trainable via cryptocurrency rewards. Earning crypto for the poorest could be made contingent upon their bodies performing designated tasks. In principle, this could range from sexual slavery to taking part in life-or-death "entertainment" shows for the rich, the idea for which has been seeded via the *battle royale* genre, including films such as *The Hunger Games* (2012) and Netflix series such as *Alice in Borderland* (2020) and *Squid Game* (2021).

In Nazi Germany, "your body was not your own. It belonged to the national community. Reproductive policy was a matter of state" (Epstein, 2015, p. 76). Similarly, the threat of "vaccine" mandates today potentially means that "You will have no autonomy over your own body, which will be owned by the State, and you will 'officially' be a slave" (Davis, 2020).

Ecofascism

Grabbing Land
The Nazi concept of *Lebensraum* (living space) was originally linked to organic land use planning and sustainability, especially in forestry (Lekan, 2005, p. 73). In time, however, it came to provide "green camouflage for the colonization of Eastern Europe" (Staudenmaier, 2011, pp. 29–32). For example, Himmler's decree, "On the Treatment of the Land in the Eastern Territories" (1942), states that if "the new *Lebensräume* (living spaces) are to

become a homeland for our settlers, the planned arrangement of the land-scape to keep it close to nature is a decisive prerequisite." Nazi Agriculture Minister Darré claimed that the Nazi "blood and soil" concept implied a "moral right to take back as much land in the East as is necessary to estab-lish a harmony between the body of our *Volk* and the geopolitical space." *Generalplan Ost* was sold to the German public as bringing humans and nature into harmony in the creation of an agrarian way of life for "Aryan" colonists (Brüggemeier et al., 2005, p. 13).

Today's "green" agenda masks a land grab on a global scale. The 30x30 initiative, for example, backed by $5 billion of private foundation funding in September 2021, aims to designate 30 percent of the world's land and oceans as "protected areas" by 2030, ostensibly to halt and reverse biodi-versity loss. This means that nearly a third of the world will be off limits to ordinary people, or accessible only with permission (like Antarctica), by the end of the decade. Given that 80 percent of biodiversity is found on land managed by indigenous peoples (United Nations Development Program, 2011, p. 54), "protecting biodiversity" has the potential to remove such peo-ples from their lands (Institute of Development Studies, 2021). While the UN speaks of "stewardship of the global commons," such discourse is really a "diversion to facilitate a robbery," involving "the theft of everything," a "worldwide heist" (Davis, 2021a, 2021b), continuous with a longstanding tradition of conservation via dispossession (Lurie, 2021).

Over half of humanity now lives in cities, set to rise to two thirds by 2050 (Okai, 2022). As more and more people come to live in cities whose footprint accounts for only 2 percent of the Earth's land surface, the remain-ing 98 percent of land increasingly becomes the preserve of the global rul-ing class—a global reincarnation of the Inclosure Acts passed in England and Wales centuries ago, which steadily removed peasant access to common land, forcing laborers into factories in towns and cities. The aim, now as then, is that "people should be rounded up off of the land and packed into human settlements" (Koire, 2011, p. 16), the current model for which is smart cities where everyone and everything can be digitally monitored and controlled.

Ulterior Financial Agendas

Natural Asset Companies (NACs), developed by the Rockefeller-funded Intrinsic Exchange Group (IEG), were created as a new asset class on the New York Stock Exchange in September 2021. NACs are described as "sustainable enterprises that hold the rights to ecosystem services produced by natural, working or hybrid lands" (Segal, 2021). Their purpose is the financialization of nature. According to IEG, existing asset classes globally, i.e. the total financial value of everything, is approximately $512 trillion; but the new asset class will be $4,000 trillion, promising a feeding frenzy for Wall Street and the financial oligarchy (Webb, 2021b). The global commons are being privatized: only NACs will have the "right" to determine who gets access to nature's resources and at what cost. In principle, entire ecosystems could be disregarded if they are not seen to turn a profit.

"Net zero" refers to the dubious idea that net CO_2 emissions must be reduced to zero to avoid environmental catastrophe—even though CO_2 only accounts for 0.04 percent of the Earth's atmosphere. The "net zero" agenda is in fact about creating centralized control over the global economy, such that businesses can only survive and prosper provided they operate within the parameters set by global technocrats. "Every company and every industry," BlackRock CEO Larry Fink (2022) threatens, "will be transformed by the transition to a net zero world"; those who fail to adjust to this new reality "do so at their peril," for "access to capital is not a right. It is a privilege." In other words, finance capital will be withheld for those who do not toe the line. Mark Carney, then Governor of the Bank of England, issued a similar ultimatum in July 2019: "Companies that ignore climate change and don't adapt will go bankrupt without question" (cited in Davis, 2021b). Achieving net zero, according to Carney, "requires a whole economy transition," i.e. economic *Gleichschaltung*. ESG ratings, awarded by the newly established International Sustainability Standards Board (ISSB), will be used to force compliance.

Control of the Food Supply

Those who control the food supply control society. Why is Bill Gates, an alleged software developer (Corbett, 2020) turned global "vaccine" pusher, the owner of the most farmland in the United States (Shapiro, 2021; Brown, 2023)? (Ted Turner, who, like Gates, calls for global depopulation [Harlow, 2009; Frank, 2009], is second on the list.) Why does the World Economic Forum promote the benefit of eating insects (Hubert, 2021), which would effectively reduce the diet of the "developed" world to that of the most "underdeveloped"? Why do Gates and the WEF promote genetically modified, lab-grown food in place of natural food such as red meat (Whiting, 2020)? Why are "rewilding" policies reducing the amount of land available for agriculture? Why are English farmers being offered lump sum payments to leave their land (Beck, 2024)? Why has the cost of food increased significantly in so-called "advanced" economies, such as the UK, where food prices were 30 percent higher in October 2023 than in October 2021 (Office for National Statistics, 2023)? Why are food manufacturing plants being destroyed (Hoft, 2023; Corbett, 2023)?

The answer to these questions is not "sustainability," otherwise measures would be taken to improve food sovereignty around the world, rather than relentlessly undermining it in favor of Agribusiness. Rather, the food supply, *like everything else*, is under attack and is being weaponized against the population (cf. my "Omniwar" concept in Hughes [2024], Chapter 1). The "European Green Deal," for instance, places extreme regulations on farmers, forcing them out of business (Vanheuckelom, 2023), while propaganda seeks to stigmatize farming as environmentally damaging (Harvey, 2023).

These are early warning signs. Totalitarianism historically has been willing to starve tens of millions of people to death to achieve its objectives. For example, as the Nazis swept into Eastern Europe, the so-called "Hunger Plan" was developed by Herbert Backe and Heinrich Himmler to feed the advancing war machine and the expanding Reich at the expense of conquered territories. Famine became an act of policy: it meant that tens of millions of Soviet citizens would face starvation (Kay, 2006, p. 128), worse even than the Holodomor (the man-made famine in the Soviet republic of Ukraine in 1932–33, which claimed 3–5 million lives). Even though the Nazis were defeated at Stalingrad, an estimated 3.3 million Soviet POWs died in German captivity, mostly through starvation (Snyder, 2010). Knowing that totalitarianism operates in this ruthless manner, it is conceivable that the global war for technocracy (Hughes, 2024, Chapter 1) could result in the deaths of hundreds of millions of people if control of the food supply is lost to the technocrats.

Ecologism, Eugenics, Extermination

The term "ecology" was coined in 1867 by zoologist Ernst Haeckel, a racial eugenicist who promoted a form of social Darwinism that saw social and political life as governed by the same laws that govern nature (Staudenmaier, 2011, pp. 18–19). If humans are no different from any other part of nature, however, human society may as well be managed according to the same principles as, say, forestry: "only healthy specimens of native, site-adapted species" are to be tolerated; anything foreign or sick is to be excised (Imort, 2005, p. 56). The Law Concerning the Protection of the Racial Purity of Forest Plants (1934) highlighted the practice of selective breeding, foreshadowing the Nuremberg Race Laws of 1935, and Nazi ecologism thereby bled into eugenics. What today goes by the name of "ecocentrism" is, therefore, not an innocent idea in the totalitarian context of the emergent biosecurity state.

The Nazi commitment to inhuman racist violence, massive political repression, and worldwide military domination, Staudenmaier (2011, pp. 39–40) observes, was "deepened and radicalized" by environmental politics, in a configuration that was "directly and substantially responsible for organized mass murder." Plimer (2021, p. 543) reaches a similar conclusion with respect to today's ecopolitics:

> I charge the greens with murder. They murder humans who are kept in eternal poverty without coal-fired electricity. They support slavery and early deaths of black child miners. They murder forests and their wild-life by clear felling for mining and wind turbines. They murder forests and wildlife with their bushfire policies. They murder economies producing unemployment, hopelessness, collapse of communities, disrupted social cohesion and suicide [. . .] They terrify children into mental illness with their apocalyptic death cult lies and exaggerations.

In sum, "green" politics today, as during the Third Reich, aids and abets some very dark agendas.

The Camp

Nazi Concentration Camps

Nazi concentration camps were originally set up by the SA to deal with political opponents and terrorize would-be dissidents (Shirer, 1991, p. 271). They were sites of arbitrary detention and cruelty: prisoners were malnour-ished, left to the ravages of disease, tortured, and murdered (Koonz, 2003, p. 228). After Himmler and the SS took control of the camps in 1934, most inmates were declared rehabilitated, and the number of prisoners fell from 90,000 in 1933 to under 10,000 by the mid-1930s. Prior to World War II, apart from a brief period in 1938, the prisoners were rarely Jews; rather, they were "mostly leftists, clergymen, and non-Jewish groups deemed racially inferior" (Epstein, 2015, p. 66).

The key stage in the "transition from social death to physical annihila-tion" of Jews was the ghetto (Kaplan, 1999, p. 184). Following the outbreak of World War II, 1,143 Jewish ghettos were established in Nazi-occupied

Central and Eastern Europe, whence German Jews were deported, though not with extermination originally in mind (Browning, 1986, pp. 344–345). Squalid living conditions claimed the lives of some, but most were murdered when the Final Solution saw the ghettos systematically destroyed and their inhabitants sent to death camps (cf. stage eight of Stanton's [2016] ten stages of genocide). Six main camps were used for industrial-scale extermination, namely: Auschwitz (1940–1945), Belzec (1942–1943), Chelmno (1941–1945), Majdanek (1941–1944), Sobibor (1942–1943), and Treblinka (1942–1943). Four of these were purpose-built to administer death.

Homo Sacer

For Agamben (1998, pp. 166–167), the camp constitutes a space in which the rights of citizenship, founded in belonging to a sovereign nation-state (the model inaugurated with the French Revolution) do not apply. In the camp, the citizen is reduced to the figure of *homo sacer*, or "bare life," whereby the state exercises power directly over biological bodies (biopower) (Agamben, 1998, p. 148). Concentration camp inmates, for example, had no legal protection and were "at the whim of the Death's Head units. They had no recourse to courts, media, or other potential intervening authorities" (Epstein, 2015, p. 66). The camp, Agamben (1998, pp. 175–181) argues, reveals "the fundamental biopolitical paradigm of the West" that will emerge as the modern nation state system breaks down and "the state decides to assume directly the care of the nation's biological life as one of its proper tasks."

Events since 2020 have confirmed that the political system of the modern nation state is finished. The core liberal principle of the separation of powers is no longer tenable:

What need for a judiciary when the rule of law has been superceded [sic] by a totalitarian system of surveillance, control and punishment administered by artificial intelligence? What need for an executive when the powers of the state have been placed under the dictates of global technocracies? Indeed, as an emergent paradigm of governance, the global biosecurity state represents the end of the classical model of politics. (Elmer, 2022)

According to van der Pijl (2020), "The social and political system of the original liberal West has run its historic course and after three hundred years has dropped all pretense of a social contract other than the state of emergency." The specter of mandatory vaccination for entire populations threatens to mark the "violent end" of European liberalism (O'Neill, 2021).

The aim of a totalitarian system, Elmer (2022) writes, "is not to build so many camps that the whole population can be housed in them—something not even the People's Republic of China could achieve—but to turn the social space itself into a camp," cf. Huxley's (1959, p. 226) notion of a "kind of painless concentration camp for entire societies." Today, the biodigital gulag is being invisibly constructed all around us: Big Tech companies and the intelligence agencies—which have always been one and the same (Corbett, 2019)—know virtually everything about us. Human beings are being herded into "smart cities" capable of monitoring their every movement. All of society is being turned into a gigantic biodigital camp, where we are all increasingly tagged and traced. Without expropriation of the relevant technologies from the ruling class, there is no escaping technocracy: the worldwide *web*, the Inter*net*, has ensnared us all.

"Covid-19" and the Logic of the Camp

The "Covid-19" operation primed the public to accept the logic of the camp in multiple ways, beginning with the "lockdown" metaphor, which is a prison term, as entire populations were placed under "a form of house arrest" (Sumption, 2020, p. 1). McDowell (2020) quickly understood that "In the global biosecurity state on any given day the border could very well end up being your front door." For residents confined to apartment blocks in New South Wales, this proved to be no exaggeration (Nilsson & O'Doherty, 2021). The Shanghai "lockdown" in April 2022 saw 25 million people confined to their homes, policed by drones using facial recognition software and broadcasting the message "Control your soul's desire for freedom" (Browning, 2022).

New legislation, such as the UK Coronavirus Act, meant that the public could be "removed, isolated and detained against their will by Government order" (K. Corbett, 2020). Powers to remove people to detention facilities, Sumption (2020, p. 4) notes, far exceed the Public Health Act, which makes no provision to "confine or control the movements of healthy people." Similar legislation was enacted transnationally (c.f. New York State Senate, 2021; Brown, 2021), with *Vox* urging the "almost unthinkable" in the United States, i.e. "centralized isolation of people who test positive for Covid-19 and their close contacts" (Yglesias, 2020).

The idea of forced relocation was seeded via the idea of "green zones," i.e. "dedicated areas at either the household, extended family or neighborhood level, in which high-risk individuals (the elderly and those with chronic, underlying conditions) are relocated temporarily [. . .]" (Favas et al., 2020). "Protecting the most vulnerable," however, soon acquired a cruel twist as UK care home residents were isolated in their rooms for months on end and prohibited from having physical contact with family members. For many, the care home became a prison: "residents were transformed into a form of bare life, in which most of their human rights had been removed on the justification of keeping them alive at whatever cost" (Elmer, 2022).

In February 2021, so-called "quarantine hotels" were introduced for certain travelers who had to pay large sums of money for their own detention, with conditions being described as "prison-like" (Thorburn, 2021; Curzon, 2021). As in a prison, residents of "quarantine hotels" were confined to their room for most of the time except for a short exercise period, they were given substandard food, and were guarded. Upsetting footage emerged of some residents breaking down psychologically. One woman in New Zealand refused to take a PCR test and was not allowed out of her room for twenty-two days (solitary confinement); her food was withheld while a soldier stood guard outside her door, and she was threatened with deportation (UK Column, 2021, 01:07:44—01:14:56). As "bare life," her attempt to assert bodily autonomy was seen as noncompliance and as punishable.

So-called "quarantine camps" were set up in Australia and New Zealand. In the Northern Territories, for example, the Army transported "positive Covid cases" to the Howard Springs "COVID quarantine camp" (McPhee, 2021), whose modern facilities blur the boundary with a hotel and normalize the camp as a residence space (Elmer, 2022). In March 2020, the Howard Springs camp was named a "Centre for National Resilience," and other such centers were built in Melbourne, Brisbane, and Perth.

In sum, not only is the biodigital gulag being invisibly constructed all around us, but the public is being psychologically conditioned to accept life in the camp.

Imprisoning Dissidents and Judicial Murder

The Expansion of UK Prison Capacity

Moves to criminalize dissent (see Chapter 2) mean that questions need to be asked about the UK Government's commitment to building 20,000 new prison places for England and Wales by the mid-2020s (Prison Reform Trust, 2023). To put this figure in context, the current UK prison population is 95,500 (Sturge, 2023, p. 4), so the new prison places will increase it by over 21 percent when also accounting for Scotland and Northern Ireland. According to Walker (2022), incarceration levels in the UK rose by 60 percent over the last thirty years, yet by 2026—within just four years—they are forecast to rise by a further 23.7 percent. This is in line with Ministry of Justice projections for a rising UK prison population up to 2027. The MoJ

(2023, p. 2) attributes the projected rise to numerous factors, but the main ones are: the Government's aim to increase the number of police officers, which will lead to an increased number of charges; the impact of new sentencing policies, including the Police, Crime, Sentencing and Courts Act (2022)—plus the Public Order Act 2023; and increased custody time for violent and sexual offenders.

In the decade prior to the "pandemic," the UK prison population "flattened off, even falling in Scotland and Northern Ireland" (Sturge, 2023, p. 4). Correspondingly, since 2010, the number of new prison places created in the UK (11,000) roughly matched the number of closed prison places (10,700) (Prison Reform Trust, 2023). Although 61 percent of UK prisons today are overcrowded (Sturge, 2023, p. 15), this was not previously used as an excuse to surge prison capacity. The planned surge, therefore, represents a significant departure from the status quo and is largely driven by executive and legislature measures, in particular swelling the ranks of the police force, plus introducing new legislation to create more crimes, especially around protest and dissent. According to Criminology Professor Francis Pakes (2021), this has nothing to do with "predicted or experienced rise in crime," it being "well established that prison rates and crime rates operate largely independent from each other." Put bluntly, there appears to be an agenda to imprison more people.

Of the 20,000 new prison places, around half are to be provided by six new "mega prisons" (five of them privately managed), the first of which, HMP Five Wells (1,700 capacity), opened in Wellingborough in 2021. For perspective, most UK prisons have 100 to 1,000 cell spaces (Walker, 2022). Community resistance against the new mega prisons has meant that progress on the 20,000 plus target lags behind schedule (5,200 new places as of June 2023) (Prison Reform Trust, 2023). To compensate, prefabricated "Rapid Deployment Cells" with an intended fifteen-year life span are being added to existing prison sites. Any measure will do, it seems, to increase capacity—but to what end?

For whom are the new prison places intended? Five in six Parole Board recommendations for transfer to lower security prisons are now being rejected by the MoJ, whereas over 90 percent were previously approved (Prison Reform Trust, 2023). This suggests that the new prison places are intended for the least dangerous offenders who are deemed unlikely to attempt escape (Categories C and D). HMP Five Wells, for instance, is Category C, and it has been remarked that its "interior is more reminiscent of a budget hotel than a quarter-of-a-billion-pound prison" (Harris & Aspinall, 2021). If the new prison places being created are primarily for low-risk offenders, this would be consistent with the criminalization of dissent and the incarceration of nonviolent dissidents.

The Politicization of the Criminal Justice System

Once dissent becomes criminalized, the criminal justice system becomes politicized, with the courts being used to advance political agendas. In Nazi Germany, new courts to try political enemies were established, whose judges were "fervent Nazis, not trained lawyers" (Epstein, 2015, p. 67). Roland Freisler, who was appointed President of the People's Court in 1942, declared: "For the enemy of the state and the community of the *Volk* there is only one course in prosecution and sentencing: unflinching severity and, if necessary, total annihilation" (cited in Müller, 1991, p. 77). Nazi legal theorists provided the courts with "the means to subvert justice and commit judicial murder": an estimated 40,000–50,000 death sentences were handed out, excluding verdicts in the summary proceedings of the military and the police, of which ca. 80 percent were carried out (Müller, 1991, pp. 81, 196).

Thankfully, we have not yet reached a comparable stage in our own time, but we should be clear-eyed regarding where the criminalization of dissent—which is starting to creep in (see Chapter 2)—eventually leads under totalitarianism. One of the more chilling aspects of Nazi rule was that brutality had to be lawful. For example, the arbitrary brutality of the SA was quickly stamped out with the murder of its leadership in 1934 (Gellately, 1991, p. 35). In July 1935, Hitler forbade Nazi Party members from engaging in unauthorized behavior against individual Jews, including unauthorized signs and graffiti. "To be 'worthy' of Nazism," Koonz (2003, p. 181) explains, "militias were admonished to remain within the law," and so the Nazi supervisor of Jewish cultural organizations "called for restraint and reminded Nazi militants that Jewish organizations had sworn their loyalty to the regime and therefore operated legally." The cruel reality, unfathomable to those accustomed to the rule of law, was that "lawful, orderly persecution would turn out to be more deadly than random cruelty," epitomized in the round-up of Jews to concentration camps and, once there, "the replacement of arbitrary violence with systematic cruelty" (Koonz, 2003, pp. 224–228). Under totalitarianism, "the law" offers no defense against the descent into barbarism and can even exacerbate it. It would, therefore, be unwise today, under conditions of emergent totalitarianism, to expect the judiciary to provide any meaningful checks on executive power.

Eugenics

Euthanasia

The ultimate expression of biopower is euthanasia, which is why Hitler was immediately keen to promote it despite there being no economic or eugenic requirement to do so (Agamben, 1998, p. 141). In this context, the reappearance of euthanasia in the West since 2020 is troubling (see Chapter 2). Notoriously, the Nazi euthanasia program expanded beyond its original remit, from the seriously ill to "virtually anyone whose death was desired" (Lifton, 1986, p. 255). So-called "mercy killing" and "deaths of grace" soon morphed into "killing the sick" (Foth, 2014). The Aktion T4 program (1939–1941) killed an estimated 250,000–300,000 disabled people—first children, then adults. The Special Action 14f13 program went on to murder other "undesirable" groups from the spring of 1941, gassing 10,000–20,000 concentration-camp inmates "unable to perform labor" (Epstein 2015, p. 156). The path from here to the Final Solution is not hard to fathom.

Medical Experimentation

Once euthanasia had been normalized, Nazi medical experimentation, masquerading as a research program to benefit humanity, was an "easy subsequent step for the regime to implement" (Haque et al., 2012, p. 477). That experimentation, however, particularly at Auschwitz, did not benefit humanity. On the contrary, it constituted a series of crimes against humanity, involving:

> artificially inflicted burns with phosphorous incendiary bombs; experiments on the effects of drinking sea water; experiments with various forms of poison, by ingestion as well as in bullets or arrows; widespread experiments on artificially induced typhus, as well as with epidemic hepatitis and with malaria; experiments in cold immersion ("in freezing water") to determine the body's reactions and susceptibilities; experiments with mustard gas in order to study the kinds of wounds it can cause; experiments on the regeneration of bone, muscle, nerve tissue, and on bone transplantation, involving removal of various bones, muscles, and nerves from healthy women. (Lifton, 1986, p. 302)

The Nuremberg Code, with its emphasis on informed consent, originated largely in response to such crimes.

Today, transhumanism—the latest iteration of eugenics—promises to "augment" or "upgrade" humanity, helping to compensate for physical and mental disabilities (Roco & Bainbridge, 2002, p. 4) and to "raise human abilities above the norm, whether via drugs, nutritional supplements, prosthetics, or neurotechnologies" (Policy Horizons Canada, 2020). Gene editing technologies such as CRISPR, Gates (2018) claims, could help humanity "overcome some of the biggest and most persistent challenges in global health and development." As with Nazi eugenics, it is all for the good of humanity.

Even a cursory glance at transhumanist pronouncements, however, indicates that a primary goal is not addressing human suffering, but, rather, increasing workforce productivity. At the 2017 World Government Summit, for instance, Elon Musk claimed that if humans want to "add value to the economy," they must "augment their capabilities through a merger of biological intelligence and machine intelligence" (cited in Solon, 2017). According to the UK Ministry of Defense (2021, p. 60), "wearables and analytics" can "improve productivity and workforce health, while augmentations could mitigate disabilities thereby allowing more people to work." Webb (2021a) observes a Welcome Leap project aimed at treating depression in which only those aspects of depression that interfere with a person's work are targeted, helping to ensure "perfect worker" behavior.

Contrary to Gates' (2018) claim that gene editing raises "no special safety concerns," CRISPR Cas-9 has been found to cause "large deletions and more complex genomic rearrangements" in mouse embryonic stem cells and a human differentiated cell line (Kosicki et al., 2018). It has been found to risk chromothripsis, "an extremely damaging form of genomic rearrangement" (Sheridan, 2021) that may potentially cause cancer or inherited disease (Robinson, 2021). In mouse embryos, it has been found to cause "whole chromosome loss and genomic instability" (Papathanasiou et al., 2021). Jennifer Doudna, who invented CRISPR Cas-9, claims to have awoken in a cold sweat after dreaming about Hitler asking her how that technology works (Knoepfler, 2015), suggesting a troubled conscience.

If this is the safety profile of CRISPR Cas-9, what about that of so-called "mRNA vaccines," which do not technically qualify as vaccines (Hughes, 2022a, p. 210)? According to Doctors for COVID Ethics (2023), all "mRNA vaccines" are toxic from the first principles of immunology and should be banned. We are yet to find out what the long-term implications of the experimental "Covid-19 vaccines" are in terms of health and fertility, but preliminary indications do not look good. Official reports of serious adverse reactions quickly reached unprecedented levels (OpenVAERS, n.d.; MHRA, n.d.; WHO, n.d. [search "COVID-19 vaccine" for over 5.2 million reports]) and may only account for 1–10 percent of the total (Ross et al., 2010; MHRA, 2019). Birth rates have fallen transnationally since the "Covid-19 vaccine" rollout began (Pfeiffer, 2022; Bujard & Andersson, 2022; Swiss Policy Research, 2022; Naked Emperor, 2023), disturbingly bringing to mind Heinrich Himmler and Viktor Brack's 1941 vision of "sterilization [. . .] on a massive scale" (Lifton, 1986, p. 278).

There appears to be a concerted effort to use "vaccines" to "program" human bodies for eugenics purposes. According to Moderna CEO, Stéphane Bancel, "mRNA is like software" (Garde, 2017), and Moderna's Chief Medical Officer, Tal Zaks (n.d.), claimed in a TEDx talk that "we are actually hacking the software of life." This resembles Harari's (2017) claim that "we are learning [. . .] how to hack humans, how to engineer them, how to manufacture them." On its website, Moderna describes their "Covid-19 vaccine" as "an operating system on a computer." President Biden's Executive Order of September 12, 2022, calls for the development of "genetic engineering technologies and techniques to be able to write circuitry for cells and predictably program biology in the same way in which we write software and program computers [. . .]" (White House, 2022b).

The patent for Moderna's "Covid-19 vaccine" claims to "safely direct the body's cellular machinery to produce nearly any protein of interest, from native proteins to antibodies and other entirely novel protein constructs that can have therapeutic activity inside and outside of cells" (Ciaramella & Himansu, 2017). There are obvious safety concerns, however, not only in light of the above morbidity and mortality data, but also given the strange rubbery "clots," often huge, which are being pulled out of dead "vaccinated" bodies by embalmers such as Richard Hirschmann (Tice, 2022); they do not appear to be natural blood clots (Mihalcea, 2023).

To the extent that mRNA technology can cause the human body to produce artifacts that are nonhuman, it blurs "what is considered natural or organic and what is digital, engineered, or synthetic," prompting us to "redefine what we consider human or natural" (Policy Horizons Canada, 2020). Moreover, "synthetic biology machines" can be programmed to create "entirely new organisms." This amounts to an attack on Nature/ Creation itself, a kind of Frankenstein's monster technology. The Rockefeller Foundation (2013) envisages the "re-engineering of humans through genetic engineering or mixed human-robots," nanobots and nanotechnology, synthetic biology and "human-designed life." The potential for disaster with such technologies, delivered worldwide, is immeasurable and could make Nazi eugenics pale in comparison.

The Role of Doctors

In Nazi Germany, not only were doctors the most eager professional group to join the Party (Haque et al., 2012), but many proved willing to carry out so-called "mercy deaths" or "deaths of grace" if absolved of legal culpability; the Nazis thus found that it was "easy to recruit professional killers" (Epstein, 2015, p. 155). In time, doctors became "the unseen generals in Hitler's war against the Jews and other Europeans deemed inferior"; they devised the eugenics formulas and hand-selected the victims for "sterilization, euthanasia, and mass extermination" (Black, 2003). According to a 1945 Foreign Office telegram, over 90 percent of top-level medics were involved in human experiments in which "the subject was either sacrificed or permanently wounded [. . .] in German hospitals, universities and concentration camps" (cited in Drobniewski, 1993, p. 541). Doctors who began their medical career by taking the Hippocratic Oath "later in cold blood inflicted the most horrible tortures on their concentration-camp victims" (Meerloo, 1953, p. 133). They facilitated the "medicalization of genocide" (Haque et al. 2012, 478).

It therefore does not bode well that, in the Covid era, doctors hypnotized by propaganda and incentivized by £12.58 a jab in the UK (rising to £15 and £20 on Sundays [McFadden, 2021]) abandoned the core medical principles of informed consent and "first do no harm" and instead injected most of the population with unlicensed experimental technologies lacking any safety data beyond a few months, under conditions of duress by the government and the media. There is, therefore, good reason to think that the medical profession will remain thoroughly complicit, as it enjoys its privileged status under the emergent biosecurity regime—unless it realizes what it has become part of and is willing to learn the lessons of history.

Syringes

In a chapter titled "Killing with Syringes: Phenol Injections," Lifton (1986, p. 254) notes that phenol injections were initially associated with the direct medical killing of the Nazi euthanasia project. Other substances, such as benzine, gasoline, hydrogen peroxide, cyanide, and air were also experimentally "injected into the vein," but phenol injected directly into the heart provided "greater killing efficiency," i.e. death within fifteen seconds (Lifton, 1986, pp. 257–258). Huge quantities of phenol were ordered on the pretext of being a legitimate medical preparation, turning the hospital into "a place of mass extermination." The T4 euthanasia operation saw hospitals experiment with various means of extermination, including Zyklon B, which was later used in the death camps (Sharav, 2022). Phenol injections thus anticipated the development of the gas chambers (Lifton, 1986, p. 255). At Auschwitz, there were some 20,000 phenol murders, representing "the most literal example of the entire healing-killing reversal" by doctors (Lifton, 1986, pp. 260–261).

The midazolam scandal in the UK in the spring of 2020 saw huge amounts of midazolam ordered and administered to those over the age of sixty-five, to give them what Conservative MP Luke Evans called "a good death" (a euphemism for euthanasia, see Chapter 2). Meanwhile, billions of syringes were being manufactured as part of a campaign to inject the entire global population with products still officially in development; as Gates (2020a) put it, "we need to make the vaccine available to almost every person on the planet." Those "vaccines," which are in fact military rather than pharmaceutical products (Hughes, 2024, Chapter 6), have so far been shot into a reported 5.55 billion people (Holder, 2023), yet are known to contain undisclosed ingredients (Hughes, 2022c) whose purpose can only be nefarious (cf. Hughes, 2024, Chapter 8). They, too, seem to have been deployed experimentally: one batch in every two hundred is over fifty times more deadly than the rest (Hill, 2022; Wilson, 2022b; cf. Schmeling et al., 2023), which is too radical a discrepancy to be attributed to bad manufacturing processes. It seems that some batches were more toxic than others by design, perhaps to calibrate the tolerance of different groups of people to different levels of whatever is in the shots. This all bodes darkly for the "era of pandemics" which the ruling class expects us to believe is coming (cited in Fleming, 2021), despite its scientific absurdity (Hughes, 2024, Chapter 4), and to which the solution only ever seems to be more and more harmful injections.

To ordinary, decent people, it is inconceivable that the "vaccines" delivered under a global public health program in the name of "protecting" the public and keeping people "safe" may in fact be nothing of the kind. Yet, once it is understood that the transnational deep state which controls governments traces its methods back to the Nazis, an altogether different mentality must be recognized: "Through T4, the Nazis learned the importance of subterfuge in killing operations. Patients were told that they were being transferred to a new hospital. Just before their murder, they entered what they believed to be shower rooms" (Epstein, 2015, p. 155). This is not to draw a comparison between "Covid-19 vaccines" and extermination at Nazi death camps, because the stage of targeted mass killing has not yet been reached. It is, however, to draw attention to a perpetrator mindset that is willing to cloak mass murder in the guise of healthcare.

Systematic Mass Murder

Murder in the Name of Morality

Old-fashioned explanations of the Holocaust, such as that "the road to Auschwitz was built by hate, but paved with indifference" (Kershaw, 1983, p. 277), or that "mass destruction [of Jews] was accompanied not by the uproar of emotions, but [by] the dead silence of unconcern" (Bauman, 1991, p. 74) are unconvincing. Contrary to the stereotype, Nazi perpetrators were anything but blind order followers aided and abetted by an indifferent population. Rather, they worked for "a regime that could murder in the name of morality—and make its justification credible in the eyes of most Germans" (Koonz, 2003, p. 99).

This did not happen overnight; it took years of indoctrination and was achieved through supposed "facts conveyed by experts, documentary films, popular science, educational materials, and exhibitions" (Koonz, 2003, p. 272). For example, discrimination against Jews had to have reached a very high level for the Holocaust to have been possible; Jews' "social death" marked the "prerequisite for deportation and genocide" (Kaplan, 1998, p. 5).

Nazi propaganda painted the *Volkskörper*, the ethnic body politic, as an organism endangered by defective members, much as an individual body might be threatened by a malignancy (Koonz, 2003, p. 130). SS doctor Fritz Klein, for example, claimed, "I am of course a doctor and I want to preserve life. I would remove a festering appendix out of reverence for human life. The Jew, however, is the festering appendix in the body of humanity" (cited in Rees, 2009, p. 75). Jews were portrayed as vermin, "maliciously recruiting the basic human revulsion of filth and pestilence into a force for [dehumanization]" (Haque et al., 2012, p. 475). Through such metaphors, it became possible to frame the extermination of Jews as a public health necessity, as a means of warding off illness and disability, and even "a fulfilment of ethical imperatives" (Haque et al. 2012, p. 474).

Conspicuously, the "Covid-19" operation assumed the form of a public health crisis in which those resisting the "measures" were castigated as a public health threat (a threat to the body politic). The "pandemic of the unvaccinated" metaphor, coined by CDC director Rochelle Walensky in July 2021 (Andone & Holcombe, 2021) and propagated by state and corporate media, painted those resisting the attack on bodily autonomy as disease spreaders, much like Jews in Nazi propaganda.

The Nazis' "new moral order" (Westermann, 2015, p. 488) ultimately entailed what Meerloo (1956, p. 217) describes as "the complete breakdown of all moral evaluations," whereby "racial persecution and murder became a kind of moral rule." According to Hilberg (1985, 55), the Final Solution was not so much a matter of "laws and commands as it was a matter of spirit, of shared comprehension, of consonance and synchronization," i.e. of manufactured *Gleichschaltung*. The perpetrators "improvised and often exceeded their orders," because they falsely intuited the ultimate goal of their actions (Koonz, 2003, pp. 10–11).

Today, if enough people, through propaganda, can be indoctrinated to believe in the reality of "global challenges" such as "pandemics" and "climate change," then they can be made to turn on those who, in good conscience and with evidence-based arguments, do not. The severity of the persecution will be a function of the perceived level of danger (which can be manufactured through propaganda and psychological warfare) and messaging by the authorities in terms of what does and does not constitute acceptable behavior.

State-sanctioned Violence against the Outgroup

Social and legal discrimination against Jews laid the groundwork for the *Kristallnacht* pogrom of November 9, 1938, which occurred two days after thousands of Polish Jews were expelled from Nazi Germany. The pogrom was initiated following the vigilante assassination of a German diplomat in Paris by the seventeen-year-old son of a Polish Jewish couple who had lived in Germany since 1911. Orders were given not to harm non-Jewish German life or property, or foreigners, and to remove archives prior to vandalizing synagogues. Police were instructed to arrest as many Jews as jails could hold, preferably healthy young men. Hundreds of Jews died from injuries sustained during the pogrom, and there were a large number of rapes and suicides. The veiled threat of another pogrom (which never came), coupled with "rational" proposals to solve the Jewish question, "set the stage for wartime genocide" (Koonz, 2003, p. 250).

In our own time, an event akin to *Kristallnacht*—i.e., state-sanctioned, society-wide violence against a specific outgroup—is yet to occur. However, the warning signs are there, such as the state's priming of the public for violence against nonconformists in the "Covid-19" era (Hughes, 2024, Chapter 7), the resultant "mask rage, vaccine rage, [and] social distancing rage" directed against those who did not comply with "the measures" (Scott, 2021), and worldwide police brutality against anti-lockdown protestors (Broudy et al., 2022).

As dissidents find their reputations smeared by spooks/the media (Hayward, 2022; Robinson, 2023), their bank accounts and/or payment processors shut down (O'Neill, 2022), their rational arguments met with thought-terminating propaganda clichés ("anti-vaxxer," "conspiracy theorist," etc.) and censorship (Shir-Raz et al., 2022; Turley, 2022), their sanity called into question (Hughes, 2024, Chapter 5), their careers destroyed (particularly in the cases of dissenting doctors), and their political views criminalized (see Chapter 2), it is beyond doubt that a specific minority is being systematically discriminated against—not on racial or religious grounds, but because it resists the *Gleichschaltung* needed to sustain the totalitarianism of the biosecurity state.

In that context, it is conceivable that a false flag event, such as "the next pandemic" repeatedly touted by Gates (2020b, 2021; Gates & Gates 2021) or "the second pandemic" let slip by President Biden (White House, 2022a), which according to the 2022 US National Security Strategy could be as contagious but more lethal than "Covid-19" (White House, 2022c, p. 28), may be used to greenlight much worse violence against dissidents than has so far been witnessed.

Stanton's Ten Stages of Genocide

The first four stages of Stanton's (2016) "ten stages of genocide"—i.e., classification, symbolization, discrimination, and dehumanization—were all fulfilled during the "Covid-19" operation, and there is reason to suspect that subsequent stages may be in progress (Hughes, 2024, Chapters 7–8). The outgroup was determined, not by nationality, ethnicity, race, or religion (as would be necessary to meet the United Nations [1948] definition of genocide), but, rather, by dissent from the official "Covid-19" narrative. Not Jews, but those resisting the transnational deep state represent the scourge that must ultimately be silenced/eliminated if technocratic totalitarianism is to triumph. "Politicide"—"the killing of people because of their political and social affiliations" (Harff, 2017, p. 112)—might be a better term than "genocide" in that respect.

As per Stanton's (2016) seventh stage, mass murder could be framed as a moral imperative, such as self-defense, e.g. to prevent the spread of a fatal new disease. The fact that WHO Director-General Tedros Adhanom Ghebreyesus stands accused of genocide when he directed the Ethiopian security services from 2013 to 2015 (Ames, 2020), and that under the WHO Pandemic Treaty he will single-handedly be able to declare a "pandemic" and the alleged necessary "countermeasures" which all governments will be legally bound to follow (Kheriaty, 2022; Knightly, 2022), is disturbing in this context.

Are the conditions for systematic mass murder of human beings deliberately being put in place? If so, then what we are looking at is *worse* than 1930s Nazi Germany, where there was no genocidal intent to begin with (Koonz, 2003, pp. 15–16). Before World War II, the Nazis aimed to get rid of Jews through "voluntary" emigration: 300,000 left, including 60,000 to Palestine, but most chose to remain because, no matter how bad things got, "they never imagined that the Nazis would outright murder them. Until it happened, the Holocaust was all but unthinkable" (Epstein, 2015, p. 91). Today, in contrast, given that Nazi Germany is demonstrably the model for so much that has been instigated transnationally since 2020 (see Chapter 2), systematic mass murder must not only have been thinkable from the very beginning, but *planned for* as a necessary stage in the road to global totalitarianism.

Systematizing Mass Murder

The systematic mass murder of Jews began with the deployment of *Einsatzgruppen* in Operation Barbarossa in the summer of 1941, and around a million Jews were killed before the Wannsee Conference of January 1942, where the formal decision to annihilate the entire Jewish population (the "Final Solution") was taken. Industrial-scale killing in the extermination camps ramped up around this time, utilizing information technologies developed by IBM to identify, round up, transport, and "process" the victims (Black, 2009, Chapter 5).

This marked the origins of what van der Pijl (2022, p. 59) calls the "information-liquidation model," with reference to British and US operations in the 1950s and 1960s to infiltrate and assassinate Communist political leaderships in Indonesia and Vietnam (Hughes, 2022b). The ARPANET (1969) originated one year after Operation Phoenix (1968), and thus the Internet was "from its very inception intended to be a tool for tracking, surveilling and, ultimately, controlling a target population" (Corbett, 2019). With such an infrastructure in place, Valentine (2017, p. 66) contends, "it is only a matter of time until we enter the next Phoenix phase of explicit terror here at home." Connecting human bodies to an external wireless network offers new possibilities for control, up to and including remote controlled torture and assassination (Hughes, 2024, Chapter 8).

Could systematic mass extermination really take place in the United States, the self-proclaimed beacon of freedom and democracy? US psychiatrist Douglas Kelley returned from the Nuremberg trials convinced that even in his country of origin, a "re-enactment of genocidal atrocities perpetrated against a dehumanized enemy" was conceivable; he saw "little in America today which could prevent the establishment of a Nazi-like state" (cited in Versluis, 2006, p. 154). Milgram reached a similar conclusion after completing his research: "If a system of death camps were set up in the United States of the sort we had seen in Nazi Germany, one would be able to find sufficient personnel for those camps in any medium-sized American town" (cited in Zimbardo, 2007, p. 281). Zimbardo, after a career spent investigating how ordinary people can be made to commit monstrous deeds, concludes that, in principle, "such deeds are reproducible at any time in any nation" (2007, p. 290).

Conclusion

When one considers the gamut of historical continuities with the Nazi past outlined in Chapter 2, it is evident the terrible course of events since 2020 has been *by design*, instigated by a ruling class seeking recourse to totalitarianism on a global scale, using the Nazi past as a template for domination. The model of using a false flag operation to suspend constitutional rights and freedoms before instigating ever more draconian legislation comes straight out of Nazi Germany. So too do revolution from above, the attack on the working and middle classes, the manufactured *Gleichschaltung*, the military-grade propaganda deployed against domestic populations, "health passports" and eugenics, euthanasia, grotesque violations of medical ethics, the hijacking of conscience, the disingenuous deployment of ecopolitics, etc.

We know from history where totalitarianism ultimately leads, and without worldwide social revolution we can expect a future involving economic slavery, lack of bodily sovereignty, judicial murder, legalized brutality, entrapment within "smart" human settlement zones (while the ruling class enjoys the world's natural resources), food dependency, coerced eugenics experiments, and systematic mass murder of those who do not "belong," among other markers of the loss of human freedom. What, then, will be the global population's response as it awakens to the nightmare future that the self-proclaimed technocrats have in store for it?

CHAPTER 8

RESISTANCE

In a totalitarian society, it can be hard to gauge what the public is really thinking and feeling, and easy to feel pessimistic about prospects for resistance. Yet, UK Health Security Agency data provides clear evidence that at least a quarter of the adult population, and probably much higher, has serious doubts about what has been unfolding since 2020 and will not, under any circumstances, knowingly allow its bodily autonomy to be violated by the state. As the truth increasingly comes to light, and class consciousness develops, massive public resistance to technocratic agendas is to be expected. That resistance will not be organized by a political Left that no longer exists in an oppositional sense, but will, rather, assume the form of a decentralized mass rejection of all aspects of technocracy. Even in Nazi Germany, there was surprising scope for resistance at the individual level. So, too, today, it is essential that everyone finds the moral courage to take lawful action in whatever way they can against the cowards, criminals, and traitors seeking to oppress and enslave them. Totalitarianism relies on public consent; once that consent disappears, it is inevitable that a global mass movement will defeat those behind the war for technocracy.

What Does the Public Really Think?

It is easy to be pessimistic about prospects for resistance in a totalitarian society. The Jewish diarist Victor Klemperer (1999, p. 214), for example, wrote: "I am slowly beginning to think that this regime can really still last for decades. There is so much lethargy in the German people and so much immorality and above all so much stupidity" (Klemperer, 1999, p. 214). One hears similar pessimism today in disparaging references to fellow citizens as "dumb herd animals" or "brainwashed sheep" who are too "asleep" to prevent the slide into tyranny. The control mechanisms can seem dismayingly effective given their crudeness: "An underlying fear of death, fed by a false but very broadly supported narrative, worked in the 1930s, worked from 2020 to 2022, and seems likely to work again" when it comes to deprivation of civil liberties (Bell, 2023).

Yet, under conditions of *Gleichschaltung*, it can be difficult to know what people are really thinking and feeling beneath their public show of conformity. In Nazi Germany, Rudolf Steiner observed, the people "put on masks. No one knows what the individual thinks [or] feels, whether he hopes for the fall of this regime" (cited in Koonz, 2003, p. 75). Even the regime's most ardent cheerleaders, Steiner adds, did not necessarily believe in Nazi ideology, making it anyone's guess what the masses were thinking. Similar was true during "Covid-19," when people literally put on masks, and it remains true today. With opinion polls manipulated (Hughes, 2024, Chapter 7), it is hard to know what proportion of the public genuinely believes in official dogma regarding "pandemics," "climate change," "the terrorist threat," etc., and what proportion is reluctant to speak out for fear of ostracization, flak, and punishment.

Still, we can make an educated guess. According to UK Health Security Agency data, 18.9 million Brits (30 percent of a cohort of 63.4 million) had not taken a first dose of a "Covid-19 vaccine" by July 2022 (UKHSA, 2022, Table 5). This includes 12.4 million responsible adults, i.e. 23 percent of the adult population of 54 million. Thus, even according to official data, almost a quarter of the UK adult population withstood the prolonged assault on its bodily sovereignty. The proportion is likely higher when one factors in routine manipulation of official "Covid-19" statistics (Crawford, 2022), creating "one of the most manipulated infectious disease events in history" (Blaylock, 2022). Even that figure does not include the increasing number of people with "vaccine regret," i.e. those people who now realize that they were duped into taking one or more dangerous experimental products into their bodies and who will not so readily place trust in authority again.

We should not forget that people repeatedly marched in their millions against the "measures" in 2021, across the world, although the media did its best to downplay the numbers and misrepresent the protestors as "far right extremists" (Hughes, 2024, Chapter 7). Similarly, the massive farmers' protests against the "European New Deal" in 2023/24, involving various forms of direct action in France, Germany, the Netherlands, and elsewhere, demonstrate a growing appetite for resistance.

As intentionally traumatic as the "Covid-19" era was, it did cause a lot of people to realize that the world is nothing like what they had been indoctrinated to believe, and to start asking critical questions. More and more people today are learning to see through propaganda and are ceasing to consume mainstream "news" and "entertainment" (psychological programming) and this poses a major threat to the control system. For as Arendt (1962, p. 363) writes, "It is in the moment of defeat that the inherent weakness of totalitarian propaganda becomes visible. Without the force of the movement, its members cease at once to believe in the dogma for which yesterday they still were ready to sacrifice their lives." Once a critical mass of people ceases to believe the ideology that is being used to legitimize the means of its oppression, it is game over.

As propaganda-induced ignorance, misunderstanding, and wrongdoing recede, the truth starts to set people free. Higham (2007, p. xv) asks some important rhetorical questions regarding the financiers and industrialists who played both sides during World War II:

What would have happened if millions of Americans and British people, struggling with coupons and lines at the gas stations, had learned that in 1942 Standard Oil of New Jersey managers shipped the enemy's fuel through neutral Switzerland and that the enemy was shipping Allied fuel? Suppose the public had discovered that the Chase Bank in Nazi-occupied Paris after Pearl Harbor was doing millions of dollars' worth of business with the enemy with the full knowledge of the head office in Manhattan? Or that Ford trucks were being built for the German occupation troops in France with authorization from Dearborn, Michigan? [. . . .] Or that such arrangements were known about in Washington and either sanctioned or deliberately ignored?

Higham's list goes on. The point, however, is that an enlightened public in full possession of the facts would never stand for such machinations, which led to a prolongation of the war and unnecessary death and suffering. Similarly, today, if the public could see through the thick web of deceit that comprises the "Covid-19" narrative (Hughes, 2024, Chapter 6), it would quickly turn against those responsible for manufacturing and propagating the lies that have led to consistently high excess mortality transnationally (US Mortality, n.d.; eurostat, n.d.; ONS, n.d., Figure 1; Australian Bureau of Statistics, 2023; Gabel & Knox, 2023).

Left vs. Right or Revolution from Above/Below?

The failure of the Left to unite and mobilize broad-based opposition to Nazism made it easy to crush. Despite underground agitation efforts between 1933 and 1935 that saw millions of illicit leaflets, newspapers, and brochures dispersed in German cities (the model for the White Rose movement and publications such as *The Light Paper* since 2020), the resistance was easily infiltrated, and by 1935, "virtually all party activists had been arrested or had fled abroad. Prior to World War II, roughly 150,000 communists endured Nazi concentration camps; 30,000 were executed" (Epstein, 2015, p. 116).

Today, the prospects for coordinated resistance by the Left appear even worse. As discussed in Chapter 2, "the Left" no longer exists as an oppositional force, and van der Pijl's (2022, p. 59) "information-liquidation model," which involves "sending agents to penetrate the resistance and then, on the basis of centralized information, moving to take out the leadership" has phenomenal potential in an age when all of our data is digitally harvested and monitored by Big Tech and the intelligence agencies (which are one and the same) in a worldwide signals intelligence operation (Corbett, 2019; cf. Hughes, 2024, Chapter 8).

On the other hand, the old Left-Right paradigm is now dead along with liberal democracy and the political system of the modern nation state, as Agamben (1998, pp. 175–181) predicted. The "Covid-19" crisis demonstrated beyond reasonable doubt that all state organs are now arrayed against the working and middle classes (Hughes et al. 2023, § V), and that "neither police nor politicians nor courts" will protect the public against the overreach of executive power (Ruechel, 2021).

The only distinction that matters is revolution from the bottom up or the top down, i.e. worldwide social revolution or the "Great Reset" and global technocracy. The former does not so much require leaders and organizers as decentralized mass noncompliance with all aspects of technocracy—something which requires *all* of us actively to play our part. Mass noncompliance can be a very powerful tool. In Romania in 1989, for instance, when the crowd lost its fear and began heckling dictator Nicolae Ceaușescu, it only took four days for his own military to court martial him and execute him by firing squad. The crowd's role was entirely peaceful; all that was required was an unmistakable indication that the public was no longer willing to accept its subjugation (Ruechel, 2021).

Finding the Courage to Act

"Even in the *gleichgeschaltet* Nazi Germany," Meerloo (1956, p. 128) writes, a resistance movement was active, and, according to Epstein (2015, p. 118), there was "surprising scope" for resistance there. Citizens without Jewish ancestry or ties to Marxism had "considerable leeway to circumvent Nazi measures of which they disapproved," as attested to in memoirs by Jews who emigrated, regarding the support they had received from non-Jewish friends who did not suffer harsh reprisals (Koonz, 2003, p. 12). Even soldiers at the front, Koonz adds, could avoid obeying orders that troubled their conscience, and thus, "not mindless obedience but selective compliance characterized Germans' collaboration with evil."

There are important lessons here in terms of possibilities for resistance. The regime—in our time, the transnational deep state that controls the political systems of most countries—is not all-powerful. There is plenty of scope for resistance in myriad ways; everyone can and must do *something* to disrupt the technocratic New World Order (see Chapter 7) that is emerging; different people bring different talents to the table. Passive bystanding is not an option: we are faced with a clear and present danger to liberty on a global scale. Remaining silent about what is happening is also not an option, for silence connotes consent (*Qui tacet consentire videtur*).

What is needed above all in the fight ahead is moral courage. Pastor Martin Niemöller famously reflected:

> First they took the Communists, but I was not a Communist, so I said nothing. Then they took the Social Democrats, but I was not a Social Democrat, so I did nothing. Then it was the trade unionists' turn, but I was not a trade unionist. And then they took the Jews, but I was not a Jew, so I did little. Then when they came and took me, there was no one left who could have stood up for me. (cited in Epstein, 2015, p. 111)

Totalitarianism comes for everyone in the end, which is why everyone needs to find the courage to oppose it before it is too late.

This is all the more true given the cowardice of our would-be oppressors. As in *The Wizard of Oz*, where the "wizard" responsible for all the satanic inversions and deceptions in the story turns out to be a man hiding behind a curtain, so those responsible for all the psychological operations waged against the public today are cowards afraid to reveal themselves. The CIA's Nelson Brickham once admitted, "A guy who has strong criminal tendencies but is too much of a coward to be one, would wind up in a place like the CIA if he had the education" (cited in Valentine, 2017, p. 38). Educated cowards and criminals are who we are up against. Moral courage is needed to defeat them.

Withdrawing Consent

Totalitarianism conjures the illusion of omnipotence, yet it is entirely reliant on public acquiescence and participation. The state of exception, for example, "cannot simply be unilaterally decreed by the sovereign"; rather, its declaration must be understood and accepted as legitimate by the public (Ahmed, 2012, p. 55). Even the feared Gestapo could not act alone; it was reliant on the collaboration of officials, as well as public participation in the enforcement process (Gellately, 1991, p. 16). To forge a racial state, the Nazis depended on contributions from virtually all professions (Epstein, 2015, p. 98).

So, too, the "Covid-19 countermeasures" were reliant on public compliance and participation—in "social distancing," mask wearing, downloading a "contact tracing" app, obeying instructions to "self-isolate," taking injections, etc. The building of the technocratic control grid is, again, only possible with the public's *consent* to smart technologies, the rollout of CBDC, "15-minute cities," facial recognition cameras, social credit scoring, "mRNA vaccines," etc. (see Hughes, 2024, Chapter 8). None of these things need be accepted, and the psychological warfare since 2020 (Hughes, 2024) was evidently intended to break the public's will to resist—meaning that resistance must now be intensified by those who value freedom.

Once technocratic agendas are rendered unenforceable by mass non-compliance, civil disobedience, and the rejection of "smart" technologies, and once it is widely understood that entire populations have been viciously abused and lied to as part of a transnational operation intended to lead to their technocratic enslavement, an irrepressible global mass movement against the actors and organizations behind the war for technocracy is sure to emerge, with the latter overwhelmingly outnumbered and facing certain defeat in the global class war which *they* initiated (Hughes et al., 2023, § 5). Contrary to calls for "Nuremberg 2.0," a form of justice far more robust than the flawed Nuremberg Trials (see Chapter 4) awaits delivery.

Conclusion

The sinister reemergence of Nazi elements in former liberal democracies offers compelling evidence that the worst elements of the Third Reich were not defeated in 1945, but were, rather, secretly incubated in preparation for their eventual return. The lynchpin for this has been the CIA, set up by Wall Street with such an eventuality in mind. As in the 1930s, the ruling class is seeking recourse to totalitarianism to deal with the acute crisis of capitalism.

One of the many shocking aspects about the attempt to engineer global totalitarianism is that knowledge about the Nazi past which was intended to prevent its recurrence (e.g. Zimbardo, 2007; Haque et al., 2012) has evidently been weaponized and deployed against populations worldwide. Such misappropriation of knowledge for malevolent purposes itself has roots in Nazi Germany. Edward Bernays, for example, was "shocked" that the Nazis "were using my books as the basis for a destructive campaign against the Jews of Germany," but he knew that "any human activity can be used for social purposes or misused for antisocial ones" (cited in Gunderman, 2015).

Today, it is essential that the public, as the unwitting enemy in the war for technocracy, also arms itself with knowledge of the Nazi past, so that it can understand who the enemy is, what its aims, motivation, and methods are, and what kind of mindset is required to perpetrate evil on a global scale.

The lessons of history are there for those with eyes to see. Will the world be plunged once more into totalitarian darkness, which this time could prove irreversible, or will each of us find the moral courage to do what needs to be done to put down the global technocratic coup and create a new social order that serves the interests of all of humanity?

REFERENCES

Chapter 1

Agamben, G. (2021). *Where are we now? The epidemic as politics.* Rowman & Littlefield.

Ahmed, N.M. (2012). Capitalism, covert action and state terrorism: Toward a political economy of the dual state. In: E. Wilson (Ed.), *The dual state: Parapolitics, Carl Schmitt, and the national security complex* (pp. 171–192). Routledge.

Alting von Geusau, C.W.J.M. (2021, November 17). Totalitarianism and the five stages of dehumanization. *Brownstone Institute.* https://brownstone.org /articles/totalitarianism-and-the-five-stages-of-dehumanization/.

Broudy, D., & Kyrie, V. (2021). Syllogistic reasoning demystifies evidence of Covid-19 vaccine constituents. *International Journal of Vaccine Theory, Research, and Practice*, 2(1), 149–171. https://doi.org/10.56098/ijvtpr.v2i1 .32.

Brüggemeier, F.-J., Cioc, M., & Zeller, T. (Eds). (2005). *How green were the Nazis? Nature, environment, and nation in the Third Reich.* Ohio University Press.

Carter, A.B., Deutsch, J., & Zelikow, P. (1998). Catastrophic terrorism: Tackling the new danger. *Foreign Affairs* 77(6), 80–94. https://www.foreignaffairs.com /articles/united-states/1998-11-01/catastrophic-terrorism.

Chancel, L., Piketty, T., Saez, E., & Zucman, G. (2022). *World Inequality Report 2022.* https://www.cadtm.org/IMG/pdf/summary_worldinequality report2022_english.pdf.

Davis, I. (2018, May 12). Operation Gladio—hard evidence of government sponsored false flag terrorism. *Iain Davis.* https://iaindavis.com/operation -gladio-false-flag-evidence/.

Davis, I. (2022a, February 22). Technocracy: The operating system for the new international rules-based order. *Unlimited Hangout.* https://unlimited hangout.com/2022/02/investigative-reports/technocracy-the-operating -system-for-the-new-international-rules-based-order-1/.

Elmer, S. (2023, April 25). Washington's puppet: The rise and fall of Volodmyr Zelenskyy. *Architects for Social Housing.* https://architectsforsocialhousing.co .uk/2023/04/25/washingtons-puppet-the-rise-and-fall-of-volodmyr-zelen-skyy/.

Fukuyama, F. (1989). The End of History? *The National Interest,* 16, pp. 3–18.

Ganser, D. (2005). *NATO's secret armies. Operation Gladio and terrorism in Western Europe.* Frank Cass.

Gill, L. (2004). *The School of the Americas. Military training and political violence in the Americas.* Duke University Press.

Higham, C. (2007). *Trading with the enemy.* Delacorte Press.

Hughes, D.A. (2022a). "COVID-19 vaccines" for children in the UK: A tale of establishment corruption. *International Journal of Vaccine Theory, Practice, and Research,* 2(1), 209–247. https://doi.org/10.56098/ijvtpr.v2i1.35.

Hughes, D.A. (2022b, July 29). Wall Street, the Nazis, and the crimes of the deep state. *Propaganda in Focus.* https://propagandainfocus.com/wall-street-the -nazis-and-the-crimes-of-the-deep-state/.

Hughes, D.A. (2024). *"Covid-19," Psychological operations, and the war for tech-nocracy.* Palgrave Macmillan.

Kaye, J. (2018, February 20). REVEALED: The long-suppressed official report on US biowarfare in North Korea. *Insurgence Intelligence.* https://medium.com /insurge-intelligence/the-long-suppressed-korean-war-report-on-u-s-use-of -biological-weapons-released-at-last-20d83f5cee54.

King, A., & Schneider, B. (1991). *The first global revolution: A report by the Council of the Club of Rome.* Pantheon Books.

Klein, N. (2007). *The shock doctrine.* Metropolitan Books.

Koonz, C. (2003). *The Nazi conscience.* Harvard University Press.

Lasswell, H.D. (2002). *The analysis of political behaviour.* Routledge.

Loftus, J. (2011). *America's Nazi secret.* Trine Day.

McCoy, A. (2007). *A question of torture: CIA interrogation, from the Cold War to the War on Terror.* Henry Holt & Company.

Pijl, K. van der. (2022). *States of emergency. Keeping the global population in check.* Clarity Press.

Project for a New American Century. (2000, September). *Rebuilding America's defences*. https://resistir.info/livros/rebuilding_americas_defenses.pdf.

Scott, P.D. (2017). *The American deep state. Big money, big oil, and the struggle for U.S. democracy*. Rowman & Littlefield.

Staudenmaier, P. (2011). Fascist ecology: The "green wing" of the Nazi party and its historical antecedents. In: J. Biehl & P. Staudenmaier (Eds.), *Ecofascism revisited: Lessons from the German experience* (pp. 13–42). New Compass Press.

Sutton, A.C. (1981). *Wall Street and the Bolshevik Revolution*. Veritas Publishing.

Sutton, A.C. (2016). *Wall Street and the rise of Hitler* (5th ed.). Clairview.

Technocracy, Inc. (2005). *Technocracy study course*. Retrieved June 13, 2023, from https://web.archive.org/web/20200716210736/https://www.technocracyinc .org/wp-content/uploads/2015/07/Study-Course.pdf.

Tunander, O. (2016). Dual state: The case of Sweden. In: E. Wilson (Ed.), *The dual state: parapolitics, Carl Schmitt, and the national security complex* (pp. 171–192). Routledge.

Valentine, D. (2017). *The CIA as organized crime. How illegal operations corrupt America and the world*. Clarity Press.

Wood, Patrick. (2018). *Technocracy: The hard road to world order*. Coherent Publishing.

Wood, P. (2022, December 19). Day 7: China is a technocracy. *Technocracy News & Trends*. https://www.technocracy.news/day-7-china-is-a-technocracy/.

Yeadon, G., & Hawkins, J. (2008). *The Nazi hydra in America. Suppressed history of a century*. Progressive Press.

Chapter 2

Adams, S., & Bancroft, H. (2020, July 12). Did care homes use powerful sedatives to speed Covid deaths? Number of prescriptions for the drug midazolam doubled during height of the pandemic. *Daily Mail*. https://www .dailymail.co.uk/news/article-8514081/Number-prescriptions-drug-midazolam -doubled-height-pandemic.html.

Agamben, G. (2021). *Where are we now? The epidemic as politics*. Rowman & Littlefield.

Ahmedzai, S.M., Dickman, A., Callistus Nwosu, A., Laird, B.J.A., Mayland, C.R., Ahamed, A., Harrison, S., Wakefield, D., Lloyd-Williams, M., Boland, J., & Fingas, S. (2020, May 19). Managing COVID-19 symptoms in the community (including at the end of life): NICE NG163 is a welcome step but needs review. *BMJ*, 369:m1461. https://doi.org/10.1136/bmj.m1461.

Aiken, A. (2018, June 12). Disinformation is a continuing threat to our values and our democracy. *Government Communication Service*. https://perma.cc/CJ8H-JKXB.

Alschner, U. (2023, November 5). "Gesucht" von deutschen Staatsanwälten—Vera Sharav, Überlebende der Shoa. *Klartext Alschner*. https://alschner klartext.de/2023/11/05/gesucht-von-deutschen-staatsanwaelten-vera -sharav-ueberlebende-der-shoa/.

Aly, G., & Roth, K.H. (2004). *The Nazi census*. Temple University Press.

Atlas, S.W. (2022, December 29). When will academia account for its Covid failures? *Wall Street Journal*. https://www.wsj.com/articles/when-will -academia-account-for-its-covid-failures-pandemic-lockdowns-stanford -ivy-league-elite-narrative-ideology-11672346923.

Austrian Science Fund. (2008). *Science gone wrong: Welteislehre*. https://www .fwf.ac.at/en/research-in-practice/project-presentations-archive/2008 /science-gone-wrong-welteislehre/.

Bagdikian, B.H. (2004). *The New Media Monopoly*. Beacon Press.

Becker, H. (1949). The nature and consequences of black propaganda. *American Sociological Review*, 14(2), 221–235. https://doi.org/10.2307/2086855.

Bell, D. (2023). Pandemic preparedness and the road to international fascism. *The American Journal of Economics and Sociology*, 82(5), 395–409. https://doi.org/10.1111/ajes.12531.

Bentham, M. (2020, October 18). Metropolitan Police counter-terror chief Neil Basu calls for action on coronavirus anti-vaxxers. *Evening Standard*. https://www.standard.co.uk/news/crime/met-police-terrorism-coronavirus-anti -vaxxers-b73161.html.

Beppler-Spahl, S. (2023, April 5). Is Germany persecuting lockdown sceptics? *Spiked!* https://www.spiked-online.com/2023/04/05/is-germany-persecuting -lockdown-sceptics/.

Bergman, F. (2023, September 28). Twitter's WEF-linked CEO boasts of "successfully" censoring "lawful but awful" speech. *SLAY*. https://slaynews .com/news/twitters-wef-linked-ceo-boasts-successfully-censoring-lawful -but-awful-speech/.

Bhattacharya, J. (2023, January 11). How Stanford failed the academic freedom test. *Tablet*. https://www.tabletmag.com/sections/arts-letters/articles/stanford -failed-academic-freedom-test.

Black, E. (2003, September). The horrifying American roots of Nazi eugenics. *History News Network*. http://historynewsnetwork.org/article/1796.

BlackRock. (2019, August 15). *Dealing with the next downturn.* https://www
.blackrock.com/corporate/insights/blackrock-investment-institute/publications
/global-macro-outlook/august-2019.

Blackstone. (2020, December 4). *Blackstone Completes Acquisition of Ancestry®,
Leading Online Family History Business, for $4.7 Billion.* https://www
.blackstone.com/news/press/blackstone-completes-acquisition-of-ancestry
-leading-online-family-history-business-for-4–7-billion/.

Blaylock, R.L. (2022). Covid update: What is the truth? *Surgical Neurology
International,* 13, Article 167. https://doi.org/10.25259/SNI_150_2022.

Booth, R. (2020, December 3). "Do not resuscitate" orders caused potentially
avoidable deaths, regulator finds. *The Guardian.* https://www.theguardian
.com/society/2020/dec/03/do-not-resuscitate-orders-caused-potentially
-avoidable-deaths-regulator-finds.

Boseley, S., & Stewart, H. (2020, May 27). Hancock: it is public's "civic duty"
to follow test-and-trace instructions in England. *The Guardian.* https://www
.theguardian.com/world/2020/may/27/government-unveils-covid-19
-test-and-trace-strategy-for-england.

Broudy, D., Hughes, D.A., & Kyrie, V. (2022, December 10). The psychology
of Covid-19 atrocities. *Doctors For Covid Ethics.* https://doctors4covidethics
.org/session-iv-understanding-tactics-of-oppression-2/.

Broze, D. (2021, April 29). Bill Gates, China, 23andMe, and your DNA.
The Last American Vagabond. https://www.thelastamericanvagabond.com
/bill-gates-china-23me-and-your-dna/.

Brüggemeier, F.-J., Cioc, M., & Zeller, T. (Eds). (2005). *How green were the
Nazis? Nature, environment, and nation in the Third Reich.* Ohio University
Press.

Butler, P. (2020, December 9). Covid-driven recession likely to push 2m UK families into poverty. *The Guardian.* https://www.theguardian.com/society/2020
/dec/09/covid-driven-recession-likely-to-push-2m-uk-families-into-poverty.

Campbell, D. (2023, November 20). NHS England gives key role in handling
patient data to US spy tech firm Palantir. *The Guardian.* https://www
.theguardian.com/society/2023/nov/20/nhs-england-gives-key-role-in
-handling-patient-data-to-us-spy-tech-firm-palantir.

Coates, S.D. (2008). *Neural interfacing.* Springer Cham. https://doi.org/10
.1007/978–3-031–01640-0.

Commons Project. (2019, September 5). CommonHealth will enable android™ phone users to access and share their electronic health record data with trusted apps and partners. *PR Newswire*. https://www.prnewswire.com /news-releases/commonhealth-will-enable-android-phone-users-to-access -and-share-their-electronic-health-record-data-with-trusted-apps-and-partners -300912580.html.

Corbett, J. (2020, May 1). Who is Bill Gates? *The Corbett Report*. https://www .corbettreport.com/gates/.

Corbett, K.P. (2021, August 7). The "Nazification" of the NHS. *The Light Paper*. https://thelightpaper.co.uk/assets/pdf/Light-12h.pdf.

Covert Human Intelligence Sources (Criminal Conduct) Act 2021, c.4. https: //www.legislation.gov.uk/ukpga/2021/4/introduction/enacted.

Covid-19: Everyone "has to play their part" in lockdown easing, says Hancock. (2021, February 23). *BBC News*. https://www.bbc.co.uk/news /uk-56164098.

Covid-19: PM announces four-week England lockdown. (2020, October 31). *BBC News*. https://www.bbc.co.uk/news/uk-54763956.

Culbertson, A. (2021, October 21). Tony Blair: Getting vaccine is "civic duty" and govt should bump boosters to 500,000 a day. *Sky News*. https://news .sky.com/story/tony-blair-getting-vaccine-is-civic-duty-and-govt-should -bump-boosters-to-500–000-a-day-12440200.

Davis, I. (2021a, December 14). The UK New Normal dictatorship. *UK Column*. https://www.ukcolumn.org/article/the-uk-new-normal-dictatorship.

Davis, I. (2021b, May 3). Buying a single version of the truth. *UK Column*. https://www.ukcolumn.org/article/buying-a-single-version-of-the-truth.

Davis, I. (2021c, October 12). Seizing everything: The theft of the global commons—Part 1. *Iain Davis*. https://in-this-together.com/global-commons -part-1/.

Davis, I. (2021d, November 7). Seizing everything: The theft of the global commons—Part 2. *Iain Davis*. https://in-this-together.com/global-commons -part-2/.

Davis, I. (2024, February 10). Richard D. Hall—A travesty of justice. *Iain Davis*. https://iaindavis.com/richard-d-hall-a-travesty-of-justice/.

Delpher. (n.d.). *Verordeningenblad voor het bezette nederlandsche gebied 06–07-1940*. https://www.delpher.nl/nl/kranten/view?coll=ddd&identifier=ddd:0 10318217:mpeg21.

Digital Citizen. (2003, September 25). 9/11 official theory. Are you brain-washed? *Phil Taylor's Papers*. https://universityofleeds.github.io/philtaylor papers/vp01eff8.html.

Dodsworth, L. (2021, December 18). A week of life under the Ministry of Fear. *Laura Dodsworth*. https://lauradodsworth.substack.com/p/a-week-of-life-under -the-ministry.

Eckersely, R. (2007). Green theory. In: T. Dunne, M. Kurki, & S. Smith (Eds.), *International Relations Theories* (pp. 247–265). Oxford University Press.

Edward, F. (2021, February 8). The papers daren't bite the Whitehall hand that feeds them. *TCW*. https://www.conservativewoman.co.uk/the-papers -darent-bite-the-whitehall-hand-that-feeds-them/.

Ehrenreich, E. (2007). *The Nazi ancestral proof*. Indiana University Press.

Ehret, M. (2021, March 16). "Nazi healthcare revived across the Five Eyes: Killing useless eaters and Biden's COVID relief bill." *OffGuardian*. https: //off-guardian.org/2021/03/16/nazi-healthcare-revived-across-the-five -eyes-killing-useless-eaters-and-bidens-covid-relief-bill/.

Elmer, S. (2021, January 8). Our default state: Compulsory vaccination for Covid-19 and human rights law. *Architects For Social Housing*. https: //architectsforsocialhousing.co.uk/2021/01/08/our-default-state-compulsory -vaccination-for-covid-19-and-human-rights-law/.

Elmer, S. (2022, November 11). Why did the Left fail so utterly to resist the global biosecurity state? *The Daily Sceptic*. https://dailysceptic.org/2022/11/11 /why-did-the-left-fail-so-utterly-to-resist-the-global-biosecurity-state/.

Epstein, C.A. (2015). *Nazi Germany: Confronting the myths*. John Wiley & Sons.

European Commission. (2019). *Roadmap for the implementation of actions by the European Commission based on the Commission communication and the Council recommendation on strengthening cooperation against vaccine pre-ventable diseases*. https://ec.europa.eu/health/sites/health/files/vaccination /docs/2019–2022_roadmap_en.pdf.

Fahrenkrug, H. (1991). Alcohol and the state in Nazi Germany, 1933–1945. In: S. Barrows & R. Room (Eds.), *Drinking. Behaviour and Belief in Modern History* (pp. 315–335). University of California Press.

Fink, L. (2022). The power of capitalism. *Blackrock*. https://www.blackrock .com/corporate/investor-relations/larry-fink-ceo-letter.

Fisher, L., & Smyth, C. (2020, November 9). GCHQ in cyberwar on anti-vaccine propaganda. *The Times*. https://www.thetimes.co.uk/article/gchq-in-cyberwar -on-anti-vaccine-propaganda-mcjgjhmb2.

Fleet Street Fox. (2021, September 20). "Anti-vaxxers want to kill your babies, stage a coup and cause another lockdown." *Daily Mirror*. https://www.mirror.co.uk/news/politics/anti-vaxxers-kill-your-babies-25025422.

FRED. (n.d.-a). *Unemployment rate*. https://fred.stlouisfed.org/series/UNRATE.

FRED (n.d.-b). *Real gross domestic product*. https://fred.stlouisfed.org/series/GDPC1.

Frick, W.M., Baerwald, E.F., Pollock, J.F., Barclay, R.M.R., Szymanski, J.A., Weller, T.J., Russell, A.L., Loeb, S.C., Medellin, R.A., & McGuire, L.P. (2017). Fatalities at wind turbines may threaten population viability of a migratory bat. *Biological Conservation*, 209, 172–177. https://doi.org/10.1016/j.biocon.2017.02.023.

Friedlander, H. (1995). *The origins of Nazi genocide: From euthanasia to the Final Solution*. University of North Carolina Press.

Fromm, E. (1942). *Fear of freedom*. Kegan Paul.

Gates, Bill. (2020, December 22). These breakthroughs will make 2021 better than 2020. *GatesNotes*. https://www.gatesnotes.com/About-Bill-Gates/Year-in-Review-2020.

Geissler, H. (2022, August 22). Terminally ill cancer patient urges next PM to change law on assisted dying. *The Express*. https://www.express.co.uk/life-style/health/1655895/assisted-dying-terminal-cancer-health-news-latest.

Gellately, R. (1991). *The Gestapo and German society*. Oxford University Press.

Goldberg, K. (2021, December 28). Mass formation: How the Left got duped. *Kim Goldberg*. https://kimgoldbergx1.substack.com/p/mass-formation-how-the-left-got-duped.

Hantanasirisakul, K., & Sawangphruk, M. (2023). Sustainable reuse and recycling of spent Li-ion batteries from electric vehicles: Chemical, environmental, and economical perspectives. *Global Challenges*, 7(4), Article 2200212. https://doi.org/10.1002/gch2.202200212.

Haque, O.S., De Freitas, J., Viani, I., Niederschulte, B., & and Bursztajn, H.J. (2012). Why did so many German doctors join the Nazi Party early? *International Journal of Law and Psychiatry*, 35(5–6), pp. 473–479. https://doi.org/10.1016/j.ijlp.2012.09.022.

Harari, Y.N. (2017). *Homo Deus*. Harwill Seeker.

Harradine, K. (2022, December 30). The new Nazis are on the march. *TCW*. https://www.conservativewoman.co.uk/the-new-nazis-are-on-the-march/.

Harrity, P. (2023, November 4). Reiner Fuellmich update following his arrest. *Daily Exposé*. https://expose-news.com/2023/11/04/reiner-fuellmich-update-following-his-arrest/.

Health and Social Care Committee. (2020, April 17). Oral evidence: Preparations for coronavirus, HC 36. *House of Commons*. https://committees.parliament.uk/oralevidence/288/default/.

Hett, B.C. (2014). *Burning the Reichstag: An investigation into the Third Reich's enduring mystery*. Oxford University Press.

Hitchens, P. (2020, September 5). Protest against our new State of Fear is banned . . . by order of a dead parrot Parliament. *Mail on Sunday*. https://www.dailymail.co.uk/debate/article-8701699/PETER-HITCHENS-Protest-against-new-State-Fear-banned.html.

Hitler, A. (1939). *Mein Kampf* (J. Murphy, Trans.). Hurst and Blackett.

HM Government. (2021). *Social Distancing Review: Report*. https://assets.publishing.service.gov.uk/government/uploads/system/uploads/attachment_data/file/999413/Social-Distancing-Review-Report.pdf.

Hodgson, J. (2023, October 25). MAiD statistics from 2022 released, show 31% increase. *Western Standard*. https://www.westernstandard.news/news/maid-statistics-from-2022-released-show-31-increase/49712.

Hookham, M. (2021, July 17). Church of England vicar, 52, faces the sack for breaking Covid rules after hugging a mourner, singing a hymn with no mask on and putting out Bibles. *Daily Mail*. https://www.dailymail.co.uk/news/article-9798687/Church-England-vicar-52-faces-sack-breaking-Covid-rules.html.

Hope, C. (2021, May 1). Matt Hancock takes first steps towards legalising assisted suicide. *The Telegraph*. https://www.telegraph.co.uk/politics/2021/05/01/matt-hancock-takes-first-steps-towards-legalising-assisted-suicide/.

Hopkins, C.J. (2020a, September 2). New Normal *Gleichschaltung*, or: The storming of the Reichstag building on 29 August, 2020. *Consent Factory*. https://consentfactory.org/2020/09/02/new-normal-gleichschaltung-or-the-storming-of-the-reichstag-building-on-29-august-2020/.

Hopkins, C.J. (2020b, November 22). The Germans are back! *Consent Factory*. https://consentfactory.org/2020/11/22/the-germans-are-back/.

Hopkins, C.J. (2021a, March 30). The "unvaccinated question." *Consent Factory*. https://cjhopkins.substack.com/p/the-unvaccinated-question.

Hopkins, C.J. (2021b, May 3). The criminalization of dissent. *Consent Factory*. https://consentfactory.org/2021/05/03/the-criminalization-of-dissent/.

Hopkins, C.J. (2023a, August 24). The road to totalitarianism (part 3). *Consent Factory.* https://consentfactory.org/2023/08/24/the-road-to-totalitarianism -part-3/.

Hopkins, C.J. (2023b, September 10). The criminalization of dissent (continued). *Consent Factory.* https://consentfactory.org/2023/09/10/the-criminalization -of-dissent-continued/.

Hopkins, C.J. (2023c, October 1). The GloboCap Nazi follies. *Consent Factory.* https://consentfactory.org/2023/10/01/the-globocap-nazi-follies/.

Hughes, D.A. (2024). *"Covid-19," Psychological operations, and the war for technocracy.* Palgrave Macmillan.

Hugo Talks. (2021, December 3). *Loudspeakers appearing all over towns.* https://hugotalks.com/2021/12/03/loudspeakers-appearing-all-over-towns -hugo-talks-lockdown/.

Human species "may split in two." (2006, October 17). *BBC News.* http: //news.bbc.co.uk/1/hi/uk/6057734.stm.

Huxley, A. (1958). *Brave New World revisited.* Harper & Row.

Huxley, J. (1946). *UNESCO: Its purpose & its philosophy.* Preparatory Commission of the United Nations Educational, Scientific, and Cultural Organisation.

Huxley, J. (1957). *New bottles for new wine.* Chatto & Windus.

Imort, M. (2005). "Eternal forest—eternal Volk." The rhetoric and reality of National Socialist forest policy." In: F.-J. Brüggemeier, M. Cioc, & T. Zeller (Eds.), *How green were the Nazis? Nature, environment, and nation in the Third Reich* (pp. 43–72). Ohio University Press.

Ingram v. Alberta (Chief Medical Officer of Health), ABKB 453. (2023).

Inman, P. (2020, April 29). Half of world's workers "at immediate risk of losing livelihood due to coronavirus." *The Guardian.* https://www.theguardian .com/world/2020/apr/29/half-of-worlds-workers-at-immediate-risk-of -losing-livelihood-due-to-coronavirus.

Institute of Development Studies. (2021, June 8). *We need to talk about 30x30.* https://www.ids.ac.uk/news/we-need-to-talk-about-30x30/.

Jayanetti, C. (2021, January 9). 70,000 households in UK made homeless during pandemic. *The Guardian.* https://www.theguardian.com/society/2021 /jan/09/70000-households-in-uk-made-homeless-during-pandemic.

Justice Centre For Constitutional Freedoms. (2021, June 24). University fires surgeon who voiced safety concerns about COVID vaccines for kids. *Children's Health Defence.* https://childrenshealthdefense.org/defender/university-fires-dr-francis-christian-covid-vaccines-kids/.

Kingsnorth, P. (2021, November 24). The vaccine moment, part one. *The Abbey of Misrule.* https://paulkingsnorth.substack.com/p/the-vaccine-moment-part-one?

Klemperer, V. (1999). *I will bear witness* (M. Chalmers, Trans.). The Modern Library.

Knightly, K. (2020, May 12). Opposing lockdown is NOT "profits before people." *OffGuardian.* https://off-guardian.org/2020/05/12/opposing-lockdown-is-not-profits-before-people/.

Knuffke, L. (2022, April 22). Obama admits COVID jab has been "clinically tested on billions" while chastising Americans who refused. *LifeSite News.* https://www.lifesitenews.com/news/obama-admits-covid-jab-has-been-clinically-tested-on-billions-while-chastising-americans-who-refused/.

Koehl, R. (1972). Feudal aspects of National Socialism. In: H.A. Turner (Ed.), *Nazism and the Third Reich* (pp. 151–174). Quadrangle Books.

Koire, R. (2011). *Behind the green mask: UN Agenda 21.* The Post Sustainability Institute Press.

Koonz, C. (2003). *The Nazi conscience.* Harvard University Press.

Kurzweil, R. (2005). *The singularity is near. When humans transcend biology.* Viking.

Lekan, T. (2005). "It shall be the whole landscape!" The Reich Nature Protection Law and regional planning in the Third Reich." In F.-J. Brüggemeier, M. Cioc, & T. Zeller (Eds.), *How green were the Nazis? Nature, environment, and nation in the Third Reich* (pp. 73–100). Ohio University Press.

Lifton, R.J. (1986). *The Nazi doctors.* Basic Books.

Light, A. (2017, August 28). Here's how you & your DNA are being targeted. *Humans Are Free.* https://humansbefree.com/2017/08/heres-how-you-your-dna-are-being-targeted.html.

Liu, P., & Barlow, C.Y. (2017). Wind turbine blade wastage in 2050. *Waste Management, 62,* 229–240. https://doi.org/10.1016/j.wasman.2017.02.007.

Malet, C. (2023, August 29). Police Misconduct: Cleaning house, or clearing the path for a one-world government? *UK Column.* https://www.ukcolumn.org/article/police-misconduct-cleaning-house-or-clearing-the-path-for-a-one-world-government.

Mayer, M. (2017). *They thought they were free* (2nd ed.). University of Chicago Press.

Menage, J. (2020, November 17). Re: Mass testing for covid-19 in the UK: Who owns the data? *BMJ*, 371:m4436. https://www.bmj.com/content/371/bmj .m4436/rr.

Miller, M.C. (2021a). A propaganda masterpiece. *Perspectives on the Pandemic XVII*, Francis Karogodins (Ed.) [Video]. Odysee. https://odysee.com /@WanderingCitizen:7/2020-A-Propaganda-Masterpiece-Perspectives-on -the-Pandemic-XVII:d?.

Miller, M.C. (2021b, August 27). With a "left press" like this, who needs fascist media? *OffGuardian*. https://off-guardian.org/2021/08/27/with-a-left-press -like-this-who-needs-fascist-media/.

Miller, M.C. (2022, February 17). What kind of "left" attacks the working class as "fascist," and pushes FOR the "vaccination" of the poor worldwide? *News From Underground*. https://markcrispinmiller.substack.com/p/what -kind-of-left-attacks-the-working.

Ministry of Defence. 2020. *Armed Forces announce launch of cyber regiment in major modernisation*. https://www.gov.uk/government/news/armed-forces -announce-launch-of-first-cyber-regiment-in-major-modernisation.

Mohamoud, A. (2021, June 4). Doctors threaten legal action to halt "unlawful" mass GP data extraction. *Pulse*. https://www.pulsetoday.co.uk/news/technology /doctors-threaten-legal-action-to-halt-unlawful-mass-gp-data-extraction/.

Morgan, C. (2018, April 17). Presentation to West Point US Military Academy [Video]. *YouTube*. https://www.youtube.com/watch?v=cTtIPBPSvOU.

Mostert, M.P. (2002). Useless eaters: Disability as genocidal marker in Nazi Germany. *Journal of Special Education*, 36(3):157–170. https://doi.org/10 .1177/00224669020360030601.

Müller, I. (1991). *Hitler's Justice. The Courts of the Third Reich* (D. L. Schneider, Trans.). Harvard University Press.

Nanu, M. (2021, August 13). Law to legalise assisted dying has enough votes to pass, claims peer. *The Telegraph*. https://www.telegraph.co.uk/news/2021/08/13 /law-legalise-assisted-dying-has-enough-votes-pass-claims-peer/.

National Health Service. (n.d.). *Choose if data from your health records is shared for research and planning—Overview*. Retrieved January 11, 2024, from https://www.nhs.uk/your-nhs-data-matters/overview/.

National Institute of Clinical Excellence. (2020, April 3). *COVID-19 rapid guideline: Managing symptoms (including at the end of life) in the community.* https://www.nice.org.uk/guidance/ng163.

Newman, J. (2021, January 25). World's richest ten people—including Elon Musk, Jeff Bezos, Bill Gates and Mark Zuckerberg—"are half a TRILLION dollars richer since Covid-19 pandemic began." *Daily Mail.* https://www.dailymail.co.uk/news/article-9182661/Oxfam-urges-radical-economic-rejig-post-COVID-world.html.

Newman, J., & Wright, J. (2021, December 22). Jesus would get a vaccine, Archbishop of Canterbury suggests as he says getting the jab is "not about me and my rights to choose—it's about how I love my neighbour." *Daily Mail.* https://www.dailymail.co.uk/news/article-10334569/Archbishop-Canterbury-says-unvaccinated-immoral-love-neighbour.html.

NHS Digital. (n.d.). *General practice data for planning and research (GPDPR).* Retrieved January 11, 2024, from https://digital.nhs.uk/data-and-information/data-collections-and-data-sets/data-collections/general-practice-data-for-planning-and-research.

O'Faolain, A. (2022, July 5). Supreme Court dismisses Gemma O'Doherty and John Waters' action over Covid-19 laws. *The Irish Times.* https://www.irishtimes.com/crime-law/2022/07/05/supreme-court-dismisses-gemma-odoherty-and-john-waters-action-over-covid-19-laws/.

Office of United States Chief of Counsel for Prosecution of Axis Criminality. (1946). *Nazi conspiracy and aggression, volume II.* United States Government Printing Office.

OpenPrescribing. (n.d.). *Midazolam hydrochloride (1501041T0).* Retrieved January 11, 2024, from https://openprescribing.net/chemical/1501041T0/.

Pijl, K. van der. (2022). *States of emergency. Keeping the global population in check.* Clarity Press.

Pijl, K. van der. (2022b, May 21). Do we need a popular front against contemporary fascism? *Propaganda in Focus.* https://propagandainfocus.com/do-we-need-a-popular-front-against-contemporary-fascism/.

Pilger, J. (2016, October 28). Inside the invisible government: John Pilger on war, propaganda, Clinton and Trump. *New Matilda.* https://newmatilda.com/2016/10/28/inside-the-invisible-government-john-pilger-on-war-propaganda-clinton-and-trump/.

Polyakova, K. (2021). Do doctors have to have the Covid-19 vaccine? *BMJ*, 372, Article n810. https://doi.org/10.1136/bmj.n810.

Proctor, R. (1988). *Racial hygiene. Medicine under the Nazis*. Harvard University Press.

Public Order Act 2023, c. 15. https://www.legislation.gov.uk/ukpga/2023/15 /enacted.

Pym, H. (2021, May 28). Covid: Surgery waiting times could be cut with specialist hubs, say surgeons. *BBC News*. https://www.bbc.co.uk/news/health -57277793.

Rate Inflation. (n.d.). *United Kingdom inflation rate*. Retrieved June 17, 2023, from https://www.rateinflation.com/inflation-rate/uk-inflation-rate/.

Real Left. (2023, October 4). *Open Letter to the Communication Workers Union*. https://real-left.com/open-letter-to-the-communication-workers-union/.

Rectenwald, M. (2021, December 26). What is the Great Reset? *Imprimis* 50(12). https://imprimis.hillsdale.edu/what-is-the-great-reset/.

Roberts, C., Maslin, M., & Parikih, P. (2023, December 1). Why are people still flying to climate conferences by private jet? *The Conversation*. https://theconversation.com/why-are-people-still-flying-to-climate-conferences -by-private-jet-218459.

Robinson, M. (2020, April 26). The British military information war waged on their own population. *UK Column*. https://www.ukcolumn.org/article /british-military-information-war-waged-their-own-population.

Rockefeller Foundation. (2020). *National Covid-19 testing action plan: Pragmatic steps to reopen our workplaces and our communities*. https://www.rockefeller foundation.org/national-covid-19-testing-action-plan/.

Röpke, W. (2008). *The German Question* (Trans. E. W. Dickes). Ludwig von Mises Institute.

Roth, C. (2021, November 1). The greatest transfer of wealth from the middle class to the elites in history. *Brownstone Institute*. https://brownstone.org /articles/the-greatest-transfer-of-wealth-from-the-middle-class-to-the-elites -in-history/.

Saunt, R., & Vincent, M. (2021, March 1). "This is not policeable": Officers say they should NOT be enforcing "unmanageable" Covid laws as walkers are questioned for going to the beach in mild weekend weather. *Daily Mail*. https://www.dailymail.co.uk/news/article-9310829/Unvaccinated-officers -NOT-want-continue-policing-coronavirus-restrictions-union-chief-says .html.

Schwab, K. (2020, June 3). Now is the time for a "Great Reset." *World Economic Forum*. https://www.weforum.org/agenda/2020/06/now-is-the-time-for-a-great-reset/.

Schwab, K., & Davis, N. (2018). *Shaping the future of the Fourth Industrial Revolution: A guide to building a better world*. World Economic Forum.

Schwab, K., & Malleret, T. (2020). *Covid 19: The Great Reset*. World Economic Forum.

Segal, M. (2021, September 17). NYSE to list new "natural asset companies" asset class, targeting massive opportunity in ecosystem services. *ESG Today*. https://www.esgtoday.com/nyse-to-list-new-asset-class-for-natural-asset-companies-targeting-massive-opportunity-in-ecosystem-services/.

Shapiro, A. (2021, January 14). America's biggest owner of farmland is now Bill Gates. *Forbes*. https://www.forbes.com/sites/arielshapiro/2021/01/14/americas-biggest-owner-of-farmland-is-now-bill-gates-bezos-turner/.

Shirer, W.L. (1990). *The rise and fall of the Third Reich*. Simon & Schuster.

Spectator. (n.d.). *The* Spectator *data tracker*. https://data.spectator.co.uk/category/sage-scenarios.

Staudenmaier, P. (2011). Fascist ecology: The "green wing" of the Nazi party and its historical antecedents. In: J. Biehl & P. Staudenmaier (Eds.), *Ecofascism revisited: Lessons from the German experience* (pp. 13–42). New Compass Press.

Steerpike. (2021, October 20). MPs extend the Coronavirus Act without a vote. *The Spectator*. https://www.spectator.co.uk/article/watch-mps-extend-the-coronavirus-act-without-a-vote/.

Stephens, M. (2021, November 14). Covid test firm "to sell swabs carrying customers' DNA." *The Telegraph*. https://www.telegraph.co.uk/news/2021/11/14/covid-test-firm-sell-swabs-carrying-customers-dna/.

Sumption, J. (2020, October 27). *Government by decree: Covid-19 and the constitution*. Cambridge Freshfields Annual Law Lecture. Retrieved June 13, 2020, from https://resources.law.cam.ac.uk/privatelaw/Freshfields_Lecture_2020_Government_by_Decree.pdf.

Sutton, A.C. (2016). *Wall Street and the rise of Hitler* (5th ed.). Clairview.

Tanzi. A., & Dorning, M. (2021, October 8). Top 1% of U.S. earners now hold more wealth than all of the middle class. *Bloomberg*. https://www.bloomberg.com/news/articles/2021-10-08/top-1-earners-hold-more-wealth-than-the-u-s-middle-class.

Todhunter, C. (2021, February 2). Viral inequality: From Jeff Bezos to the struggle of Indian farmers. *OffGuardian*. https://off-guardian.org/2021/02/02/viral-inequality-from-jeff-bezos-to-the-struggle-of-indian-farmers/.

Trendall, S. (2022, February 18). EXCL: Government withholds information on anti-disinformation unit. *Public Technology*. https://www.publictechnology.net/2022/02/18/health-and-social-care/excl-government-withholds-information-anti-disinformation-unit/.

Triggle, N., & Jeavans, C. (2021, May 13). The NHS Covid legacy—long waits and lives at risk. *BBC News*. https://www.bbc.co.uk/news/health-57092797.

Tucker, J.A. [@jeffreyatucker] (2023, October 4). *Many of us are still astounding and confused about what happened to intellectuals (even supposedly good ones) in the last* [Tweet]. Twitter. https://twitter.com/jeffreyatucker/status/1577318538838040576.

Türk, V. (2023, May 28). The Public Order Act will have a chilling effect on your civic freedoms—it must be repealed. *Office of the High Commissioner for Human Rights*. https://www.ohchr.org/en/opinion-editorial/2023/05/public-order-act-will-have-chilling-effect-your-civic-freedoms-it-must-be.

Turner, H.A. (1972). Big business and the rise of Hitler. In: H.A. Turner (Ed.), *Nazism and the Third Reich* (pp. 89–108). Quadrangle Books.

Uekötter, F. (2005). Polycentrism in full swing: Air pollution control in Nazi Germany. In: F.-J. Brüggemeier, M. Cioc, & T. Zeller (Eds.), *How Green were the Nazis? Nature, environment, and nation in the Third Reich* (pp. 101–128). Ohio University Press.

Ungoed-Thomas, J., & Townsend, M. (2023, November 4). Revealed: Plan to brand anyone "undermining" UK as extremist. *The Guardian*. https://www.theguardian.com/uk-news/2023/nov/04/plans-to-redefine-extremism-would-include-undermining-uk-values.

United Nations. (2022a). *World Population Prospects (global)* [Data set]. https://ourworldindata.org/grapher/children-per-woman-UN?tab=chart.

United Nations. (2022b). *World Population Prospects (by region)* [Data set]. https://ourworldindata.org/grapher/children-per-woman-UN?tab=chart&country=Asia+%28UN%29~Africa+%28UN%29~Europe+%28UN%29~Latin+America+and+the+Caribbean+%28UN%29~Oceania+%28UN%29~Northern+America+%28UN%29.

United Nations Development Programme. (2011, January 1). *Human Development Report*. https://hdr.undp.org/system/files/documents//human-development-report-2011-english.human-development-report-2011-english.

United Nations Secretary General. (2020, December 2). *Secretary-General's address at Columbia University: "The state of the planet."* https://www.un.org/sg/en/content/sg/speeches/2020–12-02/address-columbia-university-the-state-of-the-planet.

United States Holocaust Memorial Museum. (n.d.). Aryan. *Holocaust Encyclopedia.* https://encyclopedia.ushmm.org/content/en/article/aryan-1.

Valentine, D. (2017). *The CIA as organized crime. How illegal operations corrupt America and the world.* Clarity Press.

Weaver, K., Motion, J., & Roper, J. (2006). From propaganda to discourse (and back again): Truth, power, the public interest, and public relations. In: J. L'Etang and M. Pieczka (Eds.), *Public Relations: Critical Debates and Contemporary Practice.* Lawrence Erlbaum Associates.

Webb, W. (2021, October 13). Wall Street's takeover of nature advances with launch of new asset class. *Unlimited Hangout.* https://unlimitedhangout.com/2021/10/investigative-reports/wall-streets-takeover-of-nature-advances-with-launch-of-new-asset-class/.

Weinreich, M. (1946). *Hitler's Professors.* Yiddish Scientific Institute.

Wells, H. G., Huxley, J., & Wells, G.P. (1934). *The science of life.* The Literary Guild.

Wertheim, J. (2021, January 31). China's push to control Americans' health care future. *CBS News.* https://www.cbsnews.com/news/biodata-dna-china-collection-60-minutes-2021–01-31/.

Westermann, E.B. (2015). Political soldiers. In: P. Hayes (Ed.), *How was it -possible? A Holocaust reader* (pp. 481–494). University of Nebraska Press.

White, M.C. (2020, December 30). Wall Street minted 56 new billionaires since the pandemic began—but many families are left behind. *NBC News.* https://www.nbcnews.com/business/business-news/wall-street-s-best-year-ever-why-pandemic-has-been-n1252512.

Wickware, C. (2020, May 19). Supplies of sedative used for COVID-19 patients diverted from France to avoid potential shortages. *The Pharmaceutical Journal.* https://pharmaceutical-journal.com/article/news/supplies-of-sedative-used-for-covid-19-patients-diverted-from-france-to-avoid-potential-shortages.

Wilde, F. (2013). Divided they fell: The German left and the rise of Hitler. *International Socialism,* 137. https://isj.org.uk/divided-they-fell-the-german-left-and-the-rise-of-hitler/.

Williams, M. (2021, July 30). David Cameron met vaccines minister before firm he advises won health contracts. *Open Democracy*. https://www.open democracy.net/en/dark-money-investigations/david-cameron-met -vaccines-minister-firm-he-advises-won-health-contracts/.

Wilson, R. (2022, January 1). Pre-WWII Germany: Laws introduced for the protection of the people. *Daily Exposé*. https://expose-news.com/2022/01 /01/pre-wwii-germany-laws-introduced-for-the-protection-of-the-people/.

Wood, Patrick. (2018). *Technocracy: The hard road to world order*. Coherent Publishing.

Woodworth, E. (2022, January 22). COVID-19 and the shadowy "Trusted News Initiative." *Global Research*. https://www.globalresearch.ca/covid-19 -shadowy-trusted-news-initiative/5752930.

Workers League. (2022, February 17). The straw man: "Fascism" in the freedom movement. *Red Fire*. https://redfireonline.com/2022/02/17/the-straw-man -fascism-in-the-freedom-movement/.

Wright, R. (2019, December 30). The story of 2019: Protests in every corner of the globe. *The New Yorker*. https://www.newyorker.com/news/our-columnists /the-story-of-2019-protests-in-every-corner-of-the-globe.

Chapter 3

Aarons, M., & Loftus, J. (1998). *Unholy trinity. The Vatican, the Nazis, and the Swiss banks*. St. Martin's Griffin.

Aris, B. & Campbell, D. (2004, September 25). How Bush's grandfather helped Hitler's rise to power. *The Guardian*. https://www.theguardian.com /world/2004/sep/25/usa.secondworldwar.

Bank for International Settlements. (n.d.). *BIS history—overview*. Retrieved January 11, 2024, from https://www.bis.org/about/history_newarrow.htm #:~:text=The%20establishment%20of%20the%20BIS&text=The%20 new%20bank%20was%20to,derived%20from%20this%20original%20 role.

Black, E. (2009). *Nazi Nexus*. Dialog Press.

Epstein, C.A. (2015). *Nazi Germany: Confronting the myths*. John Wiley & Sons.

Fournier, L.T. (1932). The purposes and results of the Webb-Pomerene Law. *The American Economic Review*, 22(1), pp. 18–33. https://www.jstor.org /stable/1807256.

Friedman, J.S. (2001, March 26). Kodak's Nazi connections. *The Nation*. https://www.thenation.com/article/archive/kodaks-nazi-connections/.

Higham, C. (2007). *Trading with the enemy*. Delacorte Press.

Kinzer, S. (2014). *The brothers. John Foster Dulles, Allen Dulles, and their secret world war*. Henry Holt & Company.

Loftus, J. (2000, November 11). Unholy trinity: The Vatican, the Nazis, and the Swiss banks. *C-SPAN*. https://www.c-span.org/video/?160639–1/unholy-trinity -vatican-nazis-swiss-banks.

Loftus, J. (2011). *America's Nazi secret*. Trine Day.

Marcon, F. (2021). The quest for Japanese fascism: A historiographical over- view. In: G. Bulian & S. Rivadossi (Eds.), *Itineraries of an Anthropologist. Studies in Honour of Massimo Raveri* (pp. 53–86). Edizioni Ca' Foscari. https: //edizionicafoscari.unive.it/media/pdf/books/978–88-6969–528-5/978– 88-6969–528-5-ch-04.pdf.

Reginbogin, H.R. (2009). *Faces of Neutrality*. LIT Verlag.

Sutton, A.C. (2016). *Wall Street and the rise of Hitler* (5th ed.). Clairview.

Trento, J.J. (2001). *The secret history of the CIA*. Basic Books.

Trotsky, L. (1977). *The Transitional Program for Socialist Revolution*. Pathfinder.

Urwand, B. (2013, July 31). The chilling history of how Hollywood helped Hitler. *The Hollywood Reporter*. https://www.hollywoodreporter.com/news /general-news/how-hollywood-helped-hitler-595684/.

Chapter 4

Aarons, M., & Loftus, J. (1998). *Unholy trinity. The Vatican, the Nazis, and the Swiss banks*. St. Martin's Griffin.

Atomic Heritage Foundation. (2017, July 11). *Human radiation experiments*. https://ahf.nuclearmuseum.org/ahf/history/human-radiation-experiments/.

Barnett, A. (2002, April 21). Millions were in germ war tests. *The Guardian*. https://www.theguardian.com/politics/2002/apr/21/uk.medicalscience.

Bentley, M. (2019, July 22). The US has a history of testing biological weap- ons on the public—were infected ticks used too? *The Conversation*. https: //theconversation.com/the-us-has-a-history-of-testing-biological-weapons -on-the-public-were-infected-ticks-used-too-120638.

Blumenthal, M. (2023, September 26). Canada's honoring of Nazi vet exposes Ottawa's longstanding Ukraine policy. *The Grayzone*. https://thegrayzone .com/2023/09/26/canadas-ukrainian-nazi-ottawas-policy/.

Bode, E., & Fehlau, B. (2008, November 29). The silence of the Quandts: The history of a wealthy German family. *World Socialist Website*. https://www .wsws.org/en/articles/2008/11/quan-n29.html.

Breitman, R. (2001, April). Records of the Central Intelligence Agency (RG 263). *National Archives*. https://www.archives.gov/iwg/declassified-records /rg-263-cia-records/rg-263-report.html.

Central Intelligence Agency. (1963). *KUBARK Counterintelligence Interrogation*. https://nsarchive2.gwu.edu/NSAEBB/NSAEBB27/docs/doc01.pdf.

Cole, L.A. (1994, January 25). The worry: Germ warfare. The target: Us. *The New York Times*, p. A19. https://www.nytimes.com/1994/01/25/opinion /the-worry-germ-warfare-the-target-us.html.

de Jong, D. (2022). *Nazi billionaires*. William Collins.

Department of State. (1944). *United Nations monetary and financial conference: Bretton Woods, final act and related documents, New Hampshire, July 1 to July 22, 1944*. United States Government Printing Office. https://www.cvce.eu /content/publication/2003/12/12/2520351c-0e91–4399-af63–69e4b33 ef17a/publishable_en.pdf.

Department of the Army. (2009, August 25). *BW-I-55, Operation Big Itch, 17 November 1954*. https://documents.theblackvault.com/documents /biological/bigitch.pdf.

Engdahl, F.W. (2022, February 16). Davos and the purloined letter conspiracy. *SOTT*, https://www.sott.net/article/464568-Davos-and-the-Purloined-Letter -Conspiracy.

Feinstein, T. (2005, February 4). *The CIA and Nazi war criminals*. The National Security Archive. https://nsarchive2.gwu.edu/NSAEBB/NSAEBB146/index .htm.

Gross, T. (2019, September 9). The CIA's secret quest for mind control: Torture, LSD and a "poisoner In chief." *NPR*. https://www.npr.org /2019/09/09/758989641/the-cias-secret-quest-for-mind-control-torture-lsd -and-a-poisoner-in-chief.

Hausser, P. (1966). *Soldaten wie andere auch: Der Weg der Waffen SS*. Munin Verlag.

Heinelt, P. (n.d.). Treatment of I.G. Farben plants by the four Allies in their zones of occupation. Wollheim Memorial. http://www.wollheim-memorial .de/en/besatzungsmaechte_im_umgang_mit_igf_en.

Higham, C. (2007). *Trading with the enemy*. Delacorte Press.

Holocaust Encyclopedia. (n.d.). *Nuremberg Trials.* https://encyclopedia
.ushmm.org/content/en/article/the-nuremberg-trials.

Hughes, D.A. (2024). *"Covid-19," psychological operations, and the war for technocracy.* Palgrave Macmillan.

Human Radiation Experiments Report. (1995, October 3). *C-SPAN.* https:
//www.c-span.org/video/?67458–1/human-radiation-experiments-report.

Kaye, J.S. (2017, May 14). Department of Justice official releases letter admitting U.S. amnesty of Japan's Unit 731 war criminals. *Medium.* https:
//medium.com/@jeff_kaye/department-of-justice-official-releases-letter
-admitting-u-s-amnesty-of-unit-731-war-criminals-9b7da41d8982.

Kaye, J.S. (2018, February 20). REVEALED: The long-suppressed official report on US biowarfare in North Korea. *Insurgence Intelligence.* https:
//medium.com/insurge-intelligence/the-long-suppressed-korean-war-report
-on-u-s-use-of-biological-weapons-released-at-last-20d83f5cee54.

Kinzer, S. (2019). *Poisoner in chief. Sidney Gottlieb and the CIA search for mind control.* Henry Holt & Company.

Klein, N. (2007). *The shock doctrine.* Metropolitan Books.

Krishnan, A. (2016). *Military neuroscience and the coming age of neurowarfare.* Taylor & Francis.

Lichtblau, E. (2014, October 26). In Cold War, U.S. spy agencies used 1,000 Nazis. *The New York Times.* https://www.nytimes.com/2014/10/27/us/in-cold
-war-us-spy-agencies-used-1000-nazis.html.

Loftus, J. (2011). *America's Nazi secret.* Trine Day.

Loria, K. (2015, November 15). The Army tested "germ warfare" on the NYC subway by smashing lightbulbs full of bacteria. *Business Insider.* https://www.businessinsider.com/biological-agents-were-tested-on-the
-new-york-city-subway-2015–11.

Martin, J.M. (1950). *All honorable men.* Little, Brown, & Company.

Pilger, J. (2016, December 31). Bikini was just the beginning, bombs still threaten the islanders. *New Internationalist.* https://newint.org/features/2016
/12/01/bikini-was-just-the-beginning.

Pugliese, D. (2017, March 8). Chrystia Freeland's granddad was indeed a Nazi collaborator—so much for Russian disinformation. *Ottawa Citizen.* https://ottawacitizen.com/news/national/defence-watch/chrystia-freelands
-granddad-was-indeed-a-nazi-collaborator-so-much-for-russian
-disinformation.

Reif, E. (2023a, February 3). How a network of Nazi propagandists helped lay the groundwork for the war in Ukraine. *Covert Action Magazine*. https://covertactionmagazine.com/2023/02/03/how-a-network-of-nazi-propagandists-helped-lay-the-groundwork-for-the-war-in-ukraine/.

Reif, E. (2023b, February 17). Ukraine hawk who heads European Commission has a Nazi Pedigree she does not want you to know about. *Covert Action Magazine*. https://covertactionmagazine.com/2023/02/17/ukraine-hawk-who-heads-european-commission-has-a-nazi-pedigree-she-does-not-want-you-to-know-about/.

Richter, P. (2017, June 15). The dark side of a great company: BMW's ties to the Third Reich. *Turtle Garage*. https://turtlegarage.com/cars/the-dark-side-of-a-great-company-bmw-and-the-third-reich/.

Ryall, J. (2010, June 10). Did the US wage germ warfare in Korea? *The Telegraph*. https://www.telegraph.co.uk/news/worldnews/asia/northkorea/7811949/Did-the-US-wage-germ-warfare-in-Korea.html.

Salter, J. (2012, October 4). The Army sprayed St. Louis with toxic aerosol during a just revealed 1950s test,. *Business Insider*. https://www.businessinsider.com/army-sprayed-st-louis-with-toxic-dust-2012–10?r=US&IR=T.

Schwab, K. (2021). *Stakeholder capitalism. A global economy that works for progress, people and planet*. John Wiley & Sons, Inc.

Secret Cold War tests in St. Louis cause worry. (2012, October 3). *CBS News*. https://www.cbsnews.com/news/secret-cold-war-tests-in-st-louis-cause-worry/.

Simpson, C. (1988). *Blowback*. Weidenfeld & Nicolson.

Stedman, J.C. (1950). The German decartelization program—The law in repose. *The University of Chicago Law Review*, 17(3), pp. 441–457.

Sutton, A.C. (2016). *Wall Street and the rise of Hitler* (5th ed.). Clairview.

Swiss Policy Research. (2021, October). *The WEF and the pandemic*. https://swprs.org/the-wef-and-the-pandemic/.

Takeuchi, A. (2021, January 20). Japanese film director tells of ongoing aftermath of nuclear testing on Marshall Islands. *The Mainichi*. https://mainichi.jp/english/articles/20210119/p2a/00m/0op/033000c.

Thomas, M. (2007). *Monarch: The new Phoenix program*. CreateSpace.

U.S. Government Accountability Office. (2008, February 28). *Chemical and biological defense: DOD and VA need to improve efforts to identify and notify individuals potentially exposed during chemical and biological tests*. https://www.gao.gov/products/gao-08–366.

United States Senate Select Committee on Intelligence. (1977, August 3). *Project MKULTRA, the CIA's program of research in behavioral modification.* https://www.intelligence.senate.gov/sites/default/files/hearings/95mkultra.pdf.

Wilson, G.C. (1977, March 9). Army conducted 239 secret, open-air germ warfare tests. *The Washington Post.* https://www.washingtonpost.com/archive/politics/1977/03/09/army-conducted-239-secret-open-air-germ-warfare-tests/b17e5ee7-3006-4152-acf3-0ad163e17a22/.

Wollheim Memorial. (n.d.). *The decartelization of I.G. Farben after 1945.* http://www.wollheim-memorial.de/en/entflechtung_der_ig_farben_en.

Chapter 5

Adereth, M. (1984). *The French Communist Party: A critical history (1920–84).* Manchester University Press.

Agarossi, E., & Zaslavsky, V. (2011). *Stalin and Togliatti: Italy and the origins of the Cold War.* Woodrow Wilson Center Press.

Ahmed, N.M. (2012). Capitalism, covert action and state terrorism: Toward a political economy of the dual state. In: E. Wilson (Ed.), *The dual state: Parapolitics, Carl Schmitt, and the national security complex* (pp. 171–192). Routledge.

Anderson, P. (2017). *American foreign policy and its thinkers.* Verso.

Arendt, H. (1962). *The origins of totalitarianism.* The World Publishing Company.

Bernays, E. (1928). *Propaganda.* H. Liveright.

Botts, J. (2006). "Nothing to seek and . . . nothing to defend": George F. Kennan's core values and American foreign policy, 1938–1993. *Diplomatic History*, 30(5), 839–866. http://www.jstor.org/stable/24915049.

Braithwaite, R. (2018). *Armageddon and paranoia: The nuclear confrontation since 1945.* Oxford University Press.

Chomsky, N. (2012, October 15). The week the world stood still: The Cuban Missile Crisis and ownership of the world. *TomDispatch.* https://chomsky.info/20121015/.

Claudin, F. (1975). *The Communist movement: From Comintern to Cominform* (B. Pearce & F. MacDonagh, Trans.). Penguin.

Colás, A. (2012). No class! A comment on Simon Bromley's *American power and the prospects for international order. Cambridge Review of International Affairs*, 25(1), 39–52. https://doi.org/10.1080/09557571.2011.566550.

Corbett, J. (2019). China's suspiciously American arsenal: a closer look. *The Corbett Report*. https://www.corbettreport.com/chinas-suspiciously-american-arsenal-a-closer-look/.

Costigliola, F. (1997). Unceasing pressure for penetration: Gender, pathology, and emotion in George Kennan's formation of the Cold War. In: L. L. Bogle (Ed.), *The Cold War, Volume 2: National security policy planning from Truman to Reagan and from Stalin to Gorbachev* (pp. 113–144). Routledge.

Craig, C., & Logevall, F. (2012). *America's Cold War: The politics of insecurity*. Harvard University Press.

Davis, I. (2018, May 12). Operation Gladio—Hard evidence of government sponsored false flag terrorism. *Iain Davis*, https://iaindavis.com/operation-gladio-false-flag-evidence/.

Epp, R. (2017). Mastering the mysteries of diplomacy: Karl Marx as international theorist. *Socialist Studies*, 12(1), 78–96. https://doi.org/10.18740/S4VP8J.

Ganser, D. (2005). *NATO's secret armies. Operation Gladio and terrorism in Western Europe*. Frank Cass.

Ginsborg, P. (2003). *A history of contemporary Italy: Society and Politics, 1943–88*. St. Martins Publishing Group.

Glaberman, M., & Faber, S. (2002). Back to the future: The continuing relevance of Marx. *Critique: Journal of Socialist Theory*, 30(1), 167–177. https://doi.org/10.1080/03017600508413479.

Hett, B.C. (2014). *Burning the Reichstag: An investigation into the Third Reich's enduring mystery*. Oxford University Press.

Hoffmann, S., Huntington, S.P., May, E.R., Neustadt, R.N., & Schelling, T.C. (1981). Vietnam Reappraised. *International Security*, 6(1), 3–26. https://doi.org/10.2307/2538527.

Hughes, D.A. (2024). *"Covid-19," psychological operations, and the war for technocracy*. Palgrave Macmillan.

Hylan, J.F. (1922). The invisible government. *Brotherhood of Locomotive Engineers Journal*, 56(7–12), 659–716.

Judt, T. (2007). *Postwar: A history of Europe since 1945*. Pimlico.

Karalekas, A. (1977). *History of the Central Intelligence Agency*. Aegean Park Press.

Kennan, G. (1946, February 22). Long telegram. National Archives and Records Administration, Department of State Records (Record Group 59),

Central Decimal File, 1945–1949, 861.00/2–2246. https://digitalarchive
.wilsoncenter.org/document/116178.pdf.

Kennan, G. (1947). The sources of Soviet conduct. *Foreign Affairs*, 25(4),
566–582. https://www.foreignaffairs.com/articles/russian-federation/1947
–07-01/sources-soviet-conduct.

Kennan, G. (1948, May 4). Policy planning staff memorandum. *Office of the
Historian, US State Department*. https://history.state.gov/historicaldocuments
/frus1945–50Intel/d269.

Kennan, G. (1957, December 1). Russia, the atom, and the West. Reith
Lecture. *BBC*. https://www.bbc.co.uk/sounds/play/p00hg1nb.

Kennan, G. (1985). Morality and foreign policy. *Foreign Affairs*, 64(2), 205–
18. https://www.foreignaffairs.com/articles/united-states/1985–12-01/morality
-and-foreign-policy.

Kennan, G. (1987). Containment then and now. *Foreign Affairs*, 65(4), 885–
890. https://www.foreignaffairs.com/articles/1987-03-01/containment-40
-years-later.

Kennan, G. (2011). *E.H. Harriman: Railroad Czar*. Cosimo Classics.

Kissinger, H. (1957). *Nuclear weapons and foreign policy*. Council on Foreign
Relations.

Lippmann, W. (1987). The Cold War. *Foreign Affairs*, 65(4), 869–884.

Loftus, J. (2011). *America's Nazi secret*. Trine Day.

Marcus, L. (1974). The real CIA—the Rockefellers' fascist establishment, a
polemic. *The Campaigner*, 7(6), 5–34.

McCauley, M. (2016). *Origins of the Cold War 1941–1949*. Routledge.

Mearsheimer, J. (2014, September/October). Why the Ukraine crisis is the
West's fault. *Foreign Affairs*. https://www.mearsheimer.com/wp-content
/uploads/2019/06/Why-the-Ukraine-Crisis-Is.pdf.

Miscamble, W.D. (1993). *George F. Kennan and the making of American foreign
policy, 1947–1950*. Princeton University Press.

Morgenthau, H. (1962). *The decline of democratic politics*. University of Chicago
Press.

Norton-Taylor, R. (2010, June 25). Not so secret: Deal at the heart of UK-US
intelligence. *The Guardian*. https://www.theguardian.com/world/2010/jun
/25/intelligence-deal-uk-us-released.

Office of the Historian. (n.d.). *292. National Security Council Directive on Office
of Special Projects*. https://history.state.gov/historicaldocuments/frus1945
–50Intel/d292.

Orwell, G. (1945, October 19). You and the atomic bomb. *Tribune*. https: //www.orwell.ru/library/articles/ABomb/english/e_abomb.

Pechatnov, V.O. (2003, June). Averell Harriman's mission to Moscow. *The Harriman Review*, 1–47. https://academiccommons.columbia.edu/doi/10 .7916/d8-sa32–2490.

Peck, M. (2019, October 17). A covert ex-Nazi army helped NATO keep Stalin's troops out of West Germany. *The National Interest*. https://nationalinterest .org/blog/buzz/covert-ex-nazi-army-helped-nato-keep-stalins-troops-out -west-germany-88616.

Pijl, K. van der (2020, April 27). Health emergency or seizure of power? The political economy of Covid-19. *New Cold War*. https://newcoldwar.org /health-emergency-or-seizure-of-power-the-political-economy-of-covid-19/.

Pijl, K. van der. (2022). *States of emergency. Keeping the global population in check*. Clarity Press.

Quigley, C. (1966). *Tragedy and hope*. The Macmillan Company.

Ross, C.A. (2006). *The CIA doctors. Human rights violations by American psychiatrists*. Manitou Communications, Inc.

Sanchez-Sibony, O. (2014). Capitalism's fellow traveller: The Soviet Union, Bretton Woods, and the Cold War, 1944–1958. *Comparative Studies in Society and History*, 56(2), 290–319. https://doi.org/10.1017/S00104175 1400005X.

Schmitt, C. (1996). *The concept of the political* (G. Schwab, Trans.). University of Chicago Press.

Scott, P.D. (2017). *The American deep state. Big money, big oil, and the struggle for U.S. democracy*. Rowman & Littlefield.

Shoup, L.H., & Minter, W. (1977). *Imperial brain trust: The Council on Foreign Relations and United States foreign policy*. Monthly Review Press.

Simpson, C. (2014). *Blowback: America's recruitment of Nazis and its destructive impact on our domestic and foreign policy*. Open Road Media.

Steil, B. (2018). *The Marshall Plan: Dawn of the Cold War*. Oxford University Press.

Sutton, A.C. (1981). *Wall Street and the Bolshevik Revolution*. Veritas Publishing.

Sutton, A.C. (1972). *National suicide: Military aid to the Soviet Union*. Arlington House.

Sutton, A.C. (2016). *Wall Street and the rise of Hitler* (5th ed.). Clairview.

Tunander, O. (2016). Dual state: The case of Sweden. In: E. Wilson (Ed.), *The dual state: parapolitics, Carl Schmitt, and the national security complex* (pp. 171–192). Routledge.

Valentine, D. (2017). *The CIA as organized crime. How illegal operations corrupt America and the world.* Clarity Press.

Wall, I.M. (1991). *The United States and the making of postwar France, 1945–47.* Cambridge University Press.

Wilford, H. (2008). *The mighty Wurlitzer: How the CIA played America.* Harvard University Press.

Williams, W.A. (1992). *A William Appleman Williams Reader* (H.W. Berger, Ed.). Ivan R. Dee.

Chapter 6

Ahmed, N.M. (2012). Capitalism, covert action and state terrorism: Toward a political economy of the dual state. In: E. Wilson (Ed.), *The dual state: Parapolitics, Carl Schmitt, and the national security complex* (pp. 171–192). Routledge.

Amnesty International. (2020, May 18). *Our final plea to Obama to close Guantánamo.* https://www.amnesty.org.uk/our-final-plea-obama-close-guanta namo.

Anderson, T. (2016). *The dirty war on Syria: Washington, regime change and resistance.* Global Research.

Armstrong, C.K. (2009). The destruction and reconstruction of North Korea, 1950–1960. *The Asia-Pacific Journal,* 7(1), Article 3460. https://apjjf.org /-Charles-K.-Armstrong/3460/article.html.

Bardosh, K. (2023). How did the Covid pandemic response harm society? A global evaluation and state of knowledge review (2020–21). Preprint retrieved from http://dx.doi.org/10.2139/ssrn.4447806.

Blum, W. (2006). *Rogue state: A guide to the world's only superpower.* Zed Books.

Brown, E. (2016, March 14). Why Qaddafi had to go: African gold, oil and the challenge to monetary imperialism. *The Ecologist.* https://theecologist .org/2016/mar/14/why-qaddafi-had-go-african-gold-oil-and-challenge -monetary-imperialism.

Butz, T., Peck, W., & Porter, D. (1974). Trends. *Counter-Spy Magazine,* 2(1), 5–6.

Cavanagh, J. (1980, April 29). Dulles papers reveal CIA consulting network. *Forerunner.* http://www.namebase.net:82/campus/consult.html.

Chomsky, N. (2006). *Failed states: The abuse of power and the assault on democracy.* Metropolitan Books.

Chomsky, N. (2007). *Hegemony or survival: America's quest for global dominance.* Henry Holt & Company.

Chomsky, N. (2008). Intentional ignorance and its uses. In: A. Arnove (Ed.), *The Essential Chomsky* (pp. 300–324). The New Press.

Corbett, J. (2014, July 6). Century of enslavement: The history of the Federal Reserve." *The Corbett Report.* https://www.corbettreport.com/federalreserve/.

Corbett, J. (2018, November 19). Episode 348—The WWI conspiracy—Part two: The American front. *The Corbett Report.* https://www.corbettreport.com/episode-348-the-wwi-conspiracy-part-two-the-american-front/.

David, S. (2015, May 22). Did Britain doom the Lusitania? *History Extra.* https://www.historyextra.com/period/first-world-war/did-britain-doom-the-lusitania/.

Davidsson, E. (2013). *Hijacking America's mind on 9/11: Counterfeiting evidence.* Algora.

deHaven-Smith, L. (2013). *Conspiracy theory in America.* University of Texas Press.

de Lint, W.B. (2021). *Blurring intelligence crime: A critical forensics.* Springer.

Dowd, E. (2022). *"Cause Unknown": The epidemic of sudden deaths in 2021 & 2022.* Skyhorse.

Dyer, O. (2002). Prisoners' treatment is "bordering on torture," charity says." *BMJ,* 324, Article 187. https://doi.org/10.1136/bmj.324.7331.187.

Felton, M. (2009). *Japan's Gestapo: Murder, mayhem and torture in wartime Asia.* Pen & Sword Books.

Griffin, D.R. (2005). *The 9/11 Commission Report: Omissions and distortions.* Olive Branch.

Griffin, D.R., & Woodworth, E. (2018). *9/11 unmasked: An international review panel investigation.* Olive Branch.

Hanania, R. (2017). Tracing the development of the nuclear taboo: The Eisenhower administration and four crises in East Asia. *Journal of Cold War Studies,* 19(2), 43–83. https://doi.org/10.1162/JCWS_a_00740.

Hayward, T. (2020, March 8). Peer review vs. trial by Twitter." *Tim Hayward.* https://timhayward.wordpress.com/2020/03/08/peer-review-vs-trial-by-twitter/.

Health Advisory & Recovery Team. (2022, February 25). *Care home isolation and neglect: An urgent crisis.* https://www.hartgroup.org/care-home-isolation-and -neglect-an-urgent-crisis/.

Herman, E.S., & Peterson, D. (2014). *Enduring lies: The Rwandan genocide in the propaganda system, 20 years later.* CreateSpace.

Holder, J. (2023, March 13). Tracking coronavirus vaccinations around the world. *New York Times.* https://www.nytimes.com/interactive/2021/world /covid-vaccinations-tracker.html.

Hughes, D.A. (2015). Unmaking an exception: A critical genealogy of U.S. exceptionalism. *Review of International Studies,* 41(3), 527–551. https: //doi.org/10.1017/S0260210514000229.

Hughes, D.A. (2020). 9/11 truth and the silence of the IR discipline. *Alternatives,* 45(2), 55–82. https://doi.org/10.1177/0304375419898334.

Hughes, D.A. (2021, October 12). Questions not asked: 9/11 and the academy. *UK Column.* https://www.ukcolumn.org/video/propaganda-and-the-911 -global-war-on-terror-dr-david-hughes.

Hughes, D.A. (2022a). "Covid-19 vaccines" for children in the UK: A tale of establishment corruption. *International Journal of Vaccine Theory, Practice, and Research,* 2(1), 209–247. https://doi.org/10.56098/ijvtpr.v2i1.35.

Hughes, D.A. (2022b, July 29). Wall Street, the Nazis, and the crimes of the deep state. *Propaganda in Focus.* https://propagandainfocus.com /wall-street-the-nazis-and-the-crimes-of-the-deep-state/.

Hughes, D.A. (2022c). What is in the so-called Covid-19 "vaccines"? Part 1: Evidence of a global crime against humanity. *International Journal of Vaccine Theory, Practice, and Research,* 2(2), 455–586. https://doi.org/10.56098 /ijvtpr.v2i2.52.

Hughes, D.A. (2024). *"Covid-19," psychological operations, and the war for technocracy.* Palgrave Macmillan.

Hughes, D.A., Kyrie, V., & Broudy, D. (2022, November 29). Covid-19: Mass formation or mass atrocity? *Unlimited Hangout.* https://unlimitedhangout .com/2022/11/investigative-reports/covid-19-mass-formation-or-mass -atrocity/.

Huntington, S.P. (1965). Political development and political decay. *World Politics,* 17(3), 386–430. https://doi.org/10.2307/2009286.

Karalekas, A. (1977). *History of the Central Intelligence Agency.* Aegean Park Press.

Kaye, J.S. (2018, February 20). REVEALED: The long-suppressed official report on US biowarfare in North Korea. *Insurgence Intelligence.* https://medium.com/insurge-intelligence/the-long-suppressed-korean-war-report-on-u-s-use-of-biological-weapons-released-at-last-20d83f5cee54.

Kisielinski, K., Giboni, P., Prescher, A., Klosterhalfen, B., Graessel, D., Funken, S., Kempski, O., & Hirch, O. (2021). Is a mask that covers the mouth and nose free from undesirable side effects in everyday use and free of potential hazards? *International Journal of Environmental Research and Public Health,* 18(8), Article 4344. https://doi.org/10.3390/ijerph18084344.

Klein, N. (2007). *The shock doctrine.* Metropolitan Books.

Kolko, G. (1972). Report on the destruction of dikes: Holland 1944–45 and Korea 1953. In: U.S. Senate Committee on the Judiciary, *Problems of War Victims in Indochina. Part 1: Vietnam* (pp. 139–140). U.S. Government Printing Office.

Maddox, J.D. (2015). How to start a war: Eight cases of strategic provocation. *Narrative and Conflict: Explorations of Theory and Practice,* 3(1), 66–109. https://doi.org/10.13021/G8ncetp.v3.1.2016.601.

McCoy, A. (2007). *A question of torture: CIA interrogation, from the Cold War to the War on Terror.* Henry Holt & Company.

McCoy, A. (2015, February 15). The real American exceptionalism. *Truthdig.* https://www.truthdig.com/articles/the-real-american-exceptionalism/.

Media Lens. (2004, April 23). Burying genocide—The UN "oil for food" programme." *Media Lens.* https://www.medialens.org/2004/burying-genocide-the-un-oil-for-food-programme/.

Medicines and Healthcare products Regulatory Agency. (n.d.). *COVID-19 vaccine analysis overview* [Data set]. https://yellowcard.ukcolumn.org/yellow-card-reports.

Medicines and Healthcare products Regulatory Agency. (2019). Yellow card: please help to reverse the decline in reporting of suspected adverse drug reactions. https://www.gov.uk/drug-safety-update/yellow-card-please-help-to-reverse-the-decline-in-reporting-of-suspected-adverse-drug-reactions.

Moise, E.E. (1996). *Tonkin Gulf and the escalation of the Vietnam War.* University of North Carolina Press.

Mueller, J., & Stewart, M. (2016). *Chasing ghosts: The policing of terrorism.* Oxford University Press.

Open letter from former Guantánamo prisoners. (2013, May 4). *The Observer*. https://www.theguardian.com/world/2013/may/04/open-letter-former -guantanamo-prisoners.

OpenVAERS. (n.d.). *VAERS Covid vaccine adverse event reports*. Retrieved January 11, 2024, from https://openvaers.com/covid-data.

Oren, I. (2002). *Our enemies and US: America's rivalries and the making of political science*. Cornell University Press.

Pijl, K. van der. (2014). *The discipline of Western supremacy. Modes of foreign relations and political economy, Vol. III*. Pluto Press.

Pijl, K. van der. (2022). *States of emergency. Keeping the global population in check*. Clarity Press.

Pilger, J. (2000). Censorship by omission. In: P. Hammond & E. Hermann (Eds.), *Degraded capability: The media and the Kosovo crisis* (pp. 132–140). Pluto Press.

Rancourt, D. (2020). *All-cause mortality during Covid-19: No plague and a likely signature of mass homicide by government response*. https://denisrancourt.ca/entries.php?id=9&name=2020_06_02_all_cause_mortality _during_covid_19_no_plague_and_a_likely_signature_of_mass_homicide _by_government_response.

Rancourt, D., Baudin, M., & Mercier, J. (2021). *Nature of the Covid-era public health disaster in the USA, from all-cause mortality and socio-geo-economic and climatic data*. https://denisrancourt.ca/uploads_entries/1635189453861 _USA%20ACM%20into%202021%20-%20article—12d.pdf.

Rever, J. (2018). *In praise of blood: The crimes of the Rwandan Patriotic Front*. Random House Canada.

Rosenberg, C. (2021, May 3). Recalling the first Guantánamo detainees. *The New York Times*. https://www.nytimes.com/2021/05/03/insider/first -guantanamo-prisoners.html.

Ross, L., Klompas, M., & Bernstein, S. (2010). *Electronic support for public health—vaccine adverse event reporting system*. https://digital.ahrq.gov/sites /default/files/docs/publication/r18hs017045-lazarus-final-report-2011.pdf.

Sanderson, H. (2019, July 7). Congo, child labour, and your electric car. *Financial Times*, https://archive.ph/6xybI#selection-1765.0–1765.41.

Schlesinger Jr., A.M. (2002). *A thousand days: John F. Kennedy in the White House*. Houghton Mifflin Company.

Schmitt, C. (2005). *Political theology: Four chapters on the concept of sovereignty.* University of Chicago Press.

Schwab, K., & Malleret, T. (2020). *Covid 19: The Great Reset.* World Economic Forum.

Scott, P.D. (1996). *Deep politics and the death of JFK.* University of California Press.

Scott, P.D. (2003). *Drugs, oil, and war: The United States in Afghanistan, Colombia, and Indochina.* Rowman & Littlefield.

Scott, P.D. (2017). *The American deep state. Big money, big oil, and the struggle for U.S. democracy.* Rowman & Littlefield.

Scott, P.D., & Marshall, J. (1998). *Cocaine politics: Drugs, armies, and the CIA in Central America.* University of California Press.

Stone, I.F. (1952). *The hidden history of the Korean War.* Little, Brown & Co.

Sutton, A.C. (2016). *Wall Street and the rise of Hitler* (5th ed.). Clairview.

Urman, A., Makhortykh, M., Ulloa, R., Kulshrestha, J. (2022). Where the earth is flat and 9/11 is an inside job: A comparative algorithm audit of conspiratorial information in web search results. *Telematics and Informatics,* 72, Article 101860. https://doi.org/10.1016/j.tele.2022.101860.

Valentine, D. (2017). *The CIA as organized crime. How illegal operations corrupt America and the world.* Clarity Press.

Webb, W. (2022a). *One nation under blackmail, volume 1.* Trine Day.

Webb, W. (2022b). *One nation under blackmail, volume 2.* Trine Day.

Wood, J. (2011). *Where did the towers go? Evidence of directed free-energy technology on 9/11.* The New Investigation.

Woodworth, E., & Griffin, D.R. (2022, May 21). The "best evidence" contradicting the official position on 9/11: Excerpts from *9/11 unmasked: An international review panel investigation. Propaganda in Focus.* http://berlin-grp.org/the-best-evidence-contradicting-the-official-position-on-9–11-excerpts-from-9–11-unmasked-an-international-review-panel-investigation/.

Yemen: Why is the war there getting more violent? (2023, April 14). *BBC News.* https://www.bbc.co.uk/new/word-middle-east-29319423.

Chapter 7

Abramson, D., Fu, D., & Johnson Jr., J.E. (2020). Cryptocurrency system using body activity data. U.S. Patent No. Patent 16/138518. Washington, D.C.: U.S Patent and Trademark Office.

Agamben, G. (1998). *Homo Sacer*. Stanford University Press.

Ames, J. (2020, December 14). Tedros Adhanom: WHO chief may face genocide charges. *The Times*. https://www.thetimes.co.uk/article/who-chief-tedros-adhanom-ghebreyesus-may-face-genocide-charges-2fbfz7sff.

Andone, D., & Holcombe, M. (2021, July 16). Covid-19 "is becoming a pandemic of the unvaccinated," CDC director says. *CNN*. https://edition.cnn.com/2021/07/16/health/us-coronavirus-friday/index.html.

Australian public health chief says Covid contact tracing is part of "New World Order." (2021). *The Independent*. https://www.independent.co.uk/tv/news/australian-public-health-chief-says-covid-contact-tracing-is-part-of-new-world-order-b2181196.html.

Bauman, Z. (1991). *Modernity and the Holocaust*. Cambridge University Press.

Beck, S. (2024, February 22). A sinister agenda down on the farm. *TCW*. https://www.conservativewoman.co.uk/a-sinister-agenda-down-on-the-farm/.

Bell, D. (2023). Pandemic preparedness and the road to international fascism. *The American Journal of Economics and Sociology*, 82(5), 395–409. https://doi.org/10.1111/ajes.12531.

Biden. J. (1992, April 23). How I learned to love the New World Order. *Wall Street Journal*. https://web.archive.org/web/20131213135235/http://pennsylvaniacrier.com/filemgmt_data/files/Biden-New%20World%20Order.pdf.

Black, E. (2003, September). The horrifying American roots of Nazi eugenics. *History News Network*. http://historynewsnetwork.org/article/1796.

Black, E. (2009). *Nazi nexus*. Dialog Press.

Broudy, D. (2021). Vaccine development and social control: A psychopathology of impaired reasoning in the global push for mass compliance. *International Journal of Vaccine Theory, Practice, and Research*, 2(1), 93–124. https://ijvtpr.com/index.php/IJVTPR/article/view/29.

Broudy, D., Hughes, D.A., & Kyrie, V. (2022, December 10). The psychology of Covid-19 atrocities. *Doctors For Covid Ethics*. https://doctors4covidethics.org/session-iv-understanding-tactics-of-oppression-2/.

Brown, L. (2021, January 18). German quarantine breakers to be held in refugee camps, detention centers." *New York Post*. https://nypost.com/2021/01/18/german-quarantine-breakers-to-be-held-in-refugee-camps/.

Brown, T. (2023, May 6). Top 10 largest farmland owners in the US in 2023. *Farmland Riches*. https://www.farmlandriches.com/largest-farmland-owners/.

Browning, C.R. (1986). Nazi ghettoization policy in Poland: 1939–1941. *Central European History*, 19(4): 343–368.

Browning, O. (2022, April). Drone flying over Shanghai tells residents on balconies to comply with Covid lockdown. *The Independent*. https://www .independent.co.uk/tv/news/shanghai-china-covid-lockdown-drone -b2055301.html.

Brüggemeier, F.-J., Cioc, M., & Zeller, T. (Eds). (2005). *How green were the Nazis? Nature, environment, and nation in the Third Reich*. Ohio University Press.

Bujard, M., & Andersson, G. (2022). Fertility declines near the end of the Covid-19 pandemic: Evidence of the 2022 birth declines in Germany and Sweden. Preprint retrieved from https://su.figshare.com/articles/preprint/Fertility _declines_near_the_end_of_the_COVID-19_pandemic_Evidence_of _the_2022_birth_declines_in_Germany_and_Sweden/20975611.

Bush "Out of these troubled times . . . a New World Order" (1990, September 12). *The Washington Post*. https://www.washingtonpost.com/archive/politics /1990/09/12/bush-out-of-these-troubled-times-a-new-world-order /b93b5cf1-e389–4e6a-84b0–85f71bf4c946/.

Ciaramella, G., & Himansu, S. (2017). Combination piv3/hmpv rna vaccines. Patent No. 15/674599. Washington, D.C.: U.S Patent and Trademark Office.

Corbett, J. (2019). Episode 359—The secrets of Silicon Valley: What big tech doesn't want you to know. *The Corbett Report*. https://www.corbettreport .com/siliconvalley/.

Corbett, J. (2020, May 1). Who is Bill Gates? *The Corbett Report*. https://www .corbettreport.com/gates/.

Corbett, J. (2023, March 6). Episode 438—The future food false flag. *The Corbett Report*. https://corbettreport.com/foodfalseflag/.

Corbett, K.P. (2020, May 26). *The Covid Nazification of the National Health Service*. https://kevinpcorbett.com/onewebmedia/Nazification%20of%20 the%20National%20Health%20Servicev1.rtf.

Curzon, M. (2021, June 26). £1,750 for this! "Prison-like" conditions persist at Government-approved quarantine hotels. *The Daily Sceptic*. https: //dailysceptic.org/2021/06/26/1750-for-this-prison-like-conditions-persist -at-government-approved-quarantine-hotels/.

Davis, I. (2020, July 22). We must inoculate ourselves against the crazy anti-rationalists. *Iain Davis*. https://iaindavis.com/anti-rationalist/.

Davis, I. (2021a, October 12). Seizing everything: The theft of the global commons—Part 1. *Iain Davis.* https://iaindavis.com/global-commons-part-1/.

Davis, I. (2021b, November 7). Seizing everything: The theft of the global commons—Part 2. *Iain Davis.* https://iaindavis.com/global-commons-part-2/.

Davis, I. (2022, March 26). Is It Joe Biden's New World Order? *Iain Davis.* https://iaindavis.com/joe-biden-new-world-order/.

Doctors For Covid Ethics. (2023, January). *D4CE 5th symposium—Session IV understanding tactics of oppression.* https://doctors4covidethics.org/session-iv-understanding-tactics-of-oppression-2/.

Dowling, M. (2021, September 22). Mayor Lightfoot demands pledge of allegiance to the New World Order. *Independent Sentinel.* https://www.independentsentinel.com/mayor-lightfoot-demands-pledge-of-allegiance-to-the-new-world-order/.

Drobniewski, F. (1993). Why did Nazi doctors break their 'hippocratic' oaths? *Journal of the Royal Society of Medicine*, 86(9), 541–543.

Elmer, S. (2022, June 12). The camp as biopolitical paradigm of the state. *Architects for Social Housing.* https://architectsforsocialhousing.co.uk/2022/06/12/8-the-camp-as-biopolitical-paradigm-of-the-state-the-road-to-fascism-for-a-critique-of-the-global-biosecurity-state/.

Epstein, C.A. (2015). *Nazi Germany: Confronting the myths.* John Wiley & Sons.

Favas, C., Checchi, F., & Waldman, R.J. (2020, April 30). *Guidance for the prevention of COVID-19 infections among high-risk individuals in urban settings.* https://www.lshtm.ac.uk/media/35726.

Fink, L. (2022). The power of capitalism. *Blackrock.* https://www.blackrock.com/corporate/investor-relations/larry-fink-ceo-letter.

Fleming, S. (2021, February 28). EU must prepare for "era of pandemics," von der Leyen says. *Financial Times.* https://www.ft.com/content/fba55 8ff-94a5-4c6c-b848-c8fd91b13c16.

Foth, T. (2014). From "euthanasia killings" to the "killing of sick persons." In S. Benedict & S. Shields (Eds.), *Nurses and Midwives in Nazi Germany. The "Euthanasia Programs"* (pp. 218–242). Routledge. https://www.routledge.com/Nurses-and-Midwives-in-Nazi-Germany-The-Euthanasia-Programs/Benedict-Shields/p/book/9780415896658.

Frank, R. (2009, May 26). Billionaires try to shrink world's population, report says." *Wall Street Journal.* https://www.wsj.com/articles/BL-WHB-1322.

Garde, D. (2017, January 10). Lavishly funded Moderna hits safety problems in bold bid to revolutionize medicine. *STAT*. https://www.statnews.com /2017/01/10/moderna-trouble-mrna/.

Gates, B. (2018, May/June). Gene editing for good: How CRISPR could transform global development. *Foreign Affairs*. https://www.foreignaffairs .com/world/gene-editing-good.

Gates, B. (2020a, April 30). What you need to know about the COVID-19 vaccine. *GatesNotes*. https://www.gatesnotes.com/Health/What-you-need-to -know-about-the-COVID-19-vaccine.

Gates, B. (2020b, December 22). These breakthroughs will make 2021 better than 2020. *GatesNotes*. https://www.gatesnotes.com/About-Bill-Gates/Year-in -Review-2020.

Gates, B. (2021, December 7). Reasons for optimism after a difficult year. *GatesNotes*. https://www.gatesnotes.com/About-Bill-Gates/Year-in-Review-2021.

Gates, B., & Gates, M. (2021, January 27). The year global health went local. *GatesNotes*. https://www.gatesnotes.com/2021-Annual-Letter.

Gellately, R. (1991). *The Gestapo and German society*. Oxford University Press.

Haque, O.S., De Freitas, J., Viani, I., Niederschulte, B., & Bursztajn, H.J. (2012). Why did so many German doctors join the Nazi Party early? *International Journal of Law and Psychiatry*, 35(5–6), 473–479. https://doi .org/10.1016/j.ijlp.2012.09.022.

Harari, Y.N. (2017). *Homo Deus*. Harwill Seeker.

Harari, Y.N. (2020, January 24). Read Yuval Harari's blistering warn- ing to Davos in full. *World Economic Forum*. https://www.weforum.org /agenda/2020/01/yuval-hararis-warning-davos-speech-future-predications/.

Harff, B. (2017). R.J. Rummel: An assessment of his many contributions. In N.P. Gleditsch (Ed.), *SpringerBriefs on Pioneers in Science and Practice*, 37, 116–125. https://doi.org/10.1007/978-3-319-54463-2_12.

Harlow, J. (2009, May 24). Billionaire club in bid to curb overpopulation. *The Times*. https://www.thetimes.co.uk/article/billionaire-club-in-bid-to-curb -overpopulation-d2fl22qhl02.

Harris, M., & Aspinall, A. (2021, May 29). Inside Wellingborough mega prison with river views and windows without bars. *Northants Live*. https://www .northantslive.news/news/northamptonshire-news/inside-wellingboroughs -new-mega-prison-5471591.

Harvey, F. (2023, October 20). Impact of farming on climate crisis will be a key Cop topic—finally. *The Guardian*. https://www.theguardian.com/environment/2023/oct/20/impact-farming-climate-crisis-key-cop-topic-finally.

Hayward, T. (2022, July 29). Counter-disinformation fails: Feedback from a target. *Propaganda in Focus*. https://propagandainfocus.com/counter-disinformation-fails-feedback-from-a-target/.

Higham, C. (2007). *Trading with the enemy*. Delacorte Press.

Hilberg, R. (1985). *The destruction of the European Jews*. Holmes & Meier.

Hill, J. (2022, January 10). Researchers confirm highly variable vaccine batch toxicity despite VAERS data artifacts: Latypova. *James Hill MD's Newsletter*. https://hillmd.substack.com/p/researchers-confirm-highly-variable.

Hoft, J. (2022, June 23). Interactive map details destruction of numerous U.S. food manufacturing plants, grocery stores, etc.—compares U.S. incidents to global trends. *Gateway Pundit*. https://www.thegatewaypundit.com/2022/06/interactive-map-details-destruction-numerous-us-food-manufacturing-plants-compares-us-incidents-global-trends/.

Holder, J. (2023, March 13). Tracking coronavirus vaccinations around the world. *New York Times*. https://www.nytimes.com/interactive/2021/world/covid-vaccinations-tracker.html.

Hopkins, C.J. (2020, November 22). The Germans are back! *Consent Factory*. https://consentfactory.org/2020/11/22/the-germans-are-back/.

Howard, G.K. (1940). *America and a New World Order*. Charles Scribner's Sons.

Hubert, A. (2021, July 12). Why we need to give insects the role they deserve in our food systems. *World Economic Forum*. https://www.weforum.org/agenda/2021/07/why-we-need-to-give-insects-the-role-they-deserve-in-our-food-systems/.

Hughes, D.A. (2022a). "Covid-19 vaccines" for children in the UK: A tale of establishment corruption. *International Journal of Vaccine Theory, Practice, and Research*, 2(1), 209–247. https://doi.org/10.56098/ijvtpr.v2i1.35.

Hughes, D.A. (2022b, July 29). Wall Street, the Nazis, and the crimes of the deep state. *Propaganda in Focus*. https://propagandainfocus.com/wall-street-the-nazis-and-the-crimes-of-the-deep-state/.

Hughes, D.A. (2022c). What is in the so-called Covid-19 "vaccines"? Part 1: Evidence of a global crime against humanity. *International Journal of Vaccine*

Theory, Practice, and Research, 2(2), 455–586. https://doi.org/10.56098 /ijvtpr.v2i2.52.

Hughes, D.A. (2024). *"Covid-19," Psychological operations, and the war for technocracy.* Palgrave Macmillan.

Human species "may split in two." (2006, October 17). *BBC News.* http: //news.bbc.co.uk/1/hi/uk/6057734.stm.

Huxley, A. (1932). *Brave new world.* Chatto & Windus.

Huxley, J. (1946). *UNESCO: Its purpose & its philosophy.* Preparatory Commission of the United Nations Educational, Scientific, and Cultural Organisation.

Huxley, A. (1959). The final revolution. In: A. Simon and R.M. Featherstone (Eds.), *A pharmacologic approach to the study of the mind* (pp. 216–228). University of California Medical School.

Imort, M. (2005). "Eternal forest—eternal Volk." The rhetoric and reality of National Socialist forest policy." In: F.-J. Brüggemeier, M. Cioc, & T. Zeller (Eds), *How green were the Nazis? Nature, environment, and nation in the Third Reich* (pp. 43–72). Ohio University Press.

Institute of Development Studies. (2021, June 8). We need to talk about 30x30. https://www.ids.ac.uk/news/we-need-to-talk-about-30x30/.

Jones, H. (2020, May 22). Are we ready to embrace a New World Order? *Forbes.* https://www.forbes.com/sites/cognitiveworld/2020/05/22/are-we-ready -to-embrace-a-new-world-order/.

Kaplan, M.A. (1998). *Between dignity and despair.* Oxford University Press.

Kay, A.J. (2006). *Exploitation, resettlement, mass murder.* Berghahn Books.

Kempe, F. (2022, April 3). Op-ed: A New World Order is emerging—and the world is not ready for it. *CNBC.* https://www.cnbc.com/2022/04/03/a -new-world-order-is-emerging-and-the-world-is-not-ready-for-it.html.

Kershaw, I. (1983). *Popular opinion and political dissent in the Third Reich.* Oxford University Press.

Kheriaty, A. (2022, May 24). The WHO treaty is tied to a global digital passport and ID system. *Brownstone Institute.* https://brownstone.org/articles/who-treaty -tied-to-digital-passport-id-system/.

Klaus Schwab wants to create a "New World Order." (2023, June 29). *Wide Awake Media.* https://wide-awake-media.com/klaus-schwab-wants-to-create-a -new-world-order/.

Knightly, K. (2022, April 19). "Pandemic treaty" will hand WHO keys to global government. *OffGuardian*. https://off-guardian.org/2022/04/19 /pandemic-treaty-will-hand-who-keys-to-global-government/.

Knoepfler, P. (2015, November 18). Haunting Doudna nightmare about Hitler wanting CRISPR. *The Niche*. https://ipscell.com/2015/11/haunting-doudna -nightmare-about-hitler-wanting-crispr/.

Koire, R. (2011). *Behind the green mask: UN Agenda 21*. The Post Sustainability Institute Press.

Koonz, C. (2003). *The Nazi conscience*. Harvard University Press.

Kosicki, M., Tomberg, K., & Bradley, A. (2018). Repair of double-strand breaks induced by CRISPR–Cas9 leads to large deletions and complex rearrangements. *Nature Biotechnology*, 36(8), 765–775. https://doi.org/10.1038/nbt .4192.

Kurzweil, R. (2005). *The Singularity is near. When humans transcend biology*. Viking.

Lekan, T. (2005). "It shall be the whole landscape!" The Reich Nature Protection Law and regional planning in the Third Reich. In: F.-J. Brüggemeier, M. Cioc, & T. Zeller (Eds), *How green were the Nazis? Nature, environment, and nation in the Third Reich* (pp. 73–100). Ohio University Press.

Lifton, R.J. (1986). *The Nazi doctors*. Basic Books.

Lurie, M. (2021, June 27). Protecting 30% of the Earth by 2030 would threaten indigenous peoples. *Open Democracy*. https://www.opendemocracy.net/en /democraciaabierta/protecting-30-of-the-earth-by-2030-would-threaten -indigenous-peoples/.

Martin, B.G. (2016). *The Nazi-fascist New Order for European culture*. Harvard University Press.

Mayer, M. (2017). *They thought they were free* (2nd ed.). University of Chicago Press.

McDowell, A. (2020, October 27). Who voted in Davos? How data-driven government and the internet of bodies are poised to transform smart sustainable cities into social impact prisons. *Wrench In The Gears*. https: //wrenchinthegears.com/2020/10/27/who-voted-in-davos-how-data -driven-government-and-the-internet-of-bodies-are-poised-to-transform -smart-sustainable-cities-into-social-impact-prisons/.

McFadden, B. (2021, November 30). Covid booster jabs: GPs to be paid between £15 to £30 per vaccine administered as roll-out ramps up. *i*. https:

//inews.co.uk/news/covid-booster-jabs-gps-paid-per-vaccine-administered -rollout-ramped-up-1328159.

McPhee, S. (2021, November 24). Inside the town with the world's strictest lockdown where residents are bundled into vans, driven to a quarantine camp and banned from going for a WALK or buying food—as indigenous elders issue a frightening warning. *Daily Mail*. https://www.dailymail.co.uk /news/article-10237761/Covid-Australia-Outbreak-Indigenous-Northern -Territory-communities-spark-toughest-lockdown.html.

Medicines and Healthcare products Regulatory Agency. (n.d.). COVID-19 vaccine analysis overview [Dataset]. *UK Column*. https://yellowcard.ukcolumn .org/yellow-card-reports.

Meerloo, J.A. (1956). *The rape of the mind. The psychology of thought control, menticide, and brainwashing*. World Publishing Company.

Mihalcea, A. (2023, May 20). Visual inspection of C19 vaccinated live blood clots—rubber (hydrogel) like substance found—beware graphic images. *Dr. Ana's Newsletter*. https://anamihalceamdphd.substack.com/p/visual-inspection -of-c19-vaccinated.

Ministry of Defence. (2021, May). *Human augmentation—The dawn of a new paradigm*. https://assets.publishing.service.gov.uk/government/uploads /system/uploads/attachment_data/file/986301/Human_Augmentation _SIP_access2.pdf.

Ministry of Justice. (2023). *Prison population projections 2022 to 2027, England and Wales*. https://assets.publishing.service.gov.uk/government/uploads/system /uploads/attachment_data/file/1138135/Prison_Population_Projections_2022 _to_2027.pdf.

Morgenthau, H. (1948). *Politics among nations*. Alfred A. Knopf.

Mueller, A.P. (2020, December 8). No privacy, no property: The world in 2030 according to the WEF. Mises Institute. https://mises.org/wire/no -privacy-no-property-world-2030-according-wef.

Müller, I. (1991). *Hitler's justice. The courts of the Third Reich* (D.L. Schneider, Trans.). Harvard University Press.

Naked Emperor. (2023, March 4). Number of births in England falls by 11.9% in 2022. *The Daily Sceptic*. https://dailysceptic.org/2023/03/04 /number-of-births-in-england-falls-by-11-9-in-2022/.

New York State Senate. (2021, January 6). *Assembly bill A416*. https://www .nysenate.gov/legislation/bills/2021/a416.

Niebuhr, R. (1949). The illusion of world government. *Foreign Affairs*, 27(3), 379–388.

Nilsson, A., & O'Doherty, J. (2021, September 9). NSW Health limits residents of locked-down tower block to six beers per day. *News.com.au*. https://www.news.com.au/national/nsw-act/news/nsw-health-limits-residents-of-lockeddown-tower-block-to-six-beers-per-day/news-story/0e387ceccee145a611ddb6e38872d3d5.

Office for National Statistics (2023, December 4). *Cost of living insights: Food*. https://www.ons.gov.uk/economy/inflationandpriceindices/articles/costoflivinginsights/food.

Okai, A. (2022, June 27). Urban resilience: Addressing an old challenge with renewed urgency. *United Nations Development Programme*. https://www.undp.org/blog/urban-resilience-addressing-old-challenge-renewed-urgency.

O'Neill, B. (2021, December 6). The death of Europe. *Spiked!* https://www.spiked-online.com/2021/12/06/the-death-of-europe/.

O'Neill, B. (2022, February 6). Big Tech vs the working class. *Spiked!* https://www.spiked-online.com/2022/02/06/big-tech-vs-the-working-class/.

OpenVAERS. (n.d.). *VAERS Covid vaccine adverse event reports*. Retrieved January 11, 2024, from https://openvaers.com/covid-data.

Pakes, F. (2021, November 30). Prison numbers set to rise 24% in England and Wales—It will make society less safe, not more. *The Conversation*. https://theconversation.com/prison-numbers-set-to-rise-24-in-england-and-wales-it-will-make-society-less-safe-not-more-172566#:~:text=The%20Ministry%20of%20Justice%20is,high%20for%20the%20two%20countries.

Papathanasiou, S., Markoulaki, S., Blaine, L.J., Leibowitz, M.L., Zhang, C-Z., Jaenisch, R., & Pellman, D. (2021). Whole chromosome loss and genomic instability in mouse embryos after CRISPR-Cas9 genome editing. *Nature Communications*, 12, Article 5855. https://doi.org/10.1038/s41467-021-26097-y.

Pfeiffer, M.B. (2022, November 28). The missing babies of Europe. *RESCUE with Michael Capuzzo*. https://rescue.substack.com/p/the-missing-babies-of-europe?utm_campaign=post.

Pijl, K.van der (2020, April 27). Health emergency or seizure of power? The political economy of Covid-19. *New Cold War*. https://newcoldwar.org/health-emergency-or-seizure-of-power-the-political-economy-of-covid-19/.

Pijl, K. van der. (2022). *States of emergency. Keeping the global population in check*. Clarity Press.

Plimer, I. (2021). *Green Murder*. Connor Court.

Police, Crime, Sentencing and Courts Act 2022, c. 32. https://www.legislation.gov.uk/ukpga/2022/32/enacted.

Policy Horizons Canada. (2020). *Exploring biodigital convergence*. https://web.archive.org/web/20210706143933/https://horizons.gc.ca/en/2020/02/11/exploring-biodigital-convergence/.

Prime Minister's Office. (2019). *PM speech to the UN General Assembly: 24 September 2019*. https://www.gov.uk/government/speeches/pm-speech-to-the-un-general-assembly-24-september-2019.

Prison Reform Trust. (2023, June 30). *Prison capacity crisis won't be solved by newly opened HMP Fosse Way figures reveal*. https://prisonreformtrust.org.uk/new-figures-reveal-scale-of-prison-capacity-crisis/.

Public Order Act 2023, c. 15. https://www.legislation.gov.uk/ukpga/2023/15/enacted.

Rectenwald, M. (2021, December 26). What is the Great Reset? *Imprimis* 50(12). https://imprimis.hillsdale.edu/what-is-the-great-reset/.

Rees, L. (2009). *Auschwitz: Geschichte eines Verbrechens*. Ullstein.

Robinson, C. (2021, September 27). Gene editing may cause "massive damage" to chromosomes, study finds. *Children's Health Defence*. https://childrenshealthdefense.org/defender/crispr-gene-editing-damage-chromosomes-chromothripsis/.

Robinson, P. (2023, December 26). The perils of studying propaganda. *Propaganda in Focus*. https://propagandainfocus.com/the-perils-of-studying-propaganda/.

Rockefeller Foundation. (2013). *Dreaming the future of health for the next 100 years*. https://www.rockefellerfoundation.org/report/dreaming-the-future-of-health-for-the-next-100-years/.

Roco, M.C., & Bainbridge, W.S. (Eds). (2002, June). *Converging technologies for improving human performance*. https://web.archive.org/web/20041026051927/wtec.org/ConvergingTechnologies/Report/NBIC_pre_publication.pdf.

Ross, L., Klompas, M., & Bernstein, S. (2010). *Electronic support for public health—vaccine adverse event reporting system*. https://digital.ahrq.gov/sites/default/files/docs/publication/r18hs017045-lazarus-final-report-2011.pdf.

Russell, B. (2016). *The impact of science on society*. Routledge.

Schmeling, M., Manniche, V., & Hansen, P.R. (2023, March 30). Batch-dependent safety of the BNT162b2 mRNA COVID-19 vaccine. *European Journal of Clinical Investigation*, 53(8), Article 13998. https://doi.org/10.1111/eci.13998.

Scott, B. (2021, May 2). We are all Pavlov's dogs now. *UK Column*. https://www.ukcolumn.org/article/we-are-all-pavlovs-dogs-now.

Secret Nazi Speech. (1940, December 9). *Life Magazine*. pp. 43–44. https://books.google.al/books?id=QUoEAAAAMBAJ&printsec=frontcover&redir_esc=y#v=onepage&q=blitzkrieg&f=true.

Segal, M. (2021, September 17). NYSE to list new "natural asset companies" asset class, targeting massive opportunity in ecosystem services." *ESG Today*. https://www.esgtoday.com/nyse-to-list-new-asset-class-for-natural-asset-companies-targeting-massive-opportunity-in-ecosystem-services/.

Shapiro, A. (2021, January 14). America's biggest owner of farmland is now Bill Gates. *Forbes*. https://www.forbes.com/sites/arielshapiro/2021/01/14/americas-biggest-owner-of-farmland-is-now-bill-gates-bezos-turner/.

Sharav, V. (2022, August 20). Nuremberg Code is our defense against abusive experimentation. *Alliance for Human Research Protection*. https://ahrp.org/transcript-vera-speech-nuremberg75/.

Sheridan, C. (2021). CRISPR therapies march into clinic, but genotoxicity concerns linger. *Nature Biotechnology*, 39, pp. 897–899. https://doi.org/10.1038/d41587–021-00017–3.

Shirer, W.L. (1991). *The rise and fall of the Third Reich*. Simon & Schuster.

Shir-Raz, E.E., Martin, B., Ronel, N., & Guetzkow, J. (2022, November 1). Censorship and suppression of Covid-19 heterodoxy: Tactics and counter-tactics. *Minerva*. https://doi.org/10.1007/s11024–022-09479–4.

Slaughter, A-M. (2004). *A new world order*. Princeton University Press.

Snyder, T. (2010, October 21). The Reich's forgotten atrocity. *The Guardian*. https://www.theguardian.com/commentisfree/cifamerica/2010/oct/21/secondworldwar-russia.

Solon, O. (2017, February 15). Elon Musk says humans must become cyborgs to stay relevant. Is he right? *The Guardian*. https://www.theguardian.com/technology/2017/feb/15/elon-musk-cyborgs-robots-artificial-intelligence-is-he-right.

Stanton, G. (2016). The ten stages of genocide. *Genocide Watch*. http://genocidewatch.net/genocide-2/8-stages-of-genocide/.

Staudenmaier, P. (2011). Fascist ecology: The "green wing" of the Nazi party and its historical antecedents. In: J. Biehl & P. Staudenmaier (Eds.), *Ecofascism revisited: Lessons from the German experience* (pp. 13–42). New Compass Press.

Sturge, N. (2023, September 8). UK prison population statistics. *House of Commons Library.* https://researchbriefings.files.parliament.uk/documents /SN04334/SN04334.pdf.

Sumption, J. (2020, October 27). *Government by decree: Covid-19 and the constitution. Cambridge Freshfields Annual Law Lecture.* https://resources.law .cam.ac.uk/privatelaw/Freshfields_Lecture_2020_Government_by_Decree .pdf.

Swiss Policy Research. (2022, June). *Covid vaccines and fertility (2022).* https: //swprs.org/covid-vaccines-and-fertility/.

Thorburn, J. (2021, June 24). How can the Government sleep at night? Travellers tell of "prison-like" conditions at £1,750 quarantine hotel as they share images of "inedible" food served in polystyrene boxes. *Daily Mail.* https://www.dailymail.co.uk/news/article-9721043/Travellers-complain -prison-like-1–750-quarantine-hotel-share-images-inedible-food.html.

Tice, A. (2022, July 30). "Concerned for humanity": Alabama embalmer discovers strange clots in people since release of Covid vaccine. *1819 News.* https://1819news.com/news/item/embalmer-discovers-over-100-cases-of -strange-clots-in-people-since-release-of-covid-19-vaccine.

Transcript: George Soros Interview. (2009, October 23). *Financial Times.* https://archive.ph/mSaKx#selection-1857.0–1857.17.

Turley, J. (2022, September 27). New Zealand Prime Minister calls for a global censorship system. *ZeroHedge.* https://www.zerohedge.com/geopolitical /new-zealand-prime-minister-calls-for-a-global-censorship-system.

UK Column. (2021, July 19). *UK Column news—19th July 2021.* https://www .ukcolumn.org/ukc-column-news/uk-column-news-19th-july-2021.

United Nations. (1948). *Convention on the Prevention and Punishment of the Crime of Genocide.* https://www.un.org/en/genocideprevention/genocide .shtml.

United Nations Development Programme. (2011, January 1). *Human development report.* https://hdr.undp.org/system/files/documents//human-development-report -2011-english.human-development-report-2011-english.

Valentine, D. (2017). *The CIA as organized crime. How illegal operations corrupt America and the world.* Clarity Press.

Vanheuckelom, T. (2023, November 29). Not just the farmer's fight. *European Conservative.* https://europeanconservative.com/articles/commentary/not -just-the-farmers-fight/.

Versluis, A. (2006). *The new inquisitions: Heretic-hunting and the intellectual origins of modern totalitarianism.* Oxford University Press.

Walker, B. (2022, January 25). The UK's mega prison: if they build it, they'll fill it. *Screenshot.* https://screenshot-media.com/politics/human-rights/uk-mega -prison/.

Webb, W. (2021a, June 25). A "Leap" toward humanity's destruction. *Unlimited Hangout.* https://unlimitedhangout.com/2021/06/investigative-reports/a-leap -toward-humanitys-destruction/.

Webb, W. (2021b, October 13). Wall Street's takeover of nature advances with launch of new asset class. *Unlimited Hangout.* https://unlimitedhangout .com/2021/10/investigative-reports/wall-streets-takeover-of-nature-advances -with-launch-of-new-asset-class/.

Westermann, E.B. (2015). Political soldiers. In: P. Hayes (Ed.), *How was it possible? A Holocaust reader* (pp. 481–494). University of Nebraska Press.

White House. (2022a, June 21). *Remarks by President Biden on Covid-19 vaccines for children under five.* https://www.whitehouse.gov/briefing-room /speeches-remarks/2022/06/21/remarks-by-president-biden-on-covid -19-vaccines-for-children-under-five/.

White House. (2022b, September 6). *Press briefing by White House Covid-19 response team and public health officials.* https://www.whitehouse.gov /briefing-room/press-briefings/2022/09/06/press-briefing-by-white-house -covid-19-response-team-and-public-health-officials-88/.

White House. (2022c, October). *National Security Strategy.* https://www.white house.gov/wp-content/uploads/2022/10/Biden-Harris-Administrations -National-Security-Strategy-10.2022.pdf.

Whiting, K. (2020, October 16). How soon will we be eating lab-grown meat? *World Economic Forum.* https://www.weforum.org/agenda/2020/10/will -we-eat-lab-grown-meat-world-food-day/.

Wilson, R. (2022a, January 1). Pre-WWII Germany: Laws introduced for the protection of the people. *Daily Exposé.* https://expose-news.com/2022/01/01 /pre-wwii-germany-laws-introduced-for-the-protection-of-the-people/.

Wilson, R. (2022b, January 11). Dr Mike Yeadon: The variability in serious adverse events by vaccine lot is the "calibration of a killing weapon." *Daily Exposé*. https://expose-news.com/2022/01/11/mike-yeadon-the-variability-in-serious-adverse-events/.

World Health Organisation. (n.d.). *VigiAccess*. Retrieved January 11, 2024, from https://vigiaccess.org/.

Yad Vashem. (n.d.). *Architecture of Murder*. https://www.yadvashem.org/yv/en/exhibitions/through-the-lens/auschwitz-blueprints.asp.

Yglesias, M. (2020, April 28). The successful Asian coronavirus-fighting strategy America refuses to embrace. *Vox*. https://www.vox.com/2020/4/28/21238456/centralized-isolation-coronavirus-hong-kong-korea.

Zimbardo, P. (2005). Mind control in Orwell's *Nineteen eighty-four*: Fictional concepts become operational realities in Jim Jones's jungle experiment. In: A. Gleason, J. Goldsmith, & M.C. Nussbaum (Eds.), *On* Nineteen eighty-four*: Orwell and our future* (pp. 127–154). Princeton University Press.

Zimbardo, P. (2007). *The Lucifer effect: Why good people turn evil*. Random House.

Chapter 8

Agamben, G. (1998). *Homo Sacer*. Stanford University Press.

Ahmed, N.M. (2012). Capitalism, covert action and state terrorism: Toward a political economy of the dual state. In: E. Wilson (Ed.), *The dual state: Parapolitics, Carl Schmitt, and the national security complex* (pp. 171–192). Routledge.

Arendt, H. (1962). *The origins of totalitarianism*. The World Publishing Company.

Australian Bureau of Statistics. (2023). *Provisional mortality statistics*. https://www.abs.gov.au/statistics/health/causes-death/provisional-mortality-statistics/jan-dec-2022.

Bell, D. (2023). Pandemic preparedness and the road to international fascism. *The American Journal of Economics and Sociology*, 82(5), 395–409. https://doi.org/10.1111/ajes.12531.

Blaylock, R.L. (2022). Covid update: What is the truth? *Surgical Neurology International*, 13, Article 167. https://doi.org/10.25259/SNI_150_2022.

Corbett, J. (2019). Episode 359—The secrets of Silicon Valley: What big tech doesn't want you to know. *The Corbett Report*. https://www.corbettreport.com/siliconvalley/.

Crawford, M. (2022, May 9). Proof of statistical sieves in VE data, Part 2: ONS data. *Rounding the Earth Newsletter*. https://roundingtheearth.substack.com /p/proof-of-statistical-sieves-in-ve.

Epstein, C.A. (2015). *Nazi Germany: Confronting the myths*. John Wiley & Sons.

eurostat. (n.d.). *Excess mortality by month* [Data set]. https://ec.europa.eu /eurostat/databrowser/view/DEMO_MEXRT__custom_309801/bookmark /line?lang=en&bookmarkId=26981184–4241-4855-b18e-8647fc8c0dd2.

Gabel, J., & Knox, C. (2023, February 20). New Zealand records biggest increase in registered deaths in 100 years. *nzherald*. https://www.nzherald.co.nz/nz /new-zealand-records-biggest-increase-in-registered-deaths-in-100-years /BQERSTKIANCKRNNA7IL42RD52U/.

Gellately, R. (1991). *The Gestapo and German society*. Oxford University Press.

Gunderman, R. (2015, July 9). The manipulation of the American mind: Edward Bernays and the birth of public relations. *The Conversation*. https: //theconversation.com/the-manipulation-of-the-american-mind-edward -bernays-and-the-birth-of-public-relations-44393.

Haque, O.S., De Freitas, J., Viani, I., Niederschulte, B., & Bursztajn, H.J. (2012). Why did so many German doctors join the Nazi Party early? *International Journal of Law and Psychiatry*, 35(5–6), 473–479. https://doi .org/10.1016/j.ijlp.2012.09.022.

Higham, C. (2007). *Trading with the enemy*. Delacorte Press.

Hughes, D.A. (2024). *"Covid-19," Psychological operations, and the war for tech-nocracy*. Palgrave Macmillan.

Hughes, D.A., Broudy, D., & Kyrie, V. (2023, February 22). Global class war and the politics of a hatchet job: A reply to John Waters. *The Solari Report*. https://constitution.solari.com/global-class-war-and-the-politics-of-a -hatchet-job-a-reply-to-john-waters/.

Klemperer, V. (1999). *I will bear witness* (M. Chalmers, Trans.). The Modern Library.

Koonz, C. (2003). *The Nazi conscience*. Harvard University Press.

Meerloo, J.A. (1956). *The rape of the mind. The psychology of thought control, menticide, and brainwashing*. World Publishing Company.

Office for National Statistics. (n.d.). *Deaths registered weekly in England and Wales, provisional*. https://www.ons.gov.uk/peoplepopulationand community/birthsdeathsandmarriages/deaths/bulletins/deathsregistered weeklyinenglandandwalesprovisional/latest.

Pijl, K. van der. (2022). *States of emergency. Keeping the global population in check*. Clarity Press.

Ruechel, J. (2021, July 17). The emperor has no clothes: Finding the courage to break the spell. https://www.juliusruechel.com/2021/07/the-emperor-has -no-clothes-finding.html.

UK Health Security Agency. (2022). *Weekly national influenza and Covid-19 surveillance report, week 27*. https://assets.publishing.service.gov.uk /government/uploads/system/uploads/attachment_data/file/1088929/Weekly _Flu_and_COVID-19_report_w27.pdf.

U.S. Mortality (n.d.). *Weekly all-cause excess mortality (percentage)*. https://www .usmortality.com/excess-mortality/percentage.

Valentine, D. (2017). *The CIA as organized crime. How illegal operations corrupt America and the world*. Clarity Press.

Zimbardo, P. (2007). *The Lucifer effect: Why good people turn evil*. Random House.

INDEX

Media
  control of, 2, 11, 26–28
  as a war zone, 11, 16, 20, 22, 24,
    38, 90, 146, 149, 150, 157
Medical ethics, 2, 21, 23, 153
Medical profession, 20, 25, 121, 146
Midazolam, 33, 34, 146
Middle classes (attack on), 2, 11, 19,
  20, 153, 159
MKULTRA, 78, 96, 116, 117
Morality
  Inversion of, 2, 38, 39, 121, 148
  Moral collapse, 2, 20, 23, 156
  Moral courage, 155, 160, 161, 163
Morgan, J.P., 6, 32, 43–47, 54, 56, 59,
  68, 99, 102, 112
mRNA, 34, 143–145, 161
Mussolini, Benito, 5, 6, 20

National Health Service (NHS), 31,
  33–35
National Institute of Clinical
  Excellence, 33
National Socialism, 4, 5, 17, 21, 22,
  40, 41, 45, 60
NATO, 69, 91–93, 104, 110
Natural asset companies, 121, 131
Nazification, 20, 34
Nazis, 1, 3–5, 7, 13, 14, 18, 19, 21–23,
  25, 35, 39–41, 43, 45, 47–49,
  51–59, 63–69, 71–72, 79–81, 85,
  95, 96, 101, 105, 108, 122, 124,
  127, 128, 133, 140, 141, 145, 147,
  149, 151, 152, 158, 161–162
Net Zero, 39, 41, 121, 131
New Deal, 5, 6, 157
New Order, 123, 124
New World Order, 121, 123–127, 160
Non-compliance, 119, 150

Nuremberg Code, 23, 73, 142
Nuremberg Trials, 15, 63, 64, 66, 73,
  153, 162

Office of Policy Coordination, 72,
  86, 87
Omnicom, 26
Operation Gladio, 80, 92–94, 105
Operation PAPERCLIP, 73
Operation Phoenix, 109, 152
Pandemic, 8, 12, 18, 19, 24, 26,
  30–32, 37, 105, 111, 116, 117,
  120, 127, 139, 147, 149–151, 156

Parliament, 12–15, 34, 80, 115, 126
Pearl Harbor, 8, 53, 54, 56, 158
Persecution, 12, 24, 25, 57, 121, 141,
  149
Police brutality, 15, 150
Politicians, 17, 95, 159
Political economy, 1, 11, 41, 120
Professions, the, 2, 11, 20, 23, 34, 57, 161
Professors, 20, 23
Project BLUEBIRD (renamed
  ARTICHOKE), 77, 78, 96
Propaganda, 1, 2, 11–13, 17, 25–30,
  38, 54, 69, 86, 96, 104–106, 114,
  115, 120, 122, 132, 145, 148–150,
  153, 157
Property rights, 18
Protective custody, 12
Protests, 8, 15, 17, 21, 22, 79, 103,
  116, 139, 150, 157
Pseudoscience, 12, 37
Psychological operations/warfare, 13, 86,
  105, 106, 117, 118, 120, 149, 161
Public health, 12, 32–34, 41, 126,
  137, 147–149
Puhl, Emil, 5, 47, 66

UK Covert Human Intelligence
(Criminal Conduct) Act, 15
UK Fusion Doctrine, 28
UK Online Safety Act, 16, 25
UK prison capacity, 138–140
UK Public Order Act, 15, 139
Unemployment, 22, 24, 128, 134
UNESCO, 37, 124
Unit 731, 63, 74, 75

"Vaccines", 12, 16, 21–23, 30, 34, 35,
38, 119, 129, 132, 143–144, 147,
150, 156, 157, 161
"Vaccine passports", 11, 20, 30, 80
Vatican, 21, 43, 49, 63, 67, 81
Vinciguerra, Vincenzo, 94, 115
Volk, 17, 18, 22, 130, 140, 148
von der Leyen, Ursula, 80–81

Wall Street, 1, 4–7, 43–48, 50, 60, 34,
65, 68, 83, 86–89, 99, 100, 104,
106, 120, 124, 131, 162

Wall Street crash, 17, 19, 48
War crimes, 63, 64, 71, 72, 85,
105–110
War on Terror, 8, 95, 114, 116
Weimar Constitution, 12, 16
Western, 3–5, 8, 16, 18, 23, 30,
67–73, 80, 83, 85, 90–104, 107,
115, 119, 125, 135, 136, 141
Westrick, Gerhardt, 5
Woke, 25
Working classes, 4, 5, 7, 17, 18, 22,
23, 43, 45, 92, 93, 97, 98, 103, 104
World Economic Forum, 17–18, 26,
30, 79–81, 126, 128, 132
World Health Organization, 19, 30,
127, 144, 151

Young Plan, 43, 46